Faith and Freedom

Faith and Freedom

Women's Human Rights in the Muslim World

Edited by
Mahnaz Afkhami

I.B.TAURIS PUBLISHERS
LONDON · NEW YORK

Published in 1995 by
I.B. Tauris & Co Ltd
45 Bloomsbury Square
London WC1A 2HY

A full CIP record for this book is available from the British Library

ISBN 1 86064 008 7

Typeset by Philip Armstrong, Oxford
Printed and bound in Great Britain by
WBC Ltd, Bridgend, Mid Glamorgan

Contents

Contributors

Mahnaz Afkhami is executive director of the Sisterhood Is Global Institute and executive director of the Foundation for Iranian Studies. Her latest publication is *Women in Exile* (University Press of Virginia, 1994).

Abdullahi An-Na'im is professor of law at Emory University in Atlanta, Georgia. He holds degrees in law from the universities of Khartoum, Sudan, and Cambridge, England, and a Ph.D. in law from Edinburgh University, Scotland. He is the author of *Toward an Islamic Reformation: Civil Liberties, Human Rights, and International Law* (Syracuse University Press, 1990).

Karima Bennoune is an attorney practicing with Wayne County Neighborhood Legal Services in Detroit, Michigan. She is a graduate of the University of Michigan Law School and author of numerous articles on women in Algeria.

Eleanor Abdella Doumato teaches in the department of history at the University of Rhode Island. She is the author of a forthcoming book on women in the Arabian peninsula. Her numerous articles have appeared in *The Encyclopedia of the Modern Islamic World*, *The Encyclopedia of the Modern Middle East*, and *The Columbia Encyclopedia* among others. She is editor of the Association for Middle East Women's Studies (AMEWS) Newsletter.

Nancy Gallagher is professor of history at the University of California, Santa Barbara. Her latest publication is *Approaches to the History of the Middle East: Interviews with Leading Historians* (Ithaca/Garnet, 1994). She is currently working on a history of the international women's human rights movement.

Shahla Haeri is an assistant professor in the Department of Anthropology at Boston University, specializing in Iran and Pakistan. She is the author of *Law of Desire: Temporary Marriage in Shi'i Iran* (Syracuse University Press, 1989, 1993).

Deniz Kandiyoti is senior lecturer in the Department of Anthropology and Sociology of the School of Oriental and African Studies, University of London. She is the editor of *Women, Islam and the State* (Temple University Press, 1991) and *Gendering the Middle East* (I.B. Tauris, forthcoming).

Ann Elizabeth Mayer is an associate professor of legal studies at the Wharton School of the University of Pennsylvania. She has written on various aspects of Islamic law in contemporary Middle Eastern legal systems and human rights issues in the Middle East and authored *Islam and Human Rights: Tradition and Politics* (Westview Press, 1991 and 1995).

Fatima Mernissi is professor of sociology at Mohammed V University in Rabat, Morocco. She has reinterpreted classical Islamic texts from a feminist perspective and supervised publication of a series of books on the legal status of women in Morocco, Algeria and Tunisia. Her latest publication is *Dreams of Trespass* (Addison-Wesley, 1994).

Bouthaina Shaaban is a professor in the English Department at Damascus University, Syria, and Executive Editor of *Foreign Literature Quarterly*. She is the author of *Both Right and Left Handed: Arab Women Talk About Their Lives* (Women's Press, 1988 and Indiana University Press, 1991).

Farida Shaheed is a sociologist working at Shirkat Gah, a women's resource center in Pakistan, and one of the coordinators of Women Living Under Muslim Laws, an international network for information, solidarity and support. She is the coauthor of *Two Steps Forward, One Step Back? Women of Pakistan* (Zed, 1987).

Sima Wali is the President/CEO of Refugee Women in Development (RefWID), Inc., an international NGO devoted to helping Third World refugee women attain social and economic independence. She has written numerous articles on issues of refugee and displaced women.

Preface

This book is about Muslim women's quest for rights. It is in part
the outcome of the Washington Dialogue, a conference on
'Religion, Culture, and Women's Human Rights in the Muslim
World,' organized by the Sisterhood Is Global Institute (SIGI) in
Washington, DC in September 1994. It also contains articles
contributed by scholars and activists who were not on the panels,
but participated in the Dialogue in spirit and in sisterhood.

The Washington Dialogue, the first of three conferences SIGI
convened in 1994 as precursors of the 1995 UN World Conference
on Women at Beijing, was structured to bring the views of women
from the Muslim world to the international debate on women's
human rights and to ensure their participation in identifying
problems and recommending corrective actions. Activists, experts,
internationalists, and academicians were invited to share
experiences and to discuss subjects they considered important but
not adequately emphasized in international forums. The Dialogue
took place shortly after the UN Conference on Human Rights in
Vienna in 1993 and almost simultaneously with the 1994 UN
Conference on Population and Development in Cairo. The Vienna
Conference highlighted the seriousness of the challenge Muslim
women face as they approach the twenty-first century. Many
Muslim governments which had wholly or partly supported the
Universal Declaration of Human Rights in 1948 (and subsequent
universalist documents) reneged in Vienna. More important, rather
than justify their actions on grounds of political expediency, they
argued that universal human rights are Western parochial concepts
used as weapons of cultural imperialism, that to judge Muslim
societies by these standards injures Muslim communal rights, and
that for Muslim countries Islam provides the basic elements of a
just society, including the fundamental rights of women. In short,
they rejected women's human rights, as defined in international
documents, even as aspirations. At the Cairo Conference,
fundamentalist positions on women coalesced across cultures and

religions as Islamists joined forces with representatives from the Vatican against women's human rights.

The two events, manifesting the international community's position on women's status and rights, informed both the process and substance of the debates. Two points were particularly salient. First, rights are largely a result of empowerment and are therefore dependent on the nature and form of the prevailing politics. Second, women of the South are structurally under-represented in governmental and nongovernmental international forums on rights and therefore ought to seek, and be granted, greater opportunity for participation in the universal dialogue of rights. This volume sets the framework for debates on these two points.

The Washington Dialogue also emphasized that rights and empowerment are connected to the values that give the prevailing culture its particular moral texture. Those who have the right to define these values have power. Indeed, to be able to define these values *is* to have power. Since in Muslim societies many of these values stem from Islam, it follows that if Muslim women are to have rights, they must gain the ability to participate in determining what these values are and how they will affect human life. To paraphrase Michel Foucault, they need to control life in the extremities of social relations – between man and wife, father and daughter, sister and brother, manager and worker, teacher and student. This volume is also sensitive to this point.

Finally, the Washington Dialogue also focused on the issue of violence against women, including the systematic violence perpetrated against Muslim women in times of conflict. The majority of the refugees and displaced persons in the world are women and their children, a majority of them, by far, Muslim women and children. These are the helpless people against whom the most heinous of crimes – rape as political weapon and strategy of war, arbitrary incarcerations, practical enslavement as unpaid forced labor, and summary executions – are committed. This volume addresses this issue as well.

It is a truism that all intellectual and organizational endeavors are achieved as a result of many and varied individual and institutional contributions. The Washington Dialogue and this book are no exceptions. The Dialogue could not have taken place without the support of the Shaler Adams Foundation and the personal encouragement of its president, Margaret Knowles Schink, to whom I am most thankful. I am particularly indebted to Clovis

Maksoud and the Center for the Study of the Global South for their cosponsorship of the Dialogue. A considerable share of the smooth working of the Dialogue is owed to the Center's Suzie Nemazee and her organizational skills. My thanks to Yvonne Haddad, Leila Fawaz, Barbara Stowasser, and Hala Maksoud, who as chairs of the panels were instrumental in the blossoming of a very lively and spirited debate. I thank Miriam Cooke and Ann Elizabeth Mayer for their encouragement and many helpful suggestions on the structure, content, and participants of the Dialogue.

The book, of course, was made possible by the contributors. They participated in this collective endeavor with enthusiasm and dedication. They brought to the project superb scholarship as well as commitment to Muslim women's human rights. I have thoroughly enjoyed working with every one whose contribution has helped produce this volume. My special thanks are due to Anna Enayat, my editor at I. B. Tauris and Cynthia Maude-Gembler, my editor at Syracuse University Press, for their help and encouragement. Anna's enthusiasm and constant support has been a determining factor in the preparation and publication of the volume in time for the Beijing Conference. I would like to thank Diane Landino, my assistant at SIGI, who worked diligently against the clock to prepare the manuscript for publication. I wish to acknowledge the dedicated and steadfast cooperation and administrative support I have received from my long-time colleague and friend Ezzat Aghevli of the Women's Center of the Foundation for Iranian Studies for both the Dialogue and the book.

My husband Gholam Reza Afkhami has been my partner, closest friend, and keenest critic. His support and encouragement have been vital in this as in all other work I have done in my life.

M.A.

---------- I ----------

Introduction

Mahnaz Afkhami

There are over half a billion women in the Muslim world. They
live in vastly different lands, climates, cultures, societies, economies,
and polities. Few of them live in a purely traditional environment.
For most of them modernity means, above all, conflict – a spectrum of values and forces that compete for their allegiance and
beckon them to contradictory ways of looking at themselves and
at the world that surrounds them. The most taxing contradiction
they face casts the demands of living in the contemporary world
against the requirements of tradition as determined and advanced
by the modern Islamist world view. At the center of this conflict
is the dilemma of Muslim women's human rights – whether
Muslim women have rights because they are human beings, or
whether they have rights because they are Muslim women.[1] *Faith
and Freedom* addresses this issue.

Contemporary Islamist regimes are most lucidly identified, and
differentiated from other regimes, by the position they assign to
women in the family and in society.[2] For Muslim fundamentalists
every domestic issue is negotiable except women's rights and their
position in society. Islamist resurgence, exemplified by movements
as varied as Jama'at-i Islami in Pakistan, Ikhwan al-Muslimin in
Egypt, the Islamic Republic in Iran, and the Islamic Salvation
Front (FIS) in Algeria, insists on singling out women's relation to
society as the supreme test of the authenticity of the Islamic order.
The religious fiat, often manifested concurrently as discursive text
and naked violence, relies for its legitimacy on a tradition that it
assumes invests social structure and mores with an ethic of womanhood appropriate to Islam, symbolized historically by the institutions of *andarun* and *purdah*.[3] The ethic and the symbols, however,
are becoming increasingly porous as Muslim societies, including a
significant number of Muslim women, outgrow and transgress
traditional boundaries.

Islamist intransigence forces Muslim women to fight for their rights, openly when they can, subtly when they must. The struggle is multifaceted, at once political, economic, ethical, psychological, and intellectual. It resonates with the mix of values, mores, facts, ambitions, prejudices, ambivalences, uncertainties, and fears that are the stuff of human culture. Above all, it is a casting off of a tradition of subjection.[4]

Islamism reduces this complex, historical struggle to a metaphysical question. It does so by casting society in an idealized Platonic 'form' and by equating culture with the dogmatics of religion. This representation is functionally supported by an important strain in contemporary international discourse that takes off from Islam's assignment of private and public space to women rather than from freedom and equality as the core assumptions appropriate to modern times.[5] Akin to a presumption of guilt in a court of law, this discourse reverses a universally accepted rule. To the extent that Islam, defined and interpreted by traditionalist 'Muslim' men, is allowed to determine the context and contour of the debate on women's human rights, women will be on the losing side of the debate because the conclusion is already contained in the premise and reflected in the process. Arguably, this is the heart of the moral tragedy of Muslim societies in our time.

The Islamist position on women's human rights is advanced on two levels – one internal, the other external to the Muslim community. Internally, the argument invokes Islam and the inviolability of the text.[6] The formulation is intellectually rigid, but politically well organized and ideologically inter-connected across the Muslim world through chains of 'traditions,' clerical *fatwas,* and periodic government resolutions and legislation. Opposed to it, Muslim women in significant numbers and from all social strata are currently objecting to the fundamentalist interpretation of Islam.[7] The dimensions of the struggle are being defined as Muslim women strive for rights across the globe: what these rights are, how they relate to Islam epistemologically,[8] how they resonate with social and political power in specific Muslim societies, and how strategies that seek to promote them will or should be developed. High on the list are the ways and means of interpreting religious texts: how should women approach the issue, what sort of expertise is needed, how can the issue be bridged to grassroots leaders, how may the intelligence received from the grassroots be brought to the interpretative process?[9] Scholars and activists are also looking into ways of educating the Muslim political elite: how to identify responsive decision makers, how to communicate reinterpreted text, how to develop criteria for judging the limits of political engagement, how to help executives, legislators, and judges sympathetic to women's human rights to implement change in the condition of women. They are also searching for appropriate patterns of mobilizing grassroots support, including ways of identifying women leaders at different levels, communicating methods of pressuring political decision makers, and, most important of all, protecting women activists against moral and physical violence.[10] The list, obviously not exhaustive, nevertheless signifies the dynamics of the relationship between women's human rights, politics, and the Islamic texts.

Externally, the Islamist position meshes with the idea of cultural relativity now in vogue in the West, where relevant arguments are waged for reasons that usually transcend the problem of right in its elemental form.[11] In the West, particularly in academic circles, relativity is often advanced and defended to promote diversity. In its theoretical forms, for example as a post-structuralist critique of positivist (liberal modernization) and Marxist development theories, cultural relativism sometimes suggests that universalist discourses are guilty of reinforcing Western hegemony by demeaning non-Western experience. Whatever other merits or faults of the critique, it insists on free choice and equal access. Islamists, however, use the argument functionally to justify structural impairment of women's freedom and formal enforcement of women's inequality. This use of the argument is morally unjust and structurally flawed. As mentioned above, rather than addressing real evolving societies, Islamists abstract Islam as an esoteric system of unchanging rules and then equate it with complex, changing, and historically specific social and political conditions. As a result, they transform the practical issue of women's historical subjugation in patriarchies, which is a matter of the economic, social, cultural, and political forms power takes as societies evolve, to arcane questions of moral negligence and religious slackness. The argument becomes pernicious when it seeks to portray women who struggle for rights as women who are against Islam, which is their religion and in which they believe.[12] The Islamists confound the issue by positing men's interpretation of religion for religion itself. This book also deals with this question.

The rise in Muslim women's awareness of their identity and rights is part of a historical process in which all individuals, men and women, have increasingly appropriated their 'selves.'[13] The form of appropriation differs from culture to culture, but the essence is commonly shared. Right is a property of control a woman achieves over her person over time. It is an appropriation of individual power and acceptance of personal responsibility. It is to assume an identity that seeks perpetually to authenticate its 'self' as responsible subject. As history moves from law (the condition of obeying the framework already given) to right (the condition of acting to establish appropriate frameworks), Muslim women must forge and maintain an identity that is historically adequate, psychologically rewarding, and morally acceptable.[14] The resulting tensions, always difficult to accommodate, are intensified by the division of the world into North and South and the attractions and repulsions engendered by racial, ethnic, religious, and national cleavages and solidarities. The transition from law to right is exacting and probably never complete. The challenge is particularly hard for Muslim women because their historical memory is bound to a host of dogmatically firm but logically questionable 'traditions'[15] that emotionally and intellectually infuse and sustain their religion.

When successful, Muslim women's self-authentication becomes a transcending of history as man's signature. Specifically, it evokes a vision of reality as a world interconnected spatially and temporally, where cultures are not distillations of values, mores, and aesthetics invented by some extraordinary people at a golden point in time and inscribed in common memory as deified eternal forms, but living, changing phenomena that trace a people's evolution and a person's growth in history. Growth involves interaction with others and consequently transformations that bear the mark of the 'other.' For most of the Third World the experience of colonialism led the dialectic of encounter to an intellectual impasse by positing the 'other' as the enemy. As so much of the 'other' is appropriated in the developmental process, the enemy steals within and the impasse, intellectual and political at first, becomes a pathology of self-denial. Since the future is claimed by the 'other,' the alternative that remains is the irredeemable past. In this sense, Islamic traditionism is a scourge bequeathed by the colonial experience. Muslim women must transcend this experience if they are to accomplish their task of self-authentication. Above all, they should refuse to identify themselves as against the world outside. Rather, they ought to seek to lead in defining its issues and shaping its future.

Rights are also related to the changing properties of political culture – values, beliefs, and aesthetics that have to do with the dispositions of power. Hence, unless a substantial number of women in a community come to believe that they have rights and demand to exercise them, right remains an abstraction. Rights and empowerment are interconnected. On the one hand, rights provide individuals with choice and therefore the possibility of diversity. On the other hand, to strive for rights is *ipso facto* to be empowered. The process takes different forms and passes through different routes, but whatever the form or the path, it places women in history. The question before us is: how will Muslim women, particularly those among them who can communicate with others, influence events, and make a difference, be empowered to advance the cause of women's human rights? How can the process be enhanced, facilitated, encouraged? What possibilities exist or can be generated for women activists across the world to help Muslim women solve their problems?

The last point corresponds to the concept of global movement for women's human rights.[16] At the center of this concept is the idea that the conditions women have in common outrank and outvalue those that set them apart. As historical victims of patriarchy, they are naturally united across history; they must now transcend political and cultural divides that are contemporary effects of traditional patriarchal politics.[17] An important part of the ongoing struggle for women's human rights is the effort to find ways and means of bringing together women from different cultures to work toward solutions to common human problems. The global movement for women's human rights, therefore, is not exclusively a women's project; rather, it brings the women's rights perspective, which is fundamentally gender-inclusive, to choices that need to be made for a more productive and humane future for everyone. This historical necessity provides a reason and an opportunity for women from both South and North to cooperate in defining problems and finding solutions.

Two points deserve mention in this respect. First, because Muslim countries have not been colonial powers, Muslim women, like other women from the South, are in a better position politically to help with a global movement for women's human rights. Many among them are multicultural, familiar with the West, multilingual, and conversant with international organizations and politics.[18] Their freedom, however, is curtailed by a male-oriented hegemonic social structure at home and by their lack of access to the means of communication domestically and internationally. A consequence of this second point is that even when Muslim women are politically able and psychologically willing to participate in the international discourse on women's human rights, they are constrained in practice, because they lack access to appropriate international organizations, media, and funding. [19]

Second, international forums have been dominated by women from the North. To provide forums for women whose engagement is necessary for the enrichment of the discourse and success of the project is in the interest of all women and a great contribution to the world movement for women's human rights. Specifically, this project requires an equitable representation for the women of the South in setting the criteria, providing the context, and assigning values that will guide the global movement for human rights. Muslim women need to focus particularly on constructing a set of images that portray authentically personal and cultural diversities that exist among them and which are ignored, misconceived, or misrepresented in the West. Women from the North can help by mobilizing international support for Muslim women's struggle, particularly through the use of international media and other means of communication to facilitate interaction between Muslim women and the international community as well as among Muslim women themselves. Fair and reasonable representation of Muslim women in international debate will also help correct a debilitating tendency among Muslim women to stereotype, label, and reject women's movements in the North despite their vitality, good will, and diversity.

Part I: Women, Islam and Patriarchy

This volume – the first to emphasize Muslim women's rights as human rights – is organized in two complementary sections. Part I addresses the patriarchal structures and processes that present women's human rights as contradictory to Islam. It discusses the importance of Islam for Muslim women, the anti-woman bias in male creation and interpretation of Islamic texts throughout history, and the need to reinterpret these texts in light of the humane and egalitarian spirit of Islam as distinct from its rendition by its male guardians. It examines how social and cultural segregation of women, contradictory and conflicting legal codes, and the

monopoly held by a select group of male theologians on interpretation of religious texts result in domestic and political violence
against women and in suppression of their rights. It also focuses
on ways and means of empowering Muslim women to participate
in the general socialization process as well as in making, implementing, and evaluating public policy.

The general framework for Part I is exemplified by Deniz
Kandiyoti's critique of some of the central assumptions behind
the ongoing debates about Muslim women's rights. Noting the
recent changes in the climate of opinion on the concept of rights,
Kandiyoti makes three analytical interventions. The first demonstrates the politically contingent nature of the relationship between
Islam and women's rights from the post-colonial state-building era
to the present. The second analyzes the interplay of local and
international agendas and some of their contradictory consequences for women's movements and rights. The third evaluates
the impact of post-modern discourses on 'difference' and the multiculturalism debate in the West on our understanding of rights and
coalition-building in Muslim societies. The text concludes by
reviewing the difficulties of developing a feminist agenda that
accommodates diversity and difference without undermining the
legal and ethical grounds upon which the right to difference itself
can be upheld.

Fatima Mernissi follows by suggesting that much that comes
out of the West about Islam and Muslim societies reflects fantasy
masquerading as liberal rationality rather than actual conditions
in the Muslim world. She takes to task the proposition that Muslim
states are, or have been, 'religious' in a way that non-Muslim
states have never been, and therefore separated from non-Muslim
experience ontologically. Sunni Islam, in particular, she argues,
has never recognized an intermediary between the individual and
God. There is no established church in Islam. The caliph wields
power as secular ruler. The *imam* leads prayers, but does not stand
vis-à-vis God, the Qur'an, or the Prophet, separate from the rest
of the Muslims. That is why the *shari'a*, the law, has always been
of overriding importance in the Muslim world. Two important
points follow: (1) tuned to the law, Muslim societies are historically
and structurally receptive to democracy's motto of 'government of
law and not of men;' and (2) not being separated by an intermediary from their God and His Prophet, Muslims can, in principle, interpret the law and render it current by ordinary individual

political intervention. Mernissi wonders at how liberal Western powers that are dedicated to individual human rights cuddle up with modern oil-producing 'caliphs' who use secular means to destroy rights by falsely appealing to religion.

Abdullahi An-Na'im addresses the nature and implications of the dichotomy between religious and secular discourse on the rights of women in Islamic societies. He argues that although this dichotomy is somewhat false and often exaggerated, nevertheless it can have serious consequences for the human rights of women in these societies. He calls on human rights advocates in Muslim societies to take religious discourse seriously and to seek and articulate Islamic justifications for the rights of women. He calls for diversity and plurality of religious as well as secular advocacy strategies.

Bouthaina Shaaban discusses different interpretations in Islam of the Qur'anic verses about women, their rights and duties. Women, she argues, have been marginalized and kept out of the main stream of Islamic Studies. An example is Nazira Zin al-Din, one of the most important women interpreters in Muslim history, whose two books of interpretation of the Qur'anic texts about women, al-Sufur wa'l-hijab and al-Fatat wa'l-shiukh, published almost 70 years ago, caused a storm that resounded in many parts of the globe. Shaaban recreates in some detail Zin al-Din's position on various Qur'anic texts and her arguments on the affinity between the text fairly interpreted and women's human rights. She describes how Zin al-Din stood her ground, using unimpeachable sources and inimitable logic to answer her critics and enemies. Subsequent Muslim scholars who concur with her interpretations of the Qur'an and her reading of the *hadith*, however, have failed to mention Zin al-Din or build on her work, thus, inadvertently, helping the opponents of women's rights and equality. Zin al-Din's contemporary *ulama* engaged in a serious intellectual debate with her. There was no threat of violence or accusation of apostasy. Shaaban wonders what would have happened to her if she had lived in the last decades of our century!

Farida Shaheed examines the contextual constraints that shape women's strategies for survival and well-being in the Muslim world, the negative implications of increasingly active politico-religious groups seeking political power, and the way in which networking can support women's struggle for change. Using examples from Pakistan and other Muslim societies, she argues that the struggle for change is hampered by women's lack of knowledge of existing statutory laws and their sources, and a fear of being ostracized if they oppose their community's definition of 'Muslim' womanhood. Women's networks, she argues, can contribute to change through non-hierarchical linkages, providing women with direct access to a wealth of alternative definitions of womanhood, breaking their isolation, and creating the support mechanisms that enable women to alter their lives. The very fluidity of the network structures challenges the dichotomous choices which both the politico-religious groups and some feminist analyses present to women, placing them in an either/or situation which fails to reflect the complexity and diversity of their everyday lives.

In the last chapter of this part Ann Elizabeth Mayer examines how certain spokespersons for different regimes and religions are currently posing as supporters of women's rights while, at the same time, pursuing policies that are inimical to women's rights and that are designed to preserve traditional patterns of discrimination. She assesses the common themes in the rhetoric on women's rights – that there are certain sacred laws or laws of nature, which men are powerless to alter, that supersede international human rights and therefore must be adhered to. Comparing the rhetoric used by opponents of women's equality in Muslim countries, the US, and the Vatican, she demonstrates that all of them define women's equality so as to accommodate these supposedly compelling sacred laws or laws of nature. These definitions of equality thereby deviate from the standard of full equality for women mandated by the United Nations Convention on the Elimination of All Forms of Discrimination against Women (CEDAW), even as any intent to discriminate is being piously disavowed. Mayer labels this phenomenon 'the new world hypocrisy,' and, by showing the cross-cultural similarities in the strategies of opponents of women's rights in Muslim countries and in the West, she shows that Islam presents no unique obstacle to women's rights.

Part II: Women and Violence – Selected Cases

In Part II the book presents concrete examples to demonstrate the kind, nature, and intensity of problems women face in contemporary Muslim societies. The stories generally corroborate Anne Mayer's thesis that Muslim women's predicament is significantly exacerbated by government hypocrisy. The *shari'a* is the shield behind which the political ruler and the fundamentalist leader corroborate to check women's impulse to freedom and equality. In all cases women must endure violence and struggle against odds. The *shari'a*, however, can be used to constrain as well as expand rights, depending on the conditions of the society and the orientation of the political elite. The odds are almost insuperable in a country like Saudi Arabia, the dangers daunting in Pakistan and quite lethal in Algeria and Afghanistan. Nevertheless, everywhere women fight for their rights and in some cases, for example in Jordan, they win.

In Saudi Arabia, Eleanor Abdella Doumato states, positions on human rights in public discussion and official legal opinion are always validated by reference to the *shari'a*. The *shari'a*, however, is in many respects ambiguous, and therefore opposing political, religious, and social views can all be validated with reference to the same body of Islamic law. Similarly, when it comes to women's rights, the *shari'a* can be and is used to constrict rights for women as well as to expand them.

Interpretations of women's rights in the *shari'a* are influenced by cultural understandings about women's limited capabilities and the centrality of women's role in the family. With economic development, mass education, and the intrusion of global media, however, these understandings are changing. Doumato observes that despite growing conservatism in some sectors of society, women's actual achievements in business, arts, and academia are undermining traditional attitudes that allow validation in the *shari'a* of rules limiting women's right to work, drive, travel, study, or dress as they please. Thus, while the negative side of the *shari'a*'s ambiguity is lack of a meaningful standard for human rights, the *shari'a* may also be viewed as flexible, capable of accommodating international standards for human rights when government, religious scholars, and society at large are prepared to accept them.

Shahla Haeri discusses the politically motivated rape of specific women affiliated to the Pakistan People's Party in Karachi in 1991. Haeri argues that 'political rape' is an improvization on the theme of 'feudal honor rape,' and that the target of humiliation and shame is not necessarily a specific woman, but rather a political rival or an old enemy who is to be avenged. Specifically, in these particular cases the target of humiliation and shame was no other than Benazir Bhutto, who was the leader of the opposition in 1991. By raping female members of her party, Benazir Bhutto is 'raped' by association. Haeri suggests that, in its modern context, political rape is tacitly legitimated by the state. The idea is well corroborated by the experience of thousands of refugee women across the world and needs to be studied further in non-refugee conditions in other countries.

Sima Wali highlights the Afghan women refugees' plight as a case study of the causes and conditions of displacement of women in general and Muslim women in particular. She notes that a significant proportion of refugees, both those who have crossed international borders and those who have not, have fled from or sought asylum in Muslim societies, a great majority of them women and their children. Refugee women and children must rely on host countries, the United Nations High Commissioner for Refugees, and the international community for protection. In most cases, however, the protection is either non-existent or in-adequate. In the Muslim world, refugee women and girls suffer doubly – as displaced persons and as women – since male-dominated host countries subject them additionally to repressive social norms and practices. Wali points to the widespread practice of rape as a weapon of war, which supports Haeri's account of rape as a political act. She pleads for further attention by the international community and relevant international organizations to the problems of refugee women and children both in host countries and in the process of return and repatriation.

Karima Bennoune details violence against Algerian women by fundamentalist armed groups during the last seven years. She argues that these attacks did not begin in 1992 with the cancella-tion of the elections, but are rather tied to the fundamentalist social project for Algeria. Bennoune looks also at ways in which women have responded to the campaign against them and how they interpret its meanings. The Algerian situation may be a defining moment for the cause of women across the Middle East. Algerian women had enjoyed rights and had participated widely in Algeria's war of independence and, to a lesser extent, in sub-sequent Algerian politics.

In the last chapter of the volume, Nancy Gallagher discusses Toujan al-Faisal's campaign, and final victory, in the two most recent Jordanian elections. Faisal's story, which Gallagher places in the wider context of feminism, Islamism, and democratization in the Middle East, is encouraging for women everywhere. On 8 November 1989, Jordan held elections for the first time since the imposition of martial law during the June War of 1967. Of the 650 candidates who stood for 80 seats, twelve were women. One of the twelve, a journalist named Toujan al-Faisal, was a prominent women's rights activist noted for her television program which dealt with such topics as child abuse and wife beating. As part of her campaign, she published an article entitled 'They insult us and we elect them' in Jordan's leading newspaper (the article appears in the appendix to this volume). In November 1989 two religious leaders filed charges of apostasy against her. Citing the newspaper article, the plaintiffs asked the Islamic court to charge her with apostasy, to divorce her from her husband, to remove her children from her custody, and to grant immunity to anyone shedding her blood. The case created an enormous controversy which illuminated deep-seated social and cultural conflicts that are gaining in political importance throughout the Muslim world. While the case continued, all twelve women candidates were defeated in the elections. Rather surprisingly, 20 of the Muslim Brothers' 26 candidates were elected, and 12 other fundamentalists were also elected, even to several Christian seats. The case continued into the following year when the *qadi* (judge) of the South Amman Shari'a Court found al-Faisal innocent of all charges. On 8 November 1993, al-Faisal won election to parliament, becoming the first and only woman to serve in parliament in Jordan.

Notes

1. This is in fact the universality/relativity issue translated to the women's human rights/male-dominated Islam controversy. Although culture is usually adduced as the foundation of relativist arguments, the issue is basically political and has to do with control and power. See J. Roland Pennock, 'Rights, Natural Rights, and Human Rights – A General View,' in J. Roland Pennock and John Chapman (eds), *Human Rights: NOMOS 23*, (New York: New York University Press, 1981); Ann Elizabeth Mayer, *Islam and Human Rights: Tradition and Politics* (Boulder: Westview Press, 1991); Deniz Kandiyoti (ed.), *Women, Islam, and the State* (Philadelphia: Temple University Press, 1991).

2. For different interpretations, see Morteza Motahhari, *The Rights of Women in Islam* (Tehran: World Organization of Islamic Services, 1981); John L. Esposito, *Women in Muslim Family Law* (Syracuse: Syracuse University Press, 1982); Fatima Mernissi, *The Veil and the Male Elite: A Feminist Interpretation of Women's Rights in Islam*, trans Mary Joe Lakeland (New York: Addison-Wesley, 1991); Erika Friedl, 'Islam and Tribal Women in a Village

in Iran,' in Nancy E. Auer Falk and Rita M. Gross (eds), *Unspoken Worlds: Women's Religious Lives in Non-Western Cultures* (San Francisco: Wadsworth, 1980), pp. 159–73.

3. There is controversy about the meaning and origin of veiling in Islam. Male conservative tradition relates veiling to Qur'anic injunction (33:33) and also to the need to protect women. Liberal interpretation as well as various women's rights movements connect veiling to non-Arab aristocratic practices among ancient Persians, Romans, and Jews. Furthermore, they hold that the Qur'anic verse relates essentially to the Prophet's wives. Part of the debate is reflected in the chapter by Bouthaina Shaaban and her discussion of Muslim feminist Nazira Zin al-Din. For a discussion of the legal aspects of veil in contemporary Muslim society see Mayer, *op. cit.*, Chapter 6. See also Nawal El-Saadawi, *The Hidden Face of Eve: Women in the Arab World* (Boston: Beacon, 1981).

4. For a general survey of women's multifaceted struggle in the Islamic Republic of Iran see Mahnaz Afkhami and Erika Friedl (eds), *In the Eye of the Storm: Women in Post-revolutionary Iran* (Syracuse: Syracuse University Press, 1994).

5. There is a tendency in academe to identify culture in Muslim societies with Islam as defined by Muslim scholars. The tendency results partly from an intellectual rejection of the colonial experience, which manifests itself as a penchant for identifying traditionalism with authenticity. This leads to the paradox of the Western liberal outlook, seeking to authenticate different cultural 'realities,' ending up supporting reactionary and ahistorical positions in the Muslim world. See for examples Admantia Pollis and Peter Schwab (eds), *Human Rights: Cultural and Ideological Perspectives* (New York: Praeger, 1979) and Fernando Teson, 'International Human Rights and Cultural Relativism,' *Virginia Journal of International Law*, 25 (1985). For a discussion of modern and post-modern ethics see Zygmunt Baumann, *Postmodern Ethics* (Oxford: Blackwell, 1993).

6. This is not only prevalent in statements by Muslim religious and religiopolitical leaders (for example, the 'Draft of the Islamic Constitution' associated with al-Azhar University) but also a part and parcel of modern Muslim fundamentalist constitutions (for example, the constitution of the Islamic Republic of Iran). See, Mayer, *op. cit.*, Chapters 2 and 6.

7. The chapters in this volume attest to this. See also Yvonne Yazbeck Haddad and Ellison Banks Findly (eds), *Women, Religion, and Social Change* (Albany: State University of New York Press, 1985); Guity Nashat (ed.), *Women and Revolution in Iran* (Boulder: Westview Press, 1983); Chandra Talpade Mohanty, Ann Russo, and Lourdes Torres (eds), *Third World Women and the Politics of Feminism* (Bloomington: Indiana University Press, 1991).

8. Increasingly, women are questioning the framework within which Islamic discourse has developed. The primary question is no longer what Islam has said, but who has said what on behalf of Islam and why. Thus,

increasingly, the politics of achieving the right to interpret Islamic text becomes salient.

9. This is related to the women's human rights literacy program now being developed in a number of Muslim societies. The idea received significant support at the Sisterhood Is Global Institute's Dialogue on Religion, Culture, and Women's Human Rights in the Muslim World held in Washington, DC in September of 1994. See the Preface to this volume.

10. This is the most critical matter now. See, among others, the chapters on Algeria and Pakistan in this volume.

11. On the comparison between and interaction of right in its original liberal sense as a property of relationship between state and society and right as circumstances of the individual's relations to social groups and institutions see Gholam Reza Afkhami, 'Ideology and Genealogy in Civil Society Discourse: A Query About Some Structural Determinants of a Civil Polity in Modern Iran,' paper presented at MESA, October 1994, Phoenix, Arizona, to be published in *Iran Nameh*, 1995. See also Michel Foucault, 'Two Lectures,' in Colin Gordon (ed.), *Power/Knowledge: Selected Interviews and Other Writings, 1972–1977* (New York: Pantheon Books, 1980), pp. 78–108. By right in its elemental form I mean relative absence of religious or secular legal fetters. In most Muslim societies, women have achieved rights usually as part of government's modernization efforts. That is why anti-modernist movements are usually anti-feminist.

12. The clearest example here is that of Taslima Nasrin of Bangladesh. The problem is that once one is accused of being against Islam all possibilities of dialogue end. Furthermore, for the majority of women who seek rights, to be branded anti-Islamic is psychologically unbearable. That is why positions advocated by contemporary Iranian 'Islamist' philosopher Abdul-Karim Sorush, who maintains that Islam is essentially a personal religion and will affect the political process through the activities of individual Muslims rather than actions of formalized Islamic government, and by Abdullahi An-Na'im, whose article appears in this volume, are so attractive. See Abdullahi An-Na'im, *Toward an Islamic Reformation: Civil Liberties, Human Rights and International Law* (Syracuse: Syracuse University Press, 1990).

13. See Charles Taylor, *Sources of the Self: the Making of the Modern Identity* (Cambridge: Harvard University Press, 1989).

14. In an article in *Foreign Affairs*, Charles Maier identifies the malaise that currently afflicts public opinion in the countries of Europe, in Japan, and in North America (p. 48) as a 'moral crisis' (p. 51). 'The diagnosis of moral crisis,' he suggests, 'is highly self-reflective ... . Still one can go beyond cultural commentary to discern a profound shift of public attitude along three dimensions: a sudden sense of historical dislocation, a disaffection with the political leadership of all parties, and a recurring skepticism about doctrines of social progress. Each of these developments tend to entail the others such that they hang together as a whole' (p. 54).

'Democracy and Its Discontents,' *Foreign Affairs* (July/August 1994), pp. 48–64.

This diagnosis is largely applicable to the moral crisis in the South as well. The problem with fundamentalism is not, therefore, that it identifies malaise; it is, rather, that it prescribes ahistorical and, worse, antihistorical remedies.

15. The earliest *hadith*, or traditions, date back to the second century Islam. Although *hadith* as a discourse has its strict rules and methods, these are internal to it, that is, they have developed over the years to admit or reject statements about actions and statements of the Prophet, and in the Shi'a's case *Imams*, as determined by Muslim patriarchy. Muslim women have begun to question systematically the validity of the foundation of the *hadith*. For a concise account of the *hadith* see J. Robson's article in the *Encyclopedia of Islam*, III (Leiden: E. J. Brill, 1971), pp. 23–8.

16. In *In the Eye of the Storm, op. cit.*, I have discussed this concept as 'global feminism' and 'global feminist discourse.' See pp. 15–18.

17. The similarity in women's condition across history and the globe has been noted by most observers. See, for example, Arvind Sharma (ed.), *Women in World Religions* (Albany: State University of New York Press, 1987).

18. The first target of any empowering strategy should be the large numbers of Muslim women who have systematically penetrated potential positions of power in Muslim societies. An important example of this phenomenon is the increasing proportion of women in learning and teaching institutions. According to UNESCO statistics, women constituted 27 per cent of faculty in Egypt in 1988, higher than in France (24 per cent) and in the USA (24 per cent). The 1993 Human Rights Report states the percentage of women in technical and scientific fields as 43 per cent for Kuwait, 24 per cent for Syria, 31 per cent for Saudi Arabia, 28 per cent for Iraq, 24 per cent for Tunisia, 31 per cent for Algeria, 25 per cent for Morocco, 26 per cent for Egypt, and finally 27 per cent for Sudan. As this chapter is being completed (April 1995), in Turkey, Bangladesh, and Pakistan prime ministers are women, despite an increasingly vocal and transparent anti-woman politics.

19. The problem of Third World women's lack of access to international discourse on the future of women and women's human rights in the Third World was hotly debated at SIGI's Washington Dialogue in September 1994. The consensus was that steps should be taken to energize Third World women to demand more participation. Just as importantly, it was essential that women from the North who had the means and the know-how be made conscious of the need for significant participation by non-Western women, and to help facilitate it.

ONE

Women, Islam and Patriarchy

Reflections on the Politics of Gender in Muslim Societies: From Nairobi to Beijing

Deniz Kandiyoti

The decade that separates the United Nations Conferences on Women in Nairobi and Beijing has witnessed significant changes in thinking about human rights, with serious implications for women's rights. The first UN conference held in Mexico City in 1975 initiated a period of vigorous documentation of 'gender gaps' – in education, labor force participation, income and welfare, political and legal rights – with the explicit assumption that their elimination was a self-evident goal and that the end of the decade would be a time for stock-taking and, hopefully, self-congratulation. The 1985 Nairobi conference was also set against a developmentalist discourse which presented the achievement of parity between genders both as a lever in the fight against absolute poverty and as a distributional and human rights issue.

In the intervening period, the climate of debate was substantially modified under the impact of a complex set of global influences. In the South, the national development rhetoric of post-colonial states appeared increasingly threadbare in the face of persistent legitimacy crises and endemic economic failure. This both coincided with and stimulated a questioning of the premises and paradigms upon which notions of development and social progress are based.[1] The critique of universal narratives about social transformation – namely, modernization theory and Marxist-inspired social theory – was partly indebted to the post-structuralist turn in the social sciences which denounced not only the narrowly Western epistemological foundations of such discourses but their implication in projects of colonial domination and social engineering. This critique of modernity found echoes in a parallel body of feminist criticism which revealed the gender-biased and masculinist premises of universalist discourses about rights and citizenship in the West.[2] An affinity thus developed between post-colonial scholarship and feminist criticism in so far

as they focus on processes of exclusion and domination implicit in
the construction of the 'universal' subject.[3]

One of the by-products of this conjuncture was that the universal doctrine of human rights came under increasing attack. Indeed,
the notion of human rights itself could be identified by some as
an item of Western imperialism whereby culturally specific, Western notions of individual and society were being thrust upon
essentially different societies and polities. The debates among legal
scholars on the implications of universalist versus cultural relativist
positions for the understanding and practice of human rights
cannot be dealt with in the context of this paper.[4] What will
concern me more particularly here is that the areas of social life
singled out as privileged sites of cultural distinctiveness and identity
are, quite consistently, the family, gender relations, and women's
status. Whilst such discourses about cultural identity have a vener-
able historical pedigree,[5] current post-modernist critiques of state-
led projects of modernization and their authoritarian elitisms have
lent them a new salience and urgency. This is therefore an area
of concern for feminists trying to formulate an agenda for women's
rights centered around the necessity to accommodate diversity and
difference without undermining the legal and ethical grounds upon
which the right to difference itself can continue to be upheld. It
is more than an academic concern in countries where actual or
aspiring political regimes claim the right to define the boundaries
of the socially permissible and claim to do so in the name of a
higher religious/moral authority. The discussion to follow will
therefore concentrate on clarifying some of the central assumptions
behind ongoing debates about Muslim women's rights and probing
into some of their analytic limitations.

Revisiting an Old Debate

Contestations over gender relations, the family, and women's rights
are by no means new to the politics of Muslim societies. Such
debates have tended to gain momentum at defining moments of
history, such as periods of social reform or nationalist awakening,
and to form a central ingredient of struggles over political legitimacy. Something akin to a conventional wisdom concerning the
centrality of the 'woman question' to the politics of Muslim
societies has gradually developed. It is based on the premise that
the emphasis on Islamic forms of regulation, such as the spatial

segregation and veiling of women, has been exacerbated as a result
of encounters between Muslim societies and an imperialistic West.
The identification of Muslim women as the bearers of the 'back-
wardness' of their societies, initially by colonial administrators and
later by Western-oriented reformers, is mirrored by a reactive local
discourse which elevates the same practices into symbols of cultural
authenticity and integrity.[6] Attitudes towards modernizing local
elites often display considerable ambiguity. Such elites are frequently denied autonomous agency or forms of subjectivity that
are not a direct expression of their mimetic involvement with the
West. Their alienation from the masses they seek to modernize
inevitably means that processes of social mobility set in motion by
national development must bring to the fore a society intent upon
regaining a lost Islamic authenticity, a sort of 'return of the
repressed.' The privileged sites for such assertions of authenticity
are, once again, the dress and deportment of women.

I felt it was important to inject some historical content into this
schematic trope through a detailed examination of processes of
post-colonial state formation and analyses of specific nationalisms.[7]
This was meant, in part, to restore heterogeneity to the unhelpful
category of 'Muslim societies' which in fact span a wide variety of
political regimes, economic systems, and diverse histories of the
relationships between state, society, and imperial powers. From
this perspective, wherever the political will existed, the reform of
the family and the emancipation of women appeared primarily as
the accompaniment of the rise of the modern nation state and the
drive to create a uniform, modern citizenry that could be redefined
in terms of their allegiance to the 'nation' rather than particular-
istic ties of religion, community and ethnicity. Women's emancipation potentially could result in confronting the interests of local
patriarchs, be they tribal chiefs, village elders, or religious special-
ists, and could be used to undermine alternative foci of influence
and resistance confronting the state. There is no doubt that notions
of modern nationhood subordinated and often sought to destroy
alternative bases of solidarity and identity, with the rule of majority
communities and *dirigiste* regimes masquerading as secularism.
Nonetheless, the drive towards mass education, the creation of
local cadres, and national mobilization for development were
framed in ways that included women in novel ways, both rhet-
orically and in actual practice.

It is important to acknowledge that the relationship between

Islam and women's rights has been and remains politically contingent. Turkey's brand of cultural nationalism, for instance, propitiated a break with *shari'a* law which made formal emancipation possible as early as the 1930s. Pakistan's invocation of Islam as the *raison d'être* of the state may not have secured national unity and avoided the break with Bangladesh but it did ensure that the question of women's rights could only be debated within the confines of the *shari'a*. Likewise, throughout the Arab world, despite significant variations in actual codes, the legal equality granted to women under national constitutions is circumscribed by *shari'a*-derived personal status legislation privileging men in the areas of marriage, divorce, child custody, maintenance, and inheritance rights. As a result, many Muslim countries which have ratified the UN Convention on the Elimination of All Forms of Discrimination Against Women (CEDAW) have done so with multiple reservations since their personal status codes clearly contravene the Convention.[8] Women's claims upon the universal realm of full citizenship thus remained tenuous and fragile and could easily be sacrificed or clawed back in the name of cultural or national integrity. This is nowhere more apparent than in the Islamic Republic of Iran where Islamist women activists are still striving to recapture the ground lost since the Family Protection Law of 1975.[9] Examples abound of the non-enforcement of existing legislation protecting women's rights, in deference to communal norms, or of governments manipulating women's rights issues in opportunistic ways in order to placate internal constituencies or to posture in international forums.[10]

The initial spate of official policies geared to changing women's status in the family and the workforce generally coincided with a phase of state-led economic growth which involved the rapid expansion of locally trained cadres and public sector employment. The rhetoric of women's emancipation was invariably couched in terms of enlisting women into the national development efforts and mobilizing 'idle capacity' (sometimes quite literally, with male reformers berating women's assumed idleness or their general inadequacy as the educators of a new patriotic generation). There was undoubtedly a further ideological pay-off, namely the vision of a 'modern' nation where women's emancipation could be used to signal social progress. In any event, women's visibility in urban employment and civic life increased substantially. The post-independence era seemed to herald a period of steady expansion of women's rights even though the gains achieved were initially restricted to relatively narrow segments of the urban middle classes. Processes of social change, involving internal and international migration, produced new patterns of social mobility which rapidly changed the social and cultural landscape, with profound political consequences. Continuing ties of economic dependence and imperialist meddling in regional politics and conflicts meant that the initial discourse of national autonomy rang increasingly hollow. More recently, the economic liberalization measures advocated by the World Bank and the IMF since the 1980s have been accompanied by a significant redefinition in policy priorities: a decrease in state control over the economy, extended access to private enterprise and foreign investment, and an emphasis on export-led strategies of development.

The gender effects of such policies have been variable, ranging from calls for increased female domesticity in Egypt to a significant expansion in female employment in Tunisia. In all cases, however, economic crises set the scene for contradictory pressures with unsettling implications for gender relations; on the one hand soaring rates of male unemployment put pressure on labor markets while high rates of inflation mandated that ever larger numbers of women engage in income-earning activities to ensure the survival of their households. The ideal enshrined in *shari'a* law, that men be the sole providers thus enabling women to devote themselves exclusively to domestic tasks, became unattainable for all but the wealthiest strata where, paradoxically, women were also likeliest to have received higher education and entered prestigious professions. Mernissi notes some of the sociological indicators of these transformations: much higher average ages of marriage for both men and women, a great deal more economic insecurity for the majority of men, and an emphasis on women's education as they increasingly feel they have to fend for themselves.[11] She contends that this new landscape forms part of the conjuncture of forces that fuels fundamentalist appeals for the containment of 'trespassing' women. More generally, it must be noted that the failed promises of post-independence developmentalism could be interpreted not as mere technical failures but as moral failures requiring a complete overhaul of the world views underpinning them. It is against this background that some oppositional movements have been advocating a 'just' Islamic order, invoking notions of authentic Muslim womanhood as part of a broader critique of

Westernization and consumerism. The area of gender relations, which was always at the centre of debates about identity, emerged as an arena for renewed political contestation but in a context quite different from the era of nation building, involving a complicated set of new local and international players. In what follows, I will attempt to address the interplay between the global and the local and analyse some of its contradictory consequences.

Global Agendas, Local Responses

Since the 1970s, the framework for policy interventions affecting women and local women's movements has been shaped not only by domestic considerations but by an increasingly complex set of international influences.[12] One of the more paradoxical phenomena has been the creation of local machineries in most countries of the Middle East, North Africa and South Asia to channel international development funds into projects purportedly designed to have empowering consequences for women against a background of growing conservatism concerning their appropriate roles. For instance, in Pakistan the establishment of a Women's Division as part of the Cabinet Secretariat to safeguard women's interests and promote development programs coincided with the passage of discriminatory Islamization laws under Zia ul-Haq.[13] Likewise, in Bangladesh, successive governments performed a balancing act between the conflicting gender ideologies implicit in different aid packages: the development projects promoted by Western donors encouraged women's participation in the labor force and public life, while aid from oil-rich Muslim countries strengthened the *madrasas* and the pro-religious parties advocating stricter controls on women.[14] There is little doubt that the flow of migration to the oil-rich countries of the Gulf, and the reverse flow of cash and political influence, left its imprint on the polities of many countries, serving to strengthen the cultural and political prominence of local forces and parties with Islamist platforms. It is also the case that a wide array of regimes reached various accommodations with selected Islamist constituencies as a means of checking liberal and left-leaning political forces, of enhancing their legitimacy or upstaging more radical Islamist platforms.

On the other hand, an international 'women in development' lobby has been exerting pressure on national governments to recognize the role of women in combating poverty, illiteracy, and high birth rates ever since the International Women's Year in 1975 and the subsequent United Nations Decade for Women. Monitoring bureaucracies have been set up within the US Agency for International Development and within the foreign aid departments of the main European and Scandinavian donor nations. Private foundations have also played a prominent role in setting the agenda for research and policy intervention. The 'official' feminist rhetoric that had been the hallmark of the modernizing, post-independence state has now been appropriated by supranational bodies with contradictory effects at the local level.

However, these contradictions may be merely apparent. Donor governments and agencies attempt to harness women directly to their vision of a more effective, though not necessarily more equitable, international economic order. The very manner in which indebted countries facing the rigors of IMF-imposed reforms are integrated into that order encourages political disaffection. The policies adopted have often led to more visible disparities in wealth, higher unemployment and prices and fewer social services fuelling widespread resentment and discontent, often in the absence of adequate democratic channels of expression. The legitimacy crises engendered by these processes have favored the rise of organized oppositional movements with Islamist platforms, as well as attempts at social control by governments emphasizing their own commitment to orthodoxy.

The role of non-governmental organizations and transnational social actors in serving as conduits for funds, expertise, and lobbying capacity has yet to receive systematic attention despite its growing importance. At a time when liberalization policies have led to the retreat of the state from important areas of service delivery, especially in the health and education sectors, other actors are rapidly filling the vacuum. It seems premature to hail these developments as the harbingers of democratization and a more robust civil society. The heterogeneity of sources of funding and support, from local networks to foreign aid donors to transnational religious movements, and the diversity of the aims pursued make any simple equation between the emergence of new forms of association and greater pluralism highly problematic. Islamic associations have been attempting quite successfully to broaden their base of support by extending educational and welfare services to deprived communities, services rendered especially valuable in the absence of adequate state provision. These welfare activities constitute a solid material base from which to establish ties of patronage and networks of loyalty and influence. Groups pressing for an extension of civil liberties and women's rights typically have far fewer resources and a much lower penetrative capacity. Secular women's groups have mainly been operating in the interstices of domestic and international power structures and trying to exploit their contradictions. The Women's Action Forum in Pakistan, for instance, attempted to resist Zia's Islamization policies by invoking their un-Islamic nature and appealed to some progressive *ulama* to endorse their position. Feminists in Turkey used the ratification of the proposals of the United Nations Forum in Nairobi in 1985 by the Turkish government as the occasion for a campaign to eliminate the remaining discriminatory clauses of the Turkish civil code. In Egypt, women's groups put pressure on the government to reconsider the cancellation of the 1979 decree law revising personal status and giving women greater equality just before the Egyptian delegation was due to attend the Nairobi Forum in 1985. The existence of international solidarity networks such as Women Living Under Muslim Laws is evidence of a serious attempt to form linkages cutting across diverse contexts.[15] Although these are limited forms of action, they denote the presence of constituencies which are able to mobilize and enter into pragmatic alliances at both local and international levels.

However, the question of alliances remains a vexed one for women's movements since these range from secular feminists, who see women's emancipation as wholly incompatible with Islamic law, to groups trying to articulate indigenous forms of gender activism within a reinterpreted Islamic framework, to committed Islamist women who fully endorse the dictates of the *shari'a*. The discursive possibilities and the range of alliances available to women's groups are necessarily constrained by the type of regime they live under, as are their possibilities of organizing outside direct government sponsorship. Thus, in countries where Islamization is state-sponsored and a secular democratic alternative does not appear likely, ameliorative and reformist action within an Islamic framework is the only avenue for women seeking to press their demands. The choices are far more complex in countries such as Turkey or Egypt, where Islamist platforms may present themselves as one of the democratic alternatives and may elicit substantial support from an active female constituency. Secular feminists may be torn between their motivation to protect their hard-won civil

rights, on the one hand, and their recognition, on the other, that
some of their Islamist sisters are responding, albeit in a different
manner, to the pressures and constraints imposed by a society
where habits of heterosocial interaction are weak, at best, and
mostly fraught with tension.

These tensions are well exemplified by a debate in Turkey some
years ago over whether the municipality of Istanbul should run
women-only buses. This demand was put forward by Islamist
women, in the name of Muslim etiquette, but found favour among
some secular feminists longing to travel in peace, whereas others
could not condone a return to the days of enforced segregation.
It is interesting to note the recognition of a common predicament
among women whose lifestyles mandate exposure to public places
and daily interaction with unrelated men. It has thus been argued
that part of the interest in veiling is closely related to new patterns
of female mobility for an educated generation whose mothers
normally would have been bound to home and neighborhood.[16]
This is not to suggest that this option, when translated into
activism, may not be harnessed to the furtherance of a political
project which has as its ultimate aim the capture of the state. It
is in this sense that some Islamist women's identities[17] should not
be confused with the myriad of sub-cultural identities on display
in post-industrial societies as statements of lifestyle preference and
personal inclination. Such confusion was inadvertently encouraged
by the turn feminist theories took since the late 1980s, in the
context of debates over multiculturalism in the West. I shall now
turn my attention to these developments with the tentative suggestion that discourses, like wines, do not necessarily travel well.

Post-modernism, Multiculturalism
and Muslim Women's Rights

The appropriation of post-structuralist and post-modernist ideas
by feminists produced some contradictory outcomes.[18] On the one
hand, the demise of grand narratives accounting for the subordination of women, and the questioning of 'women' as a unitary
category sharing a common oppression, opened the way to more
context-dependent and historically sensitive analyses, as well as a
more refined understanding of coalition building. On the other
hand, these developments fostered a new relativism under the
rubric of 'difference' which could, at times, take uncritical or

unprincipled forms. This reorientation in feminist theory derived primarily from an internal critique originating in the West. In the United States, white, middle-class feminism came under attack for displaying racist and ethnocentric tendencies, obliterating the experiences of women of different class/ethnic/racial backgrounds and sexual orientation. In Europe, this critique coincided with demands by non-European migrants and ethnic minorities for their rights to cultural distinctiveness, and was punctuated by events such as the Salman Rushdie affair in England and the *foulard* debate in France. Policies of multiculturalism and identity politics in the West thus had a direct impact on feminist theorizing which has not been without consequence for feminist scholars and activists elsewhere.

The multiculturalism debate in the West was, in principle, based upon a recognition of the internal heterogeneity of modern societies and the necessity of accommodating difference within democratic polities. Multiculturalist policies, however, have not been without their paradoxes. In the case of Britain, Saghal and Yuval-Davis have argued that while aiming to legitimize the heterogeneity of national culture some policies have ended up creating a space for the development of movements which seek to impose homogeneity and uniformity on their adherents, particularly on women who are invited to comply with the strictures of their communities.[19] Lazreg suggests that in the United States terms such as 'women of color' paradoxically re-inscribe the very social relations they purport to combat.[20] Women themselves may be enthusiastic participants in the search for a new identity which they feel confers on them greater dignity in a racist society, or may resist what they perceive as attempts to disempower them. In either case, the capture of the terrain upon which claims to cultural authenticity and representational legitimacy are built passes through an intensely political process which empowers certain categories of people as cultural brokers and marginalizes others. This is not only true of minority communities, but has parallels in mainstream politics where, for instance, the electoral victory of the 'pro-life', familistic new Right in the United States would almost certainly have consequences for women.[21]

I would like to suggest here, nonetheless, that debates about multiculturalism and identity politics in the West have sometimes been inappropriately transposed to other contexts. Indeed, any parallels between the accommodation of Muslim minorities in the democracies of the West, where they do not represent a hegemonic threat,[22] and of Islamist movements in the Middle East and North Africa, where they do, can be quite misleading. As Zubaida rightly points out, dialogue and mutual accommodation can only proceed under conditions of freedom of expression and association,[23] conditions which are noticeably absent in the region. The right of Muslim women in Bradford to veil and to attend religious schools, even with the support of public funds, does not deprive any other sections of the community of the possibility of making different choices. In the Middle East and North Africa, where Islamist movements can and have made bids for alternative state projects, it is the choices and rights of all women that are affected, whether they subscribe to an Islamist world view or not. What is at stake, therefore, is not a choice of lifestyle or freedom of worship, but the conditions for the existence of a pluralist polity, which some movements freely admit they have no interest in. The position of purportedly secularist governments is seriously weakened in the face of opposition by the fact that their own democratic credentials often leave much to be desired and their human rights record is unenviable. This, however, does not make their oppositions, which partake in the same political culture, necessarily more democratic or pluralistic. This is a conjuncture which serves to deepen the conundrum of those interested in developing feminist agendas as part and parcel of an ongoing struggle for democracy.[24]

Scholars doing micro-level studies on Islamist women and their movements have performed a crucial service by recognizing their capacity for agency and interpreting their strategies as alternative forms of gender activism. However, exploring the motivations of individual social actors or discrete social movements does not, in and of itself, exhaust the task of social analysis or absolve us from the necessity of making any further judgements about the nature of the more global political contexts in which such strategies are enacted. Ultimately, it is only through such detailed, context-dependent analyses that we will arrive at a better understanding of which sorts of coalitions and alliances are likely to maximize room for manoeuvre and ensure the broadest representation of women's interests, and which, on the contrary, are not. It is also the only way we can hope to avoid the dual pitfalls of both ethnocentrism and unprincipled relativism, and work with integrity towards a conception of women's rights that does not 'give hostages to fortune, to prevarications and amendments following political and doctrinal pressures.'[25]

Notes

Acknowledgements. Special thanks are due to Mervat Hatem for her thoughtful comments on the first draft of this paper and for engaging in a stimulating scholarly dialogue which enriched me. I am also grateful to Michael Anderson for pointing me in the direction of the legal scholarship on human rights, and Mahnaz Afkhami for her persistent encouragement to pursue the topic.

1. There is a vast critical literature on this subject. See for example S. and F. Marglin (eds), *Dominating Knowledge: Development, Culture and Resistance* (Oxford: Clarendon Press, 1990); M. Hobart (ed.), *An Anthropological Critique of Development* (London: Routledge, 1993).

2. As a classic example see Carol Pateman, *The Sexual Contract* (Oxford: Polity Press, 1988).

3. For a selection of such perspectives see Patrick William and Laura Chrisman (eds), *Colonial Discourse and Post-colonial Theory* (London: Harvester Wheatsheaf, 1993).

4. See for instance A. Pollis and P. Schwab (eds), *Human Rights: Cultural and Ideological Perspectives* (New York: Praeger, 1979), A. Dundes Renteln, *International Human Rights: Universalism versus Relativism* (Newbury Park, California: Sage, 1990). More specifically on the Middle East: Kevin Dwyer, 'Universal Visions, Communal Visions: Human Rights and Traditions,' *Peuples Méditerranéens* , 58–59 (1992), pp. 205–20. For an overview of the implications of the debate for women's rights see Annie Bunting, 'Theorizing Women's Cultural Diversity in Feminist International Human Rights Strategies,' in Anne Bottomley and Joanne Conaghan (eds), *Feminist Theory and Legal Strategy* (Oxford: Blackwell, 1993).

5. Deniz Kandiyoti, 'Identity and its Discontents: Women and the Nation,' *Millennium*, 20, 3 (1991), pp. 429–43.

6. See for example Leila Ahmed, *Women and Gender in Islam* (New Haven and London: Yale University Press, 1992).

7. Deniz Kandiyoti (ed.), *Women, Islam and the State* (London: Macmillan, 1991).

8. For a full discussion of Muslim countries' positions *vis-à-vis* CEDAW, see Ann Elizabeth Mayer's contribution in this volume.

9. Parvin Paidar, 'Feminism and Islam in Iran,' in D. Kandiyoti (ed.), *Gendering the Middle East* (London: I.B. Tauris, forthcoming).

10. A particularly detailed and pertinent account of the latter may be found in Hatem's examination of the trajectory of Egyptian legislation on personal status from 1979 to 1985. Mervat Hatem, 'Economic and Political

Liberalization in Egypt and the Demise of State Feminism,' *International Journal of Middle East Studies,* 24 (1992), pp. 464–85.

11. Fatima Mernissi, 'Muslim Women and Fundamentalism,' *Middle East Report,* 153, (July–August 1988), pp. 8–11.

12. Kathleen Newland, 'From Transnational Relationships to International Relations: Women in Development and the International Decade for Women,' in Rebecca Grant and Kathleen Newland (eds), *Gender and International Relations* (Milton Keynes: Open University Press, 1991).

13. Ayesha Jalal, 'The Convenience of Subservience: Women and the State in Pakistan,' in D. Kandiyoti (ed.), *Women, Islam and the State.*

14. Naila Kabeer, 'The Quest for National Identity: Women, Islam and the State in Bangladesh,' in D. Kandiyoti (ed.), *Women, Islam and the State.*

15. Farida Shaheed, 'Controlled or Autonomous: Identity and the Experience of the Network Women Living Under Muslim Laws,' *Signs,* 19, 4 (1994), pp. 997–1019.

16. See for instance Fadwa el Guindy, 'Veiling *Infitah* with a Muslim Ethic: Egypt's contemporary Islamic Movement,' *Social Problems* 8 (1981), pp. 464–85; Arlene E. Macleod, *Accommodating Protest: Women, the new Veiling and Change in Cairo* (New York: Columbia University Press, 1991); also Leila Ahmed, *Women and Gender in Islam;* Nilufer Gole, *Modern Mahrem* (Istanbul: Metis Yayinlari, 1991); Aynur Ilayasoglu, *Ortulu Kimlik* (Istanbul: Metis Yayinalri, 1994).

17. The term 'some' is used advisedly here since this author is of the opinion that veiling can have different meanings and finalities in different contexts and among different generations and strata. For further elaboration of this point in the Egyptian context see Hatem, 'Economic and Political Liberalization.'

18. It must be noted that the implications of the post-modern turn for feminist politics is a matter of continuing controversy. See Nancy Harstock, 'Rethinking Modernism: Minority vs. Majority Theories', *Cultural Critique,* 7 (1987), pp. 187–206 and Judith Butler and Joan W. Scott (eds), *Feminists Theorize the Political* (New York and London: Routledge, 1992) for opposing views.

19. Gita Saghal and Nira Yuval-Davis (eds), *Refusing Holy Orders: Women and Fundamentalism in Britain* (London: Virago, 1992).

20. Marnia Lazreg, *The Eloquence of Silence* (New York and London: Routledge, 1994).

21. In this respect, Bunting quite rightly points out that essentializing and homogenizing the West does the same sort of disservice as stereotyping the Third World. (Bunting, 'Theorizing Women's Cultural Diversity.') Ann Elizabeth Mayer, in this volume, illustrates this point well with reference to US politics and suggests that trans-national anti-feminist alliances involving the Vatican, Muslim fundamentalists and the new Right are not inconceivable, although they cut across cultures and faiths.

22. These accommodations have been far from perfect and it is plain that the cultural entrenchment of minority communities is in no small measure due to the racism of host countries. This, in turn, exerts a destabilizing influence on host societies by increasing support for extreme right-wing political forces and racist platforms. These, however, have not yet acquired followings of a magnitude that could modify the nature of their political regimes.

23. Sami Zubaida,'Human Rights and Cultural Difference: Middle Eastern Perpectives,' *New Perspectives on Turkey*, 10 (Spring 1994), pp. 1–12.

24. I am particularly impressed by the fact that it is in the Middle East and North Africa that feminism is presented as one of the most powerful antidotes to deep-seated authoritarian tendencies in political culture. This is quite explicitly stated in the work of Fatima Mernissi, *Islam and Democracy: Fear of the Modern World* (London: Virago, 1993) and Hisham Sharabi (ed.), *Theory, Politics and the Arab World* (London: Routledge, 1990).

25. Sami Zubaida, 'Human Rights and Cultural Difference,' p. 11.

3

Arab Women's Rights and the Muslim State in the Twenty-first Century: Reflections on Islam as Religion and State[1]

Fatima Mernissi

Few words in contemporary political and ideological lexicons have been as misused, and abused, as 'Islam' by both Muslims and non-Muslims alike. The term, meaning peace and submission, now invokes images of violence, totalitarianism, and irrationality. Speculation on the chances for peace in the Middle East usually centers on an embarrassingly racist question: are Islam and democracy compatible? The question is racist not only because it reduces a set of complex, multifaceted, and global contradictions between Muslim and Western states to an opposition between a medieval *religion* and a modern political system, but also because when a Westerner asks such a question, he automatically assigns rationality to democracy and irrationality to Islam.[2] This approach is wrong for a variety of reasons, one of which is that it creates 1.2 billion potential enemies, more or less the number of Muslims living in the world today.

Creating enemies in such massive numbers is suspiciously warlike, belonging more in the realm of irrationality than cold analysis. Samuel Huntington, Ernest Gellner, and some other Western intellectual leaders and Islamic experts have come close to this kind of unreasonable bellicosity by producing putative 'scientific' and 'philosophical' grounds that encourage crusade-like trends in Western academic circles at a time when right-wing attacks in Western streets and parliaments have made Muslim migrant workers easy targets of violence.[3] It seems to me that we need to reformulate the question of Islam and democracy away from political violence and racist overtones and closer to the realm of reason. The first step is to compare what is logically comparable: liberal democracy and the Muslim state as forms of government, rather than liberal democracy and Islam as culture or religion.

The Nature of the Muslim State

What is the nature of the Muslim state? Is the Muslim state rational? Is it theocratic? Is the Muslim ruler's authority divine like that of the Christian Church? If it is, the Muslim state will be irremediably irrational. Montesquieu, for example, maintained that the Muslim despot's authority was divine. 'Dans les empires Mahometans,' says Montesquieu, 'c'est de la religion que les peuples tirent en partie le respect étonnant qu'ils on pour leur prince ... . Dans le gouvernement despotique, le pouvoir passe tout entier dans les main de celui à qui on le confie. Le visir est le despote lui-même; et chaque officier particulier est le visir.'[4]

If we believe that the Muslim ruler, Montesquieu's model of the 'oriental despot,' had divine authority, then how do we explain that when medieval Europe was marked by widespread ignorance and intellectual stagnation, science flourished in the Muslim territories, whence it was exported to Christendom as strange, heretical ideas like those of Averroes (d. 1198) who, among other things, demonstrated rationally that no after-life was possible.[5] Whatever the Muslim political system, its nature was different from the Church. According to Montgomery Watt, 'by the 11th and 12th centuries much Greek science had been assimilated, the great Islamic scholars, thinkers and scientists had reached the highest spheres of intellectual life, and were superior to the intellectuals of Christendom at that period.'[6] How can we explain also that while for centuries the Christian Church practiced religious inquisition as an official policy, Muslim states resorted to it only exceptionally? Official Muslim inquisition, such as the persecution of the zendiq (heretic) by the Abbasid Caliph al Mahdi in 780/163, is rare in Muslim history and stands out as an anomaly.[7] Furthermore, if a Muslim ruler's authority is divine, why would Khomeini declare 'his' Iran a republic as soon as he gained power? How can we explain that Algerian fundamentalists justify their claim to power today by their electoral success in the early 1990s? If the Islamic power is divine, why do modern politicians need elections, an evidently Western institution, while they are preaching that the West is the corrupting devil itself?

This idea of a God-like Oriental despot, so central to the development of Western ideas of liberal democracy, has been identified by many as the source of confusion in the West about Islam, particularly as Islam is associated with irrational government and fatalistic and submissive believers. In *Structure du sérail: la fiction du despotisme asiatique dans l'occident classique*, Alain Grosrichard shows how Montesquieu created his 'oriental' phantasm, not only in the literary *Lettres Persanes* but also in the magisterial *Esprit des Lois*, because he needed 'his' oriental despot to be like a God so that he could see clearly what form of government would help Europeans free themselves.[8] In her introduction to *Western Republicanism and the Oriental Prince*, Patricia Springborg points to the extent of the confusion that existed about Islamic institutions among such key figures of Western political thought as Max Weber and Karl Marx.[9] 'It is worth pointing out,' remarks Springborg,

> that each of the instances Max Weber gives in his Preface to *The Protestant Ethic and the Spirit of Capitalism* for the administrative, scientific, and technical superiority of the West over the East is erroneous ... . On the subject of the compilation and dissemination of knowledge, Weber claims that Western universities are superior to those of China and Islam, 'superficially similar,' but lacking 'the rational, systematic, and specialized pursuit of sciences with trained and specialized personnel' – he neglects to point out that Islamic universities like al-Azhar were older than those of the West, which did not begin life as scientific institutes either.[10]

The identification of Islam with 'oriental despotism' in Western discourse may be studied and disposed of by examining Montesquieu's question: is the Muslim ruler's authority divine? If it is, secularization, that is rationalization of decision making, is impossible; and the war between liberal democracies and the East, as well as other calamities Huntington predicts for the twenty-first century, becomes nearly unavoidable. But if it is not, if the ruler's authority is secular, we are then left with a puzzle: why do Muslim rulers and their militant Islamic opposition both claim religion as their base and source of legitimacy? The answer, I suggest, is that because the Muslim ruler's authority is inherently secular, he is not threatened by science, but by pluralism. Because his legitimacy rests on this earth and his ability to serve the Muslim *umma*'s practical interests, he can monopolize power only if he creates the fiction that his 'will' coincides with the *umma*'s. He needs therefore to coax the people into believing that the *umma* is homogeneous. The concocted homogeneity, however, comes into conflict with the real, actual, and concrete socio-economic groups: women;

religious, racial, and ethnic minorities; and others whose interests are contradictory, and whom the ruler tries to veil and silence with whatever means he has or can mobilize. But the Muslim ruler has a problem: he can sustain the fiction of a homogeneous *umma* only by negating the reality of the conflict, which leaves him only one practical device: the political suppression of dissent in the community.

The Law and the Muslim State

The Muslim state cannot perform as a world power because, needing the fiction of homogeneity, it can neither allow free initiative among citizens nor mobilize their creative energies. Caught in this dilemma, the frustrated citizens, for their part, dream of Harun al-Rashid's 'efficient Muslim state,' because their desired model is that of a ruler who competes with the Roman emperor and wins. Thus, whereas pluralism is the Muslims' only hope for facing the challenges of a ferociously competitive global market, Muslim state and society collude to produce increasingly monistic structural forms and social conditions. On the other hand, the competitive impulse pushes the citizen and state each to seek rational ways of solving their problems by self-empowerment, which is an eminently modern and rational quest.

If we define *irrationality* as basically the intolerant behavior of a person or a system that believes in 'certainty,' thinks there is only one truth and therefore those who think otherwise ought to be suppressed, and hence rejects pluralism, *rationality* then may be defined as the opposite. Rationality is to accept conflict as the philosophical foundation of society, and to adhere to what Ralph Dahrendorf calls the ethics of uncertainty: 'The ethics of uncertainty are the ethics of liberty, and the ethics of liberty are the ethics of conflict, of antagonism generated and institutionalized.'[11] Rationally, we must assume that some Western citizens and institutions identify their interests and act on them irrationally, if interests and actions are examined in the light of liberal standards of rationality. To assume otherwise is to eliminate the 'uncertainty' principle, which comes uncannily close to a Muslim *imam*'s *fatwa*. We hear daily about all kinds of Mafia activity, corruption, and illegal privileges. Aberrations in the ethical rules supposed to regulate the liberal market and to assure representative democracy's smooth functioning are assumed to be part of the reality;

the divine will, and moreover, that a person was summoned to nothing else ... . There could be no question of a church ministering God's grace to humans, nor of priests whose ritual acts mediated between a group of worshippers and God. It was symbolically correct that in public worship, the leader, the Imam (who might be any one of the faithful), performed the same acts as anyone else, only standing in front of others, who made their gestures in time with his. With the rejection of Arabism as the basis of Islam, there could not even be a chosen people. Though Muslims were set off from others, it was only in that they had chosen personally to obey God, a duty incumbent upon everyone else as well.[22]

The fact that the law is above everyone, the Caliph included, rendered the power hierarchies juridically fragile, forcing the government to rely on brutal force. The result was that the Muslim state became somewhat like the Christian Church, but for the opposite reasons. Bertrand Russell's comparison of Christianity and other religions captures some of the nuances that are particularly pertinent to the understanding of the difference between the nature and scope of power in Christian and Muslim political ideology, process, and organization.[23] Russell makes a distinction between three aspects of religion: creed, church, and moral conduct. He explains:

> The relative importance of these three elements has varied greatly in different times and places. The ancient religions of Greece and Rome, until they were made ethical by the Stoics, had not very much to say about personal morals: In Islam the Church has been unimportant in comparison with the temporal monarch; in modern Protestantism there is a tendency to relax the rigors of the creed. Nevertheless, all three elements, though in varying proportions, are essential to religion as a social phenomenon, which is what is chiefly concerned in the conflict with science. A purely personal religion, so long as it is content to avoid assertions which science can disprove, may survive undisturbed in the most scientific age.[24]

This distinction is the key to understanding why Islam, which as a creed had tolerated sciences, as state ideology has problems with modernity: it needs to silence conflict so as to maintain the fiction of the unfragmented *umma*. The Algerian political sociologist Lahouari Addi summarizes the idea quite well when he explains why fundamentalist Islam today cannot survive long, since it can only exist as long as its power to kill dissenters is unchallenged:

The Islamist social consciousness does not acknowledge the division of society into divergent interests, whether economic, ideological, or what have you. Religion can become a means to hide these divisions. Thus religion is mobilized in order to avoid the creation of institutions that can express social and ideological differences within the community. But all this rests upon the view that religion can make social divergences disappear, and that those who wield power can be restrained purely by the fear of God ... . The mobilization of Islam bespeaks a rejection of political modernity to the extent that modernity, resting upon individual freedom, recognizes, institutionalizes, and regulates social and ideological divergence within society.[25]

Significantly, the medieval official inquisition in Islam was organized only when the creed overlapped with a minority problem. The heretic hunt under the Abbasids was in fact aimed at the Persians who rejected Arab supremacy. The inquisition began when a number of brilliant intellectuals, who had contributed greatly to Islamic culture as well as to the court's administrative apparatus, claimed, in an evidently ethical movement called the Shu'ubiyya, that their culture was superior to that of the Arabs. 'Shu'ubiyya ... was essentially a literary movement in whose writings non-Arabs and especially Persians were praised and the faults and weaknesses of the Arabs emphasized ... . '[26] The Abbasid Caliph installed the official inquisition tribunals in 163/ 780, appointed the *qadis* (judges) with the title of *arif*, and ordered them to hunt down, arrest, try, and eventually execute the *zindiq*s or heretics.[27]

Zindiq (plural *zanadiqa*) was the Iranian term used in Muslim criminal law to describe the heretic whose teaching was deemed a danger to the state.[28] It started as a strictly technical term designating then recently converted Persians, suspected of 'Mananiya' (the Manicheans or followers of Mani) and only later did the word expand to include other enemies of the regime. *Zindiq*s were condemned as adepts of Mani, a resurgence of the old Persian Zoroastrian religion among newly converted Iranians. The *zindiq*s had the right to a trial and the possibility to repent and repudiate their crime (a heretical faith) and return to Islam. If they repented, they were set free. The nature of the test administered by the Muslim judges to repenting *zindiq*s was quite revealing.

To make sure that the *zindiq* had really renounced his heresy, Caliphs used many tests, the most famous among which were those used by *qadis* under Caliph Ma'mun, and which consisted of asking the *zindiq* to spit on a representation of Mani and to kill a sea bird called tadaruj, because killing birds or animals or any living creature was forbidden by Mani.[29]

What is sacred in Islam is the *shari'a*, the religious law, and this very fact dwarfs the Caliph's authority.

> The Islamic Shari'a law was largely an expression of the responsibility of individuals not only for their personal life but for the whole ordering of society: public offices, as such, were ruled out; everything became the responsibility of the community as a whole and therefore of the individuals who made it up. The Caliph might have a function, but it was, in principle, minimal.[30]

It is because the Caliph's function is so unimportant, dwarfed by an overwhelmingly transcending God and a community-based law, that the Caliph needs to negate social conflict, that the use of violence to assure his authority is inescapable.

Reclaiming the Future

Violence against women was common during economic crisis. Al-Hakim forced women to veil and forbade mixing when irregularities in the Nile flow brought about inflation and social unrest.

> Quand al-Hakim, le fatimide qui a commandé aux mathématiciens de régler les eaux du Nil, a vu que leur tentative échoua, il se tourna vers des mesures plus réalisables pour calmer les masses lorsque la baisse des eaux persista et provoqua une inflation gigantesque. En 405, il se décida à agir, il donna ordre d'enfermer les égyptiennes. En cette année al-Hakim interdit à jamais aux femmes de sortir de chez elle, et leur interdit de se rendre dans les *hammam*, et mit fin à l'industrie de la chaussure pour femmes (*khifaf*). Beaucoup s'opposèrent à ses ordres et furent tuées ... . Quelques décennies plus tard en 487, mais cette fois-ci la scène se passe à Baghdad, sous le règne d'une dynastie rivale, le Khalife 'Abbasside al-Muqtadi, vingt-huitième de la dynastie, ordonna d'exiler les chanteuses (*moughaniyates*) et les pêcheresses (*Mufsidates*) de Baghdad. Leurs maisons furent vendues et elles mêmes exilées et on interdit aux gens de rentrer au bain sans un *mi'zar* (Tissu fin qu'on enroule autour des hanches) ... . On interdit également aux marins de transporter hommes et femmes ensemble ... .[31]

Destroying wine stocks, preventing men from traveling with women on the same boats (which created much hardship in cities

like Baghdad and Cairo where rivers were used for public trans-
portation and communication), forcing women to wear veils,
forcing Christians and Jews to wear special crosses and belts –
such impositions are a common feature of Muslim politics in times
of economic crisis. The need for the troubled political leader to
mask difference and negate diversity at the very moment when
economic crisis erodes all kinds of legitimacy continues today. The
fundamentalist leader Shaykh Abbas Madani, for example, has
made long speeches explaining how women are the roots of all of
Algeria's troubles.

> Notre religion nous recommande de porter conseil. Et le prophète,
> que le salut soit sur lui, a dit 'la religion est conseil' ... . Nous avons
> donc essayé en toute circonstance de porter conseil à nos frères, pour
> travailler ensemble au bien être de cette communauté et de ce pays
> ... . Nous avons vu les calamités morales qui n'ont aucun lien avec la
> religion, ni les traditions de l'Algérien. La consommation du vin
> devenue licite, la mixité dans les écoles, les lycées et les universités ont
> eu pour conséquence la prolifération des bâtards. La dépravation s'est
> répandue et nous voyons la femme ne plus se cacher et étaler aux yeux
> de tout le monde son corps maquillé et nu, à l'intérieur et à l'extérieur.
> Où est donc la dignité de l'Algérien après que son honneur ait été
> bafoué publiquement ... . [32]

The Saudi king has to put the veil on women to mask their
differences in order to create a theatrical credibility that his male
authority stems from a homogeneous *umma*. The symbolism of the
veil is spatial: the veil refers to the harem and identifies the woman
trespassing beyond her assigned private space as someone who
does not belong.[33] The Sudanese Hasan al-Turabi, despite his
claim to transcendent spirituality, seems at a loss about how to
smooth his conflict with his Christian co-citizens. And women
and minorities are one of the indigestible huge chunks of that
defiant and challenging reality an Islamic state can neither deny
without asphyxiating itself, as the Islamic Republic's experience
demonstrates, nor affirm without democratizing its decision-
making processes and by so doing destroying itself. As Olivier Roy
has pointed out, the dilemma has more to do with Muslim states'
capacity to face reality, than with the false issue of secularism
versus religion:

> In Islamic societies, the power was always secular. It is true that it
> gives itself a religious legitimacy, but the functioning mode of politics

was always perfectly secular … . When I hear that secularism does not
exist in Islamic society, I do not understand what it means … . In the
very functioning of the social and the political, secular fields are wide
open … . The problem of Islam is not to accept a secularization which
exists, but to 'think' the reality it negates.[34]

The real underlying problem of a modern Muslim state is
inefficiency and mediocre performance, as by masking conflict it
cuts itself from the very roots of vitality and creativity. And a
Muslim state which does not fulfill the promise which brought it
to power, that is to make Muslims richer and more powerful, can
indeed not last. Empowerment is what brings the poor to engage
in militant Islam. Bombarded with publicity and hungry to con-
sume, they see in religion a means to give them what modernity
has so far refused them – a decent citizenship of the global market,
or, rather, 'the global *suk*.' Efficiency is the test of any Islamic
state. If it does not provide what the masses need and want, it will
last only as long as the people's fear to contest it lasts. But the fear
will evaporate, and the risk of popular contention is today, for a
whole combination of reasons much more than yesterday, very
much a feature of the future.

To equate Islam with irrationality is probably as absurd as it is
to equate liberal democracy with rationality. The reasonable question to ask is: how can we increase the chances of rationality in
the Muslim world? The 'we,' of course, is any individual or group,
regardless of culture and nationality, interested in nurturing the
chances of rational discourse and government in the next century.
It represents virtually millions of people within and without the
Muslim world, because no serious thinker can any longer reason-
ably separate East and West in the Kiplingesque tradition. One
cannot imagine a USA without the precious Arab oil, or the Emir
of Kuwait without his Pentagon friends.

Thus posed, the question has at least two advantages: first, it
liberates us from the racist bias inherent in polarizing the debate
about which cultural group is rational and which is not. Second,
it empowers us, both Westerners and Muslims, by helping us
identify key factors which can increase the chances of rational
problem solving and reduce the need for violent methods of
conflict resolution.

It may be added that, on the practical level at least, Francis
Fukuyama's supposed conflict between universalist liberal democracies and nationalist authoritarian states does not explain con-

temporary Western–Arab relations. For example, since 1945 liberal democracies have allied themselves with the Saudi Wahhabism, which is one of the most extreme religious regimes in the Middle East. This kind of alliance shifted the balance of power against the secular forces, which were very active and strong after the Second World War throughout the Middle East. A case in point is the resultant fate of minorities and women, probably the best secularization indicators anywhere, in conservative Arab states.

Minorities, women, and slaves are the groups that have historically constituted a challenge and a limitation to Islam's claim to universality and equality. They were objects of special legal dispositions that defined and protected their special inferior status within the Muslim *umma*. The Islamic state thus rested on a contradiction between the legal inferiority of some groups and the philosophical principle of equality of all beings, which is central to Islam as a universal religion. Since the abolition of slavery, only women and minorities are left as a test for the state to modernize itself and to bring its laws into conformity with the principle of equality it claims as a fundamental value. This is why most of the debate on democracy in the Muslim world circles endlessly around the explosive issue of women's liberation, and also why a piece of cloth, the veil, is so loaded with symbolic meaning and so powerful as a source of violence within, and now also without, Muslim territories.[35]

Despite the obvious relationship between democratization, the development of civil society, and women and minority status in the community, the liberal democracies' oil lobbies and arms interests have persistently undermined women and minority rights in the Arab world. The alliance with conservative and reactionary rulers, of course, is not inconsistent with the 'rationality' theory. It controls 'uncertainty,' which in turn allows the capitalist states to develop the systems of hierarchy necessary to the development and management of power in colonial settings. A democratically run secular Arab world, where millions of citizens, including women who constitute more than half of the population, have the right to vote and to criticize political actors, would have created intolerable 'uncertainties' in the oil and arms markets.

However, rampant population growth in recent times has dramatically transformed societal conditions in Arab countries. It has produced severe threats to both oil-rich fundamentalist regimes and their Western allies by destabilizing governments, fomenting

religious dissent, internationalizing terrorism, and promoting clan-
destine emigration. It has thus forced both Western and Arab
rulers to reconsider their strategies. If choking civil society and
investing in fundamentalism was a profitable strategy up to the
mid-1980s, recent dislocations resulting from demographic pressure, unemployment, skyrocketing debt, the closing of Europe's
immigration doors, and the IMF-induced state withdrawal from
social services have made democratization in the Arab world the
only feasible scenario for the twenty-first century. The key factor
shaping the future will be whether all states, Eastern and Western,
will accept 'global' responsibility for promoting freedom, pluralism,
gender equality, and democracy, with the richest nations taking
the lead. If Fukuyama's thesis that universalization is a compelling
inclination of liberal democracies is correct, perhaps liberal bank-
ers and arms producers may yet magically shift gear and begin
funding Muslim women's free initiative to unveil, after having
invested for decades in veiling pluralism in the Middle East.

Notes

1. I began to prepare this paper in the spring of 1994 for the Dialogue
on Religion, Culture, and Women's Human Rights in the Muslim World,
convened by the Sisterhood Is Global Institute in Washington, DC in
September 1994. Since then it has evolved in several ways. Part of it was
specially developed and presented at the UNSRID Conference 'World
Summit for Social Development' in Copenhagen, 11–12 March 1995,
under the title 'Rethinking Social Development.' It is also partially an
excerpt from my coming essay on 'Arab Women's Rights and the Flow of
Oil,' a continuation of my reflections on *La Peur de Modernité* (Paris: Albin
Michel, 1992), or the English translation, *Islam and Democracy* (New York:
Addison Wesley, 1992), written after the trauma of the Gulf War, where I
predicted that the military intervention of the allies in the Gulf would
unleash fundamentalist xenophobia and violence within the Arab world,
with women as the traditional sacrificial scapegoat. For me, the Gulf was
an evident manifestation that Western liberal democracies have a strong
irrational component. But it was during my first months at the Wissen-
schaftskolleg in Berlin at the end of 1994, that I came to realize that this
irrational dimension escapes the West: Westerners had a deep quasi-
religious belief that they were miraculously rational beings. Looking at
the world from my Berlin room, it became clear to me that 1) the West
has a religion, their God is called 'Rationality;' 2) the Westerners see
themselves, in spite of their forcing the global market on the rest of the
planet, as a miraculously separate entity, unpolluted by any strong links

to the 'Orient,' an Orient necessarily different from them, and blocked in the role they needed it to play: eternal and pure, undiluted irrationality. These two anthropological 'discoveries' helped me to advance in my own work since I realized that for me as an Arab woman such a separation does not exist: I see liberal democracies as completely 'Saudi-ized,' with an eminently oily side to them that makes them more akin to 'oriental despots' than to universally oriented civilizations. Then I decided to submit this discrepancy to cold analysis, starting with the assumption that my perception might be a fantasy. But I came to believe that fantasies are precious, at least for writers. It is worthwhile expounding my biased perception: sharing it and analyzing it might be, if not good scientific data, at least good therapy. And a cheap therapy is not a bad thing either, if one thinks in market values. This work is at its beginning; exciting and often heated intellectual debates with the fellows at the Wissenschaft-skolleg, with help from its Library (Aja Brockmann) and Editing Service (Michael Cohen) have allowed me to make substantial progress, but I am far from getting to where I want: to make the little flicker of reason shine brighter.

2. Max Weber's distinction between civilized and savage man with its colonial turn-of-century flavor reflects quite well the value condemnation which lurks behind the rationality/irrationality dichotomy: 'What gives the life of "civilized" man ... as opposed to the savage, its specifically "rational" flavor is ... 1) his general tendency to believe that the phenomena of his everyday life – a bus or an elevator, money, a court of law, military affairs, medicine – are in principle rational, i.e., that they are human artifacts accessible to rational knowledge, creation and control ... 2) his confidence that these phenomena function rationally, i.e., according to familiar rules, and not irrationally, like the powers that the savage seeks to influence with his magic, so that at least in principle one can reckon with them, calculate their effects, and base one's actions confidently on the expectations they arouse.' Max Weber, as quoted in Ralph Dahrendorf, 'Market and Plan,' *Essays in the Theory of Society* (Stanford: Stanford University Press, 1965), p. 216.

3. Samuel P. Huntington, 'A Clash of Civilizations?' *Foreign Affairs*, 72 (1993) and Ernest Gellner, *Conditions of Liberty: Civil Society and its Rivals* (London: Hamish Hamilton, 1994). Jürgen Habermas points out that 'Beyond the street attacks of extremists, it is their successes in parliaments which is shocking and constitutes a threat for liberal democracies ethical foundations ... .' The unexpected outbreak of radical right-wing violence is explosive. The 1992 year-end balance sheet of the Hamburg-based Bureau for the Protection of the Constitution (published in *Frankfurter Allgemeine Zeitung* in December 1992) is shocking. During 1992, 17 people were murdered by right-wing radicals, between 800 and 900 were injured, in total, there were 2,200 attacks. According to the Bureau, the known right-wing extremists are unevenly divided between the old and the new

Federal Republic: 2,600 in the old western states compared with 6,500 in the new eastern states, although the latter make up only one-fifth of the total population. It is certainly true that the organizational level of the groups in the former GDR is rather low, while in the west the political parties to the right of the CDU have had quite a large clientele in state parliamentary elections ever since 1988. In the last regional elections in Berlin and Bremen, 18 per cent of young male voters cast their ballots for the right-wing parties. As in all of Europe, of course, these changing voting patterns also express a general level of resentment against the established political parties ... . This rejection of the established political parties is a disturbing symptom of a dwindling acceptance of political pluralism. In *The Past as Future* (Omaha: University of Nebraska Press, 1994), p. 124. On the concern raised by extremist violence against foreigners in Europe, see the latest report of the Aspen Institute of Berlin's conference on 'Right-Wing Extremism and German Democracy' 18–19 June 1994.

4. Montesquieu, *L'Esprit des Lois* quoted by Alain Grosrichard, in *Structure du sérail: la fiction du despotisme asiatique dans l'occident classique* (Paris: Editions du Seuil, 1979), pp. 122–3.

5. Charles Lee writes: 'The audacity of these rash intruders (Christian philosophers) upon the sacred precincts increased immeasurably with the introduction of the works of Averroes (*d.* 1198) in the second quarter of the thirteenth century, constituting a real danger of the perversion of Christian thought. In the hands of the Arab commentators the theism of Aristotle became a transcendental materialism ... . In this system, matter has existed from the beginning, and the theory of creation is impossible. The universe consists of a hierarchy of principles, eternal, primordial, and autonomous, vaguely connected with a superior unity. One of these is the only form of immortality. As the soul of man is a fragment of a collective whole, temporarily detached to animate the body, at death it is re-absorbed into the Active Intellect of the universe. Consequently there are no future rewards or punishments, no feelings, memory, sensibility, love or hatred. The perishable body has the power of reproducing itself and thus enjoys a material immortality in its descendants, but it is only collective humanity that is immortal ... it was from Toledo that Michael Scot came with translations of Aristotle and Averroes, and was warmly welcomed at the court of Frederick, whose insatiable thirst for knowledge and whose slender reverence for formulas led him to grasp eagerly at these unexpected sources of philosophy. It was probably these translations which formed the body of Aristotellam distributed by him to the universities of Italy. Hermanus Alemannus continued Michael's work at Toledo and brought versions of other books to Manfred, who inherited his father's tastes, so that by the middle of the century the principal labors of Averroes were accessible to scholars ... The infection spread with rapidity almost incredible. Already in 1243, Guillaume d'Auvergne, Bishop of Paris, and the Masters of the University condemned a series of scholastic errors, not

indeed distinctively Averroist, but manifesting in their bold independence the influences which the Arab philosophy was beginning to exercise ... .' in 'Special Fields of Inquisitorial Activity,' *A History of the Inquisition of the Middle Ages, Vol. III* (New York: Russell and Russell Publishers, 1958), p. 559.

6. Montgomery Watt, 'The Religious Institution,' *Islamic Political Thought* (Edinburgh: Edinburgh University Press, 1966), p. 77.

7. Abderahman Badawi, *On the History of Heresy in Islam (Min tarikh al-ilhad fi'l-Islam)* (Beirut: al-Mu'asasa al-Arabiyya al-Dirasat wa Nashr, 1980), p. 31.

8. Grosrichard, 'Le Concept d'un fantasme: la chaîne secrète' in *op. cit.*, pp. 34–70.

9. Patricia Springborg, *Western Republicanism and the Oriental Prince* (Cambridge: Polity Press, 1992).

10. *Ibid.*, p. 9.

11. Dahrendorf, *op. cit.*, p. 247.

12. Habermas, *op. cit.*, p. 117.

13. Ethnic 'minorities' can reach as much as roughly half of the population as is the case in Iran where 'the dominant group, the Persians, comprise an estimated 55 per cent of the population. The country's ethno-linguistic minorities – Turkish-speaking Azerbaijanis, Kurds, Baluchis, Turkomen, and Arabs have many legitimate grievances and aspire to greater cultural autonomy ... ' Ali Banuazizi, 'Iran's Revolutionary Impasse: Political Factionalism and Societal Resistance,' *MERIP* (November/December 1994), pp. 2–8. The legal discrimination of the Muslim state against women is more commonly known than its discrimination against minorities (*dhimmi*), whence the need to summarize its main devices: the inferiority of the *dhimmi* is represented by the fact that he is obliged to buy off his right to live and work on a Muslim territory by paying two special taxes in return for state protection, on one hand, and by being debarred from office in government and state administration on the other. The first tax, *al kharaj*, he pays on the property he owns; the second, *al jizya*, he pays as a person, to buy the right to stay on a Muslim territory. See also Louis Millot, *Introduction à l'étude du droit musulman* (Paris: Receuil Sirey, 1970) and Watt, 'The Protected Minorities,' in *op. cit.*, pp. 49–61.

14. Bertrand Russell, *Science and Religion* (Oxford: Oxford University Press), p. 37.

15. Lee, *op. cit.*, p. 559.

16. Ali Abd al-Raziq, *al-Islam wa usul al-hukm* (Beirut: al-Mu'asasa al-Arabiyya al-Dirasat wa Nashr, 1988), p. 148. An old translation by Louis Bercher appeared in *Revue des études islamiques* in 1934–5. A new French translation by Abdou Mall and a very important introduction by the translator has just appeared from Editions Le Fennec, Casablanca, 1994; 'Le Califat ou le Grand Imamat n'est ni une institution fondée sur les articles de la foi religieuse, ni un système que justifie la raison, et que

toutes les prétendues preuves en ce sens tombent d'elles-mêmes lorsqu'on les examine attentivement' (p. 77).

17. Abd al-Raziq, *op. cit.*, p. 144. The French translation is: 'Nous avons vu que le Livre sacré n'a jamais daigné évoquer le califat, ni faire moindre allusion à son sujet, que la Tradition du Prophète l'a ignoré, qu'aucun *ijma'* ne s'est produit à son propos. Quel argument reste-t-il donc aux partisans du califat? Peut-on encore parler d'une obligation religieuse, alors qu'on ne peut s'appuyer ni sur le Livre sacré ni sur la Tradition du prophète ni encore sur un accord unanime des fidèles?' p. 82.

18. Abd al-Raziq, *op. cit.*, p. 142.

19. Abd al-Raziq, *op. cit.*, p. 140.

20. The biography of al-Hakim Bi Amri Allah (d. 411/1020) in *The Encyclopedia of Islam* is a good introduction to this bizarre ruler. His strange behavior has puzzled Muslim historians, who recorded his eccentricities in great detail in classical Islamic history books such as al-Makrizi, *Al Khitat* (Cairo: Maktabat al-taqafa al-diniya, 1987), vol. 2, p. 285; Ibn al-Athir, *al-Kamil* (Beirut: Dar al-Fikr), vol. 7, p. 477; and Ibn Khalikan, *Wafayat al-a'yan* (Beirut: Dar al-thaqafa), vol. 5, p. 375.

21. Al-Makrizi, *op. cit.*

22. Marshall G. S. Hodgson, 'The Shari'a Islamic Vision' in *The Venture of Islam: Conscience and History in a World Civilization* (Chicago: University of Chicago Press, 1959), vol. I, 'The Classical Age of Islam,' pp. 319–20.

23. Russell, *op. cit.*, p. 8.

24. *Ibid.*, pp. 8–9.

25. Lahouari Addi, 'The Islamist Challenge: Religion and Modernity in Algeria,' *Journal of Democracy*, 3, 4 (October 1992).

26. Watt, *op. cit.*, p. 83 and H. A. R. Gibb 'The Social Significance of the Shu'ubiya', reprinted in William R. Polk and Stanford Shaw (eds), *Studies on the Civilization of Islam* (London: Routledge and Kegan Paul, 1962), pp. 62–73.

27. Badawi, *op. cit.*, p. 21.

28. The article by Louis Massignon, 'Zindiq', in the *Encyclopedia of Islam* (Leiden: E.J. Brill, 1960) gives a brief introduction as well as an important bibliography.

29. Badawi, *op. cit.*, p. 31.

30. Marshall G. S. Hodgson, *Rethinking World History: Essays on Europe, Islam, and World History* (Cambridge: Cambridge University Press), p. 116. The other dimension which enhances individual responsibility is the importance accorded to contractual relations by the *shari'a*. 'Whenever Muslims were found in sufficient numbers, the shari'a laws would allow them to constitute their own fully legitimate social structure in all needful respects. And the authority of shari'a law was such that no alternative institutions, which might have neutralized its effect, could achieve legitimization and hence long-run durability ... . One consequence of this autonomy and exclusiveness in the shari'a law was an undermining of the

legitimacy of any agrarian absolutist authority, including the Caliphate itself ... . The Muslim shari'a law represented the most radical of the old entities. It was highly egalitarian, and therefore, perhaps, what may be called contractualistic. A very wide range of relations were left to contracts between responsible individuals, including in theory, even the whole range of politics. In principle, no man was properly a ruler until he had been accepted in covenant by the representatives of the Muslim community; and even then again, in principle what we would call public duties were potentially the obligation of every Muslim if no one Muslim was fulfilling them. More generally and effectively, the directive offices of society were never filled on the basis of fixed heredity, but normally by designation and/or consultation, even when they were filled from a given family. Remarkably little was left, in the shari'a law, to ascribed status, which was so very important in the two great 'idolatrous' regions that flanked the Nile to Oxus region, Europe and India.'

31. Mernissi, *op. cit.*, p. 153.

32. *Ibid.*, p. 153.

33. Fatima Mernissi, 'The Hijab' (Chapter 5) and 'The Prophet and Space' (Chapter 6) of *The Veil and the Male Elite* (New York: Addison Wesley, 1991).

34. Robert Solé and Henri Tincq, 'Penser l'Islam comme politique conduit à l'échec: entretien avec Olivier Roy,' *Le Monde*, dossier special 'La France et l'Islam,' 13 October 1994, page XII. See also Olivier Roy, *The Failure of Political Islam* (London: I. B. Tauris, 1994).

35. The heated French debate on 'le foulard Islamique,' the Islamic scarf adopted by young adolescent Muslim school girls in Paris suburbs, shakes daily the Republic of France and splits its intellectuals and politicians, not only because it confronts France as a liberal democracy with its 'unconscious' irrational racist inconsistencies, but also because it forces everyone to put their clocks on time. It forces the Muslim population to discover and deal with its own inconsistencies and clashing aspirations. And it forces the supposedly universal European liberal democracies to test their claims to rationality.

See 'La Saga des foulards: une querelle juridique, politique, quasiment philosophique,' *Le Monde*, dossier special, 'La France et l'Islam,' 13 October 1994, p. 5. On the philosophical challenge emigrant populations pose to liberal democracies, see Habermas, 'The Asylum Debate' in *op. cit.*; Gilles Kepel, 'Etre musulman en France: associations, militants et mosquées' (Presses de la Fondation Nationale des Sciences Sociales, March 1994); Bruno Etienne, *La France et l'Islam* (Paris: Le Seuil, 1987); Martine Gozian, *L'Islam et la Republique: des musulmans de France contre l'intégrisme* (Belfond, February 1994); and Emmanuel Todd, *Le Destin des immigrés* (Le Seuil, 1994).

4

The Dichotomy between Religious and Secular Discourse in Islamic Societies

Abdullahi An-Na'im

While fully realizing that there is no substitute for the experience, insight, and understanding that women bring to discussions of the issues raised in this brief paper, I believe that male advocates of the rights of women have a contribution to make. This is particularly important for forging an effective partnership between women and men advocates of the human rights of women. The real work has to be done within the Islamic societies in question, but strategies and alliances can and should be developed wherever there is the opportunity to do so.

My basic thesis in this brief paper may be summarized as follows. First, I argue that although the apparent dichotomy between so-called religious and secular discourse about the rights of women in Islamic societies is somewhat false or grossly exaggerated, its implications are too serious to ignore in practice. It is therefore imperative to reconcile and integrate the two types of discourse, or minimize the significance of differences between them, in the interest of promoting the rights of women in Islamic societies. Second, I suggest that it is conceptually possible to do so, but the advocates of the rights of women need to devise and implement appropriate strategies for realizing this possibility. In particular, they need not only to challenge traditional so-called Islamic doctrine and dogma about the rights of women, but also to develop and articulate their own Islamic justifications for the human rights of women.

The Genesis and Resolution of Dichotomy

The dichotomy between religious and secular discourses is supposed to emanate from differences in their respective frames of reference, methodology, and outcome. It is commonly assumed that since the first derives from the authority of scriptural or other religious sources and the second is premised on the supremacy of human reason and experience, the two types of discourse must also be different in their process and conclusions.

Without disputing the existence of some differences between the two types of discourse, it seems clear to me that they overlap and interact so much that it would be misleading to maintain a sharp dichotomy between them. I would also suggest that there are good reasons for diminishing, rather than emphasizing, the significance of differences between religious and secular discourse as much as possible. The danger of a strict dichotomy is that it can be manipulated either to exclude some people from the discussion or to give undue weight and authority to the views of others by virtue of their presumed 'special' qualification or status in 'religious affairs.'

On the one hand, human interpretation is unavoidable in any effort to articulate and implement the normative and practical implications of religious texts. So-called secular approaches to politics and policy making for believers, on the other hand, are internally and inherently influenced, if not conditioned, by religious understandings and motivation. In other words, it is conceptually misleading to speak of 'purely' religious or secular discourse about the rights of women because the two interact and overlap so much in practice. People do not compartmentalize the religious and secular in their minds, motivation, and behavior as the two constantly overlap and interact in their own daily lives.

There is no way for human beings to understand and relate to any religion, including a scriptural religion like Islam, and for that religion to have any impact on their lives, except through human agency.[1] As a Muslim, I believe the Qur'an to be the final and comprehensive revelation which contains all the guidance Muslims need in the public and private, individual and communal, spheres. But I also believe that the Qur'an has to be understood, and its guidance implemented, through human reason and action. In fact, the Qur'an describes itself in these terms in, for example, verses 1–4 of Chapter 43, the meaning of which can be translated as saying: 'Ha, mim. Wa'l-kitab al-mubin. (We [God] have made it [the Qur'an] in the Arabic language so that you [human beings] may understand. But in its ultimate nature, it is with Us, supreme and wise.)' That is, while one aspect of the Qur'an lies with the Divine, beyond human reason, another aspect is and should be seen as falling within the realm of human understanding and action.

Otherwise, how can Muslims draw guidance from it and be inspired by its supreme moral and spiritual power?

Once that elementary fact is appreciated, it becomes clear that all Muslims, men and women alike, have the right to debate among themselves the meaning of what the Qur'an says regarding the rights of women, or any other issue or question, challenge so-called established orthodox interpretations, and advance their own in this regard. In so doing, Muslim men and women would be drawing on their own experiences and knowledge of the world in their respective historical, economic, political, and social contexts. The arbiter of this debate and judge of its outcome should be the community of believers, and not any formal institution of government or learning. That is to say, it is the living community which should decide which view or interpretation of the Qur'an should prevail at any given time.

It should also be emphasized that this is the way in which what is commonly known as *shari'a*, the divinely ordained way of life and its legal and ethical norms, was 'constructed' by Muslim scholars and jurists of the second and third centuries of Islam.[2] To describe the founders of the *shari'a* as 'scholars and jurists' does not mean that they had formal qualifications for interpreting the Qur'an other than their own learning and integrity as judged and accepted by the community. They were neither certified by any person, body, or institution as 'qualified' interpreters to the exclusion of others, nor did they claim such a status for themselves. Rather, they were simply acknowledged as such by Muslim communities through a very gradual, spontaneous, and informal process of acceptance and following (or rejection) of their views by contemporary and subsequent generations. Thus, there should be no inclusive or exclusive criteria for participating in discourse about the rights of women, whether it is characterized as religious or secular. Nobody should be excluded from discourse, and no view should be seen as having more or less weight simply by virtue of the identity or status of the person who is expressing it.

This will not be easy to realize in practice because people tend to take the identity and standing of the author into account in evaluating a point of view. Nevertheless, it is very important to resist any effort to institutionalize or standardize this tendency into a clerical hierarchy or other exclusive elite who claim the divine right to interpret the Qur'an. To the extent that the identity and standing of the author is considered, that should be as a

matter of personal judgment and free choice in attributing credibility and weight to a point of view in light of its coherence and
rationality, and the commitment of its author to the values
articulated.

To say that the dichotomy between religious and secular discourses should be diminished does not mean that the distinction
between the two can or should be collapsed in every sense. The
religious and secular do overlap and interact, and should be seen
as doing so, but they do not coincide completely. In particular, it
is vital to maintain a distinction between the two so that religious
doctrine and dogma are not made the basis of political authority
and/or legal status and rights. My purpose here is to emphasize
the need for the advocates of the human rights of women to fully
engage in religious as well as secular discourse relevant to the
subject, rather than to suggest that there is no distinction between
the two.

If the advocates of the human rights of women fail to take
religious discourse seriously, their opponents will mobilize it in
Islamic communities, thereby denying them the vital political and
practical support of those constituencies. Furthermore, diminishing
the dichotomy between religious and secular discourse may help
in rehabilitating secularism itself from its present negative anti-
religious and colonial associations among the masses of Muslims,
thereby enhancing the prospects of maintaining the distinction
between the religious and the secular in the political and legal
spheres.

The Context and Outcome of Discourse

The dynamics of current discourse about human rights in general,
and those of women in particular, should be seen in light of local,
regional, and global contexts and circumstances. Because of a
combination of factors, including the failure of secular nationalist
projects of the immediate post-colonial era, coupled with growing
demands for cultural self-determination in terms of an Islamic
collective identity, discourse about public policy has become polarized and 'dichotomized' in most Islamic societies between so-called
Islamist and secularist perspectives. Moreover, the Islamists seem
to have succeeded in seizing the initiative and the power to define
the frame of reference and terms of the discourse with a view to
controlling its outcome. To counter this trend which, I believe, is

detrimental to the protection and promotion of the human rights of women in Islamic societies, the advocates of those rights need to understand the nature and consequences of the discourse of the Islamists in the present context.

For one thing, the discourse of the Islamists appears to be modernist in form but extremely regressive and backward-looking in content. Islamists are very effective in employing modern methods of communication and organization to carry their message to their constituencies, but the content of that message is deliberately vague and regressive for human rights, especially of women, because they advocate the implementation of archaic conceptions of the *shari'a*.[3] Instead of challenging this discourse for its obvious failings, the opponents of the Islamists tend to be defensive about their 'secular' views and apologetic for appearing to oppose the application of *shari'a* principles which the Islamists are advocating. In fact, some of them become more royal than the king by trying to be more 'Islamic' than the Islamists. In this way, the opponents of the Islamists concede much more of their position than they need to by accepting the terms of reference set by the Islamists, and their underlying assumptions and principles.

A second point about the nature and likely consequences of discourse is that because of the general conditions of political oppression and lack of respect for freedoms of expression and association in most Islamic countries, the proponents of the two sides to the issue do not have the opportunity and occasion to communicate among themselves or with each other's constituencies. In the limited space allowed for public debate, each participant tends to focus on those who share her/his point of view, and on what she/he deems to be a 'receptive constituency,' rather than engage in dialogue with proponents of the opposing point of view. Consequently, the Muslim public at large is confronted with a stark, albeit false, choice: either support the Islamists who present themselves as standing for Islam and the implementation of *shari'a*, or their opponents who are already conceding the religious high ground to their opponents, and are consequently weakened by popular perceptions of secularism as an anti-Islamic ideology.

A stark choice in these terms is false not only because of the exaggeration of the dichotomy between the religious and secular, as explained earlier, but also because the Islamists do not necessarily stand for Islam and the implementation of *shari'a*. The Islamists may claim representation of their own view of Islam and what *shari'a* ought to be today, but they should not be allowed to speak for Islam itself, or all possible perceptions of its law.

This polarization of discourse is further reinforced by the so-called confrontation with the West. In view of the history of colonialism and current experiences of Western domination and exploitation, which are deeply ingrained in the consciousness of Muslim peoples throughout the region, the issues are now often cast in terms of a struggle to define and preserve the Islamic identity of these communities. The boundaries of identity tend to be seen as more important than its content, with the Islamists claiming the right to define and defend it in those terms, while their opponents are conceding the issue as noted earlier. In my view, this is another falsely stark choice because the asserted right to cultural self-determination and Islamic identity is itself in conflict with the claim of an exclusive monopoly to exercise that right on behalf of all Muslims.

The issue of cultural identity and self-determination is particularly important for the human rights of women because, for reasons that I am unable to discuss in this limited space, the rights of women are commonly seen as a product of cultural understandings. But the pertinent question here is: how do some cultural understandings come about and prevail, while others are suppressed? All cultures not only change over time, but also offer different normative options or choices at any given time. It is therefore imperative for the advocates of the human rights of women to understand and work with the processes of the formation and transformation of cultural norms and institutions in order to use them in promoting their own cause. They need to utilize cultural discourse and the power relations within the culture in ways which make their own understandings of culture prevail, rather than allow others to impose their understandings.[4]

Islamic Foundations for the
Human Rights of Women

Once the proponents of the human rights of women begin to take a religious discourse seriously, and to educate themselves in its concepts and techniques, they will gain the confidence and competence to challenge the Islamists on their own ground. But when they do so, they will find that it is difficult to reconcile traditional conceptions of *shari'a* with the notion of human rights of women.

That is probably one of the reasons they have sought to avoid an Islamic discourse in the first place – seeing it as unlikely to support their cause.

I would suggest, however, that since *shari'a* is merely a historically conditioned human understanding of Islam, alternative interpretations in the modern context which are conducive to the human rights of women are possible, indeed imperative in my view. By emphasizing the impact of historical context on the human interpretation of Islamic sources in the construction of *shari'a*, as indicated earlier, advocates of the human rights of women can assert their own right to present alternative interpretations and participate in the development of modern principles of Islamic law in support of the human rights of women. Why is *shari'a* difficult to reconcile with the human rights of women, and how would it be possible to present alternative interpretations of Islamic sources in this regard?

It is true that *shari'a* did establish a clear set of rights for women, which in fact achieved a substantial improvement in their situation not only in contrast to what it used to be in pre-Islamic societies of the region, but also in favorable comparison to what existed under most other major religious and legal systems in the world until very recently. However, the concept of rights under a particular religious or legal system, including that of *shari'a*, is fundamentally different from that of human rights. Whereas human rights are, by definition, universal in that they are owed to all human beings by virtue of their humanity without distinction on grounds of gender or religion, the concept of rights under *shari'a* is fundamentally premised on these distinctions. That is to say, there are different rights for Muslim men, Muslim women, and non-Muslims under *shari'a*, rather than equal rights for all, regardless of gender or religion.

Some may wish to debate whether the concept of human rights itself is valid and useful, and, on this count, I personally believe that it is of vital validity and importance. But whatever view one may take of human rights as such, the concept itself must be distinguished fundamentally from any regime of rights, however favorable it may be, which distinguishes between human beings on ground of gender. It should also be noted that *shari'a* not only distinguishes between the rights of Muslim men and women, but discriminates against women in this regard.[5]

Space does not permit a full presentation of the theological and legal argument I have made elsewhere about how Islamic sources can be interpreted as fully supporting human rights for all, without distinction on grounds of gender, or religion, and so forth.[6] The essential premise of that argument, however, is simply the proposition that since *shari'a* is the product of human interpretation, alternative conceptions of Islamic law are possible.

What is commonly known as *shari'a* today was the product of a process of interpretation and elaboration of general principles and detailed rules by Muslim scholars/jurists of the second and third centuries of Islam. In fact, the term *shari'a* was unknown to the earliest generations of Muslims in the sense used today. The earliest Muslims simply took guidance from the Qur'an and living traditions of the Prophet (*sunna*) and of his companions according to their own spontaneous understanding of those sources, without being concerned with developing a comprehensive ethical and legal system. The so-called founding jurists of the second and third centuries were also not engaged in a process of laying down an immutable *shari'a* for eternity. Rather, they were responding to the immediate needs of their communities in that particular historical context, but their work came to be taken by subsequent generations as the final and conclusive interpretation of Qur'an and sunna, and application of Islamic juridical reasoning (*ijtihad*). Despite the radical rhetoric of Islamic activists today, and their calls for adapting *shari'a* to the modern context, very little has been done to articulate how that might be done in sound methodological terms.

As a product of human interpretation, *shari'a* should be seen as an inherently and constantly evolving and changing ethical and legal system, and each generation of Muslim men and women have the right, indeed obligation I believe, to contribute to that process in terms of their own historical context. It must be emphasized, however, that the process of reinterpretation of Islamic sources will not achieve significant results if it is confined to marginal 'reform' within the jurisprudential and methodological framework of *shari'a*, as established by the founding jurists, commonly known as *usul al-fiqh*, the foundations of Islamic jurisprudence. The process of reinterpretation must include the assumptions and methodology of traditional formulations, as well as the content of the principles and rules of *shari'a*.

The project briefly outlined above is perfectly feasible, I suggest, from a conceptual Islamic point of view. The modern formulation of the law I propose, including the foundation of human rights of women, will be as Islamic as *shari'a* has ever been. The primary difficulty, I believe, is psychological, sociological, and political. It is psychological in the sense that Muslim advocates of human rights are inhibited and intimidated by prevailing reverence for *shari'a* as the only valid conception of Islamic law. This lack of self-confidence is reinforced by a combination of social intolerance of dissent, especially in relation to the human rights of women, and political repression. Without under-estimating the seriousness of the sociological and political limitations, I suggest that the advocates of the human rights of women must begin by ridding themselves of their own inhibitions and educate themselves in the concepts and techniques of Islamic discourse. They must also realize that in challenging *shari'a*, they are simply disputing a historically conditioned human understanding of Islam, and not repudiating Islam itself. Efforts to create the sociological and political space for effective discourse for the protection and promotion of human rights, especially those of women, can only begin after that psychological difficulty is overcome.

In any case, the advocates of the human rights of women should realize that they have no alternative but to engage in an Islamic discourse. Whatever they may think of it, the fact of the matter is that Islamic groups have already succeeded in 'Islamizing' the terms of reference of public discourse in most Islamic societies. For a variety of factors, some of which were indicated earlier, Muslim human rights advocates are now responding to that 'Islamic' discourse rather than engaging in their own discourse or attempting to define, or to contribute to defining, its terms. This state of affairs need not be permanent or irreversible, but the way to change it is surely to engage, rather than seek to avoid, an Islamic discourse.

To emphasize the need for human rights advocates to engage in an Islamic discourse does not mean that it should be the only type of frame of reference they should adopt. As suggested by Fatima Mernissi and other scholars and intellectuals who have already elected to engage in an Islamic discourse, there is a need for diversity and plurality of approaches. It is certainly true that some human rights advocates have a stronger aptitude for, and personal inclination to engage in, an internal discourse within an Islamic frame of reference, and are better at this sort of advocacy than others. But at least some supporters of the human rights of women should peruse this type of advocacy, without denying the right of others to adopt different approaches.

In particular, I would emphasize the need to engage in a political struggle for the protection and promotion of human rights, especially those of women. Adopting appropriate types of discourse should be seen as integral to that struggle, and not as a substitute for it.

Notes

1. For a brief elaboration of this proposition in the Islamic context, see Abdullahi An-Na'im, 'Toward an Islamic Hermeneutics for Human Rights,' in Abdullahi An-Na'im *et al.* (eds), *Human Rights and Religious Values: An Uneasy Relationship?* (Grand Rapids, Michigan: William B. Eerdmans Publishing Company, forthcoming), pp. 229–42.

2. See Abdullahi Ahmed An-Na'im, *Toward an Islamic Reformation: Civil Liberties, Human Rights and International Law* (Syracuse, New York: Syracuse University Press, 1990), Chapter 3.

3. See *ibid.*, Chapters 4 to 7.

4. On issues of cultural transformation and human rights, see Abdullahi Ahmed An-Na'im and Francis M. Deng (eds), *Human Rights in Africa: Cross-Cultural Perspectives* (Washington DC: Brookings Institution, 1990) and Abdullahi Ahmed An-Na'im (ed.), *Human Rights in Cross-Cultural Perspectives: Quest for Consensus* (Philadelphia: University of Pennsylvania Press, 1992).

5. Abdullahi Ahmed An-Na'im, 'Human Rights in the Muslim World: Socio-Political Conditions and Scriptural Imperatives,' *Harvard Human Rights Journal*, 3 (1990), pp. 13–52; Abdullahi Ahmed An-Na'im, 'The Rights of Women and International Law in the Muslim Context,' *Whittier Law Review*, 9 (1987), pp. 491–516. See further, An-Na'im, *Toward an Islamic Reformation, op. cit.*, especially Chapter 4.

6. See sources cited in preceding notes.

5

The Muted Voices of Women Interpreters

Bouthaina Shaaban

There are very few women interpreters in the history of Islam because women are seen to be the subject of the Islamic *shari'a* and not its legislators. Yet even the few interpreters who have appeared during the long history of Islam have been kept at the periphery, their views never allowed to influence Islamic legislation. Moreover, even men interpreters who were open-minded about women were marginalized and, in some cases, found their authority questioned. In this chapter I shall discuss the contribution to Islam of Muslim women interpreters, the concurrence between their views and the views of later men interpreters, and the deliberate marginalization of their thought by contemporary Islamists. I will focus on Nazira Zin al-Din as one of the more serious and knowledgeable Muslim women scholars of our time.

The first person to believe the message of the Prophet and to become a Muslim was Muhammad's wife Khadija Bint Khuwaylid, of whom the Prophet said: 'She believed when people did not, and believed me when others did not, and consoled me with her money when I was abandoned by others.'[1] The first martyr for the Islamic cause was a woman (Summiyya). Women attended the first and the second Aqaba Conferences (Bay'at al-Aqaba al-Awla wa'l-Thaniyya) believed to have founded the Islamic state in Yathrib.[2]

The first Muslim woman whose views have been important to Muslims throughout Islamic history was Aisha, wife of the Prophet. Muhammad's contemporaries, among them both the *muhajerun* (emigrants who followed him from Mecca) and the *ansar* (those who helped the Prophet in Medina) considered Aisha a source of religious rules and an expert on issues of Islamic legislation. When she was mentioned to Ata Bin Abi Rabah, he said: 'Aisha was the most knowledgeable Muslim and had the best opinion in public affairs; she related 2210 sayings of the prophet Muhammad among which are 170 which have been approved and Bukhari took 54

sayings from them.'³ In *Arab Women in Jahiliya and Islam*, Abdol Sir
Afifi writes: ' Muslim women scholars are known for their honesty
in relating *hadith* and for their objectivity, which have rendered
them free of intellectual suspicion, the things that most men were
not fortunate enough to have.' In *Mizan al-I'tidal* (The Scales of
Moderation), al-Hafez al-Zahabi (died 748 IE, 1347 CE) a renowned Muslim authority on *hadith*, points to four thousand
suspect Muslim *hadith* tellers and then adds: 'I have not known of
any woman who was accused of falsifying *hadith*. To this we add,
that from the time of Aisha, the mother of believers, until the
time of al-Zahabi the sayings of the prophet Muhammad were
not kept or related by anyone as they were kept in the hearts of
women and related by them.'⁴

The wives and women relatives of the prophet Muhammad
were not an exception in their age. Many women were scholars
and teachers.⁵ Muhammad Bin Sa'id mentions over 700 women
who related *hadith* from the prophet Muhammad or from the
muhajirun and *ansar*. Men scholars and pillars of Islam quoted these
women.⁶ Thus Asma Bint Yazid bin al-Sakan al-Ansariyya is
known to have related 81 sayings from the prophet Muhammad
and her uncle Mahmud Bin Amr al-Ansari and Abu Sufian and
others reported and quoted her. She is also known to have been
a woman of science and a defender of women's rights. It is
reported that she led a delegation of women to the Prophet
Muhammad and said to him 'I am the envoy of women to you.
God has sent you to both men and women. We believed in you
and in your God, but we as women are confined to our homes,
satisfying your desires and carrying your children while you men
go out to fight, and go to *haj* and lead holy wars for the sake of
God. When one of you goes to the battle field we keep your money
for you, weave your clothes and bring up your children. Do we
deserve to share your wages?'⁷ The Prophet Muhammad acknowledged that she represented women, and he answered her and the
women who stood behind her.

Muslim women assumed political power as well as literary authority. They became queens, warriors, doctors, poets, and literary
critics. Many won reputations for valor in battle and received
praise from the Prophet and his followers. Clearly, the role of
women was not confined to encouraging men and treating their
wounds; they also played an active part in defending their tribe
and their cause. Ismat al-Din, known as Shajarat al-Dur, was the

first woman in Islam to assume a throne in her own right. Her husband, King Sala al-Din, died during the crusaders' invasion of Egypt. She continued to issue military and operational orders, keeping the news of his death secret for over two months to avoid undermining the morale of the troops. She found a man named Swab al-Suhayla who forged her husband's handwriting so well that no one doubted that the orders were issued by the king himself. She drew up plans, encouraged soldiers and instructed officers to lead the battle against the crusaders, during which King Louis IX of France (Saint Louis) was captured, making Shajarat al-Dur's victory final. Once the battle was over and victory secured, Shajarat al-Dur announced her husband's death, gave him a royal funeral, and openly assumed the throne. Shajarat al-Dur was mentioned in Friday prayers and money was coined in her name.[8] She was known as a 'knowledgeable queen who is deeply informed of matters, big and small. People felt optimistic during her rule and the poor enjoyed her good deeds. Her government was not authoritarian and she would not make a decision until she convened a council of consultants and listened to the opinions of her ministers and advisers.'[9] Women have also ruled in other Muslim countries. In Yemen there was more than one queen after the fifth/tenth century. The best known among them, Queen Orpha (died 484/1090) assumed total political authority which included planning and executing wars. In the thirteenth century many women were top leaders in Islamic countries, among them Sultana Radia in Delhi and Turkan Khatun, Safwat al-Din Malik Khatun, Sati Bik Khan and Tendo in Central Asia. In the same century, queens ruled Indonesia for 24 years without interruption and carried names such as 'Taj al-Alam' (The Crown of the World), and 'Nur al-Alam' (The Light of the World).

Muslim women were poets and literary critics. First among such critics is Sukayna Bint al-Husayn who was the ultimate judge of poetic production in her time. Poets travelled long distances in order to recite their poetry and obtain her judgement, which could affect the future course of a poetic career.[10] Aisha Bint Talha followed in the steps of Sukayna, meeting with poets and men of letters. Amra al-Jamihiya from Beni Jumah met with poets and story tellers at her home, listened to them, and judged their literary production.[11] Women also played an important role in medicine for which Arabs were renowned. They practiced in Baghdad, Qurtaba, and other cities in Iraq and Andalus.[12] However, their names and their contributions in different fields still await proper recording and authoritative documentation. The information, scattered in books, journals, and newspapers, has not been classified properly in archives and therefore is not yet a part of the mainstream historiography of Islam. Indeed, more often than not, the role of women in Muslim history has been marginalized and obscured, sometimes totally reversed, depending on the whims of men scholars.

Nazira Zin al-Din and Textual Interpreters

'As women have the right to participate in public governing they also have the explicit right to participate in Qur'anic interpretation and explanation. Women are better qualified than men to interpret the Qur'anic Verses speaking of their rights and duties because everyone is better equipped to understand his or her right and duty,'[13] writes Nazira Zin al-Din in *al-Fatat wa'l-shiukh*. Nazira Zin al-Din is the most serious and knowledgeable of the women Muslim scholars and interpreters to date. She is the daughter of Shaykh Sa'id Zin al-Din, a judge and the first president of the court of appeal in Lebanon in the 1920s. She was encouraged by her father to study. She tried to understand why Muslim women at the time were kept at home wrapped in darkness that covered not only their bodies but also their minds. The answer was that Islam was responsible. She studied the Qur'an and *hadith* and arrived at her own conclusions regarding the position of women in Islam. Although she was only 20 years of age when her books were published, her work is a significant source of reference on the relations between men and women in Islam. Very little is known about her personal life except that she is from a Druzi (Shi'i) sect. Her conclusions showed that Islam is not the reason behind the inferior status of women. The main reason is the gender-biased interpretation of the Qur'anic text by men of religion. When her first book was published, men of religion announced their stand against Zin al-Din and started distributing pamphlets against her; they incited demonstrations against the book and threatened the owners of bookshops who carried it. They accused her of atheism and treason. Her answers were sober, based on logic and clear evidence.

Nazira Zin al-Din made a thorough study of the Qur'anic texts and *hadith* concerning women, their rights, and their duties. Her two books, *al-Sufur wa'l-hijab*[14] and *al-Fatat wa'l-shiukh*, are perhaps the best scholarly studies available of Islamic texts and their interpretations dealing with women. Both are controversial, but the first is more so because it touches on the most sensitive issue in contemporary Islam, namely *hijab*.

In the introduction to *al-Sufur wa'l-hijab*, Nazira Zin al-Din writes that although she had always been interested in women's rights, what prompted her to write this book were the incidents in Damascus in the summer of 1927, in which Muslim women were deprived of their freedom and prevented from going out without *hijab*. 'I took my pen trying to give vent to the pain I feel in a brief lecture,' Zin al-Din says, 'but I could not stop writing and my pen had to follow in the trace of my injured self until the lecture became lectures too long to be delivered or attended.' In this book, Zin al-Din starts from the premise that she is a Muslim woman who believes in God, in his Prophet Muhammad, and in the holy Qur'an, and that all her arguments are informed by those beliefs.

According to Zin al-Din, the Islamic *shari'a* is not what this or that Muslim scholar says, but what is in the Qur'an and in the *hadith*. She argues that men have drawn up laws without the slightest participation by women. Yet even major interpreters of Islam such as Baydawi, al-Nusufi, and Tabari did not agree on the meaning of the Qur'anic text in such matters as geography, history, and astronomy, or, for that matter, on rituals and appropriate behavior, one should, therefore, go back to the Qur'an and the *sunna* to attain knowledge on all religious matters. She writes:

> When I started preparing my defence of women, I studied the works of interpreters and legislators but found no consensus among them on any subject; rather, every time I came across an opinion, I found other opinions that were different or even contradictory. As for the *aya(s)* concerning *hijab*, I found over 10 interpretations, none of them in harmony or even agreement with the others as if each scholar wanted to support what he saw and none of the interpretations was based on clear evidence.[15]

Zin al-Din argues that Islam is based on freedom of thought, will, speech, and action, and that no Muslim has authority over another Muslim in matters of religion, mind, and will. She cites many verses from the Qur'an to show that God did not want even his Prophet to watch over the deeds or misdeeds of Muslims: 'He who obeys the Apostle, obeys God; But if any turn away, We have not sent thee To watch Over their evil deeds' (*Sura al-Nisa'*, *Aya* 80). God also said, addressing his Apostle: 'If it had been God's Plan, they would not have taken False gods: but We Made thee not one To watch over their doings, Nor art thou set Over them to dispose of their affairs' (*Sura al-An'am*, *Aya* 107). And then in another *sura*: 'Therefore do thou give Admonition, for thou art One to admonish. Thou art not one To manage (men's) affairs' (*Sura al-Gashiya*, *Aya* 21–22). Zin al-Din then argues that if God did not allow the Prophet Muhammad to watch over people's deeds, how do other Muslims assume for themselves such a privilege? Through well-chosen and well-placed quotations from the Qur'an and *hadith*, Zin al-Din establishes that Islam is the religion of freedom and that Muslims are only accountable to their God. The claims of some Islamists to be the custodians of Islamic practices are therefore against the very spirit of Islam. The Prophet was also instructed to 'Invite all to the Way of thy Lord with wisdom And beautiful preaching; And argue with them In ways that are best And most gracious: For thy Lord knoweth best, Who have strayed from His Path' (*Sura al-Nahl*, *Aya* 125). God also said: 'And dispute ye not With the People of the Book, Except with means better (Than mere disputation), unless It be with those of them Who inflict wrong (and injury): But say, 'We believe In the Revelation which has come down to us and in that Which came down to you' (*Sura al-Ankabut*, *Aya* 46).

Through these citations and many similar ones, Zin al-Din argues that the question of belief or non-belief and the question of carrying out the instructions of Islam are matters between God and the individual. No one on earth, not even God's apostle, is responsible for those who believe or those who do not, and no measures should be taken against those who refuse to be Muslims. Only logical arguments should be used, and used kindly; true belief should stem from the heart and generate a feeling of satisfaction and inner peace, for 'If it had been thy Lord's Will, They would all have believed, All who are on earth. Wilt thou then compel mankind Against their will, to believe!' (*Sura Yunus*, *Aya* 99). In an *aya* that bears no possible other interpretation, God says 'Let there be no compulsion in religion: Truth stands out clear from Error' (*Sura al-Baqara*, *Aya* 256). In citing these and many other similar *ayas* from the Qur'an, Zin al-Din establishes that Muslims are

responsible only to their God and that no authority on earth has
the right to be God's representative, especially as God's Apostle
was not allowed to watch over the deeds of Muslims. She convincingly argues that this is a lesson to all Muslims that no one
on earth, not even the Prophet Muhammad, is authorized by God
to punish people for their lack of faith, as all Muslims are free in
will and thought; it follows, then, that Muslim women are free.
The problem lies with the laws legislated in the name of the
Islamic *shari'a*; laws that are in total contradiction to the spirit of
Islam. She complains that the practices of some religious authorities violate Islam and God's *shari'a*; 'It is a great shame that some
Muslim local authorities dare to disobey the words of God and
impose constraints on the freedom of Muslim women in towns,
while non-Muslim women in towns and Muslim women in the
countryside enjoy their full freedom.'[16]

There is no basis in the Qur'anic text for the idea that men are
better than women. God prefers the most pious regardless of
gender: 'O mankind! We created You from a single (pair) Of a
male and female, And made you into Nations and tribes that Ye
may know each other (Not that ye may despise Each other). Verily
The most honored of you In the sight of God Is (he who is) the
most Righteous of you, And God has full knowledge And is well
acquainted (With all things)' (*Sura al-Hujurat, Aya* 13). God also
stated in the Qur'an: 'O mankind! reverence Your Guardian Lord,
Who created you From a single Person, Created, of like nature,
His mate, and from them twain Scattered (like seeds) Countless
men and women' (*Sura al-Nisa', Aya* 1). Again it is stated in the
Qur'an 'It is He Who hath Produced you From a single person'
(*Sura al-An'am, Aya* 98).

Zin al-Din attributes the idea that men are superior to women
to the state of servitude to which women have been reduced
throughout the ages. She draws a parallel with slavery: 'That was
the case of each nation reduced into slavery and of each people
deprived of their freedom. No slave has ever excelled before
gaining his freedom because the injustice imposed on him exhausts
the powers of his mind and prevents its effects from emerging.'[17]
Women's inferior social status has nothing to do with their mind
or religion. Was the inequality that prevailed between the serf and
the master the result of the former's shortcomings? There is not
a single *aya* that grants men a degree over women in either mind
or religion: 'If any one do deeds Of righteousness, Be they Male

or Female And have faith, They will enter Heaven, and not the least injustice Will be done to them' (*Sura al-Nisa', Aya* 124).

Zin al-Din's advocacy against the veil does not aim at depriving women of their status as mothers, nor does she wish to lower their status to that of mere imitators of men. Her advocacy is prompted by her belief that 'knowledge rather than ignorance preserves women's dignity and morality.'[18] She cites Muslim scholars, including Shaykh Muhammad Abduh, Shaykh Badr al-Din al-Na'sani, Shaykh Yusuf al-Faqih, Shaykh Jamal al-Din al-Afghani, Muhyi' Din al-Arabi and Shaykh Mustafa al-Ghalayini, who decried the distortion of the *hadith* and insisted that Islam does not accept judgment without evidence and clear proof. Those authorities insisted that we only follow what God Himself has stated in the Qur'anic text and what his Apostle has explained.[19]

Zin al-Din divides her evidence against *hijab* into two parts: intellectual and religious. She first cites intellectual and historical arguments contending that *hijab* encourages immorality rather than morality and decent behavior. Masking identity is an obvious incentive for wrongdoing: 'Can't men see that thieves and murderers mask their true identities in order to have the nerve to commit crimes?'[20] She explains that 'fear of social disgrace is one of the strongest imperatives that restrain people from wrong doing. Why do men deny women this important imperative?'[21] She goes on to ask 'How could serfdom be an incentive to morality? Only if darkness could be the source of light and death the cause of life and annihilation the reason for existence!' Zin al-Din stipulates that the morality of the self and the cleanness of the conscience are far better than the morality of the *chador*. No goodness is to be hoped from pretence; all goodness is in the essence of the self.

Zin al-Din also argues that imposing the veil on women is the ultimate proof that men suspect their mothers, daughters, wives and sisters of being potential traitors to them. This means that men suspect 'the women closest and dearest to them. What quality of life do they live if they are in a perpetual state of suspicion about their mothers, daughters, sisters and wives, fearing all the time their betrayal?'[22] How can society trust women with the most consequential job of bringing up children when it does not trust them with their faces and bodies? How can Muslim men meet rural and European women who are not veiled and treat them respectfully but not treat urban Muslim women in the same way? She concludes this part of the book by stating that it is not an

Islamic duty on Muslim women to wear *hijab*. If Muslim legislators have decided that it is, their opinions are wrong. If *hijab* is based on women's lack of intellect or piety, can it be said that all men are more perfect in piety and intellect than all women?

Zin al-Din then wonders how some people can consider *hijab* and the total withdrawal of women from public life a sign of their honor and dignity. An honorable woman is someone who does useful things for both herself and for others. If all women are locked behind walls or behind *hijab*, how can we distinguish one from the other? The spirit of a nation and its civilization is a reflection of the spirit of the mother. How can any mother bring up distinguished children if she herself is deprived of her personal freedom? She concludes that in enforcing *hijab*, society becomes a prisoner of its customs and traditions rather than of Islam.

In the second part of the book, Zin al-Din sets out to prove that neither the text of the Qur'an nor the *hadith* require Muslim women to wear *hijab*. The *ayas* in the Qur'an concerning *hijab* are four, two of them addressed to the wives of the Prophet and two to Muslim women in general. She cites each of the two groups of *ayas*, discusses all the explanations stated in interpretive texts, cites the *ayas* against these interpretations, and finally reaches her own conclusions. The first two *ayas* about the wives of the Prophet Muhammad (32 and 53) of *Sura al-Ahzab* read as follows:

O consorts of the Prophet! Ye are not like any Of the (other) women: If ye do fear (God), Be not too complaisant Of speech, lest one In whose heart is A disease should be moved With desire: but speak ye A speech (that is) just. And stay quietly in Your houses, and make not A dazzling display, like That of the former Times Of Ignorance; and establish Regular Prayer, and give Regular Charity; and obey God and His Apostle. And God only wishes To remove all abomination From you, Members Of the Family, and to make You Pure and spotless. And recite what is Rehearsed to you in your Homes, of the Signs of God And His Wisdom: For God understands The finest mysteries and Is well-acquainted (with them). (*Ayas* 32–4, of *Sura al-Ahzab*).

The second *aya* concerning the wives of the Prophet (53) says:

Ye who believe! Enter not the Prophet's houses, Until leave is given you, For a meal, (and then) Not (so early as) to wait For its preparation; but when Ye are invited, enter; And when ye have taken Your meal, disperse, Without seeking familiar talk. Such (behavior) annoys The Prophet; he is ashamed To dismiss you, but God is not ashamed (To

tell you) the truth. And when ye Ask (his ladies) For anything ye want,
Ask them from before A screen; that makes For greater purity for Your
hearts and for theirs. Nor is it right for you That ye should annoy
God's Apostle, or that Ye should marry his widows After him at any
time. Truly such a thing is In God's sight an enormity.

Zin al-Din reviews the mainstream interpretations of these *ayas*
in the best known books of *tafsir* (the interpretation of the Qur'an),
namely *al-Tafsir al-mawsum bi-anwar al-tanzil wa asrar al-ta'wil* (The
Interpretation Characterized by the Lights of Inspiration and the
Secrets of Understanding) by the judge Baydawi, *Tafsir al-Qur'an
al-jalil* (The Interpretation of the Glorious Qur'an) by Imam Ala
al-Din al-Sufi known as al-Khazin; *Madarik al-tanzil wa haqa'iq al-
ta'wil* (Domains of the Text and Truths of Interpretation) by Imam
Abdullah al-Nasafi, which is a comment on al-Khazin's interpretation, and *Mujama' al-bayan fi tafsir al-Qur'an* (The Cluster of
Evidence in Interpreting the Qur'an) by Imam al-Tabari. They all
agree that these *ayas* are addressed to the wives of the Prophet
and not to other Muslim women, although they differ on the
reasons that caused these *ayas* to be sent by God to his Prophet.
Al-Nasafi adds that when these *ayas* were addressed to the wives
of the Prophet, other Muslim women asked why were they not
addressed by God? After that the *aya* 'Muslim men and Muslim
women, etc.' was conveyed to the Prophet. Challenging those
Muslim interpreters who claim that these *ayas* call on the wives of
the Prophet or all Muslim women to stay at home and inactive,
Zin al-Din draws upon many examples of women active in all
walks of life during the time of the Prophet and his caliphs. In *The
Status of Woman in Islam* by Prince Ali Khal and in *The Rights of
Woman in Islam* by Ahmad Agayeeve, it is stated that Fatima al-
Zahra, the daughter of the Prophet, gave lessons and lectures to
both men and women and that Shaykha Shahda (5th/11th), known
as the Pride of Women, gave lectures and lessons in the schools
and mosques of Baghdad in literature, history, *fiqh* and religion.
Imam Shafi'i learned at the hands of Nafisi, who was the grand-
daughter of Ali Bin Abi Talib and wife of Ishaq, son of Jafar al-
Sadiq. Qatar al-Nada, wife of the caliph al-Mu'tad and mother of
al-Muqtadir, met in the presence of ministers the ambassadors of
foreign countries and reviewed people's cases every Friday with
judges and advisors in her audience. In brief, Muslim women
remained in mixed company with men until the late sixth century
IE (eleventh century CE). They received guests, held meetings,

and went to wars helping their brothers and husbands defend their castles and bastions.[23]

The other two *ayas* that are usually taken to justify the imposition of *hijab* on Muslim women are *Aya* 30 from *Sura al-nur* and *Aya* 59 from *Sura al-ahzab*. The first *aya* reads:

> Say to the believing men That they should lower Their gaze and guard Their modesty: that will make For greater purity for them: And God is well acquainted with all that they do. And say to the believing women That they should lower Their gaze and guard Their modesty; that they Should not display their Beauty and ornaments except What (must ordinarily) appear Thereof; that they should Draw their veils over Their bosoms and not display Their beauty except To their husbands, their fathers, Their Husband's fathers, their sons, Their husband's sons, Their brothers or their brothers' sons, Or their sisters' sons, or their women, or the slaves Whom their right hands Possess, or male servants Free of physical needs, Or small children who Have no sense of the shame of sex; and that they Should not strike their feet In order to draw attention To their hidden ornaments.

Aya 59 from *Sura al-Ahzab* reads: 'Prophet! Tell Thy wives and daughters, And the believing women, That they should cast Their outer garments over their persons (when outside): That is most convenient, That they should be known (As such) and not molested.'

Zin al-Din reviews the interpretations of these two *ayas* by al-Khazin, al-Nasafi, Ibn Masud, Ibn Abbas and al-Tabari and finds them full of contradictions. Yet, almost all interpreters agreed that women should not veil their faces and their hands and anyone who advocated that women should cover all their bodies including their faces could not base his argument on any religious text. If women were to be totally covered, there would have been no need for the *ayas* addressed to Muslim men: 'Say to the believing men that they should lower their gaze and guard their modesty.' (*Sura al-Nur, Aya 30*). She supports her views by referring to the sayings of the Prophet Muhammad, always taking into account what the Prophet himself said, namely, that everything has to be referred back to the book of God and anything that is inconsistent with it is an ornament. 'I did not say a thing that is not in harmony with God's book.'[24] When ordering the wives of the Prophet to wear *hijab* for special reasons relating to the house of the Prophet, God, as if He feared that Muslim women might imitate the wives of the Prophet, stressed: 'O consorts of the

Prophet! ye are not like any of the (other) women' (*Ahzab*, 53). Thus it is very clear that God did not want us to measure ourselves against the wives of the Prophet and wear *hijab* like them and there is no ambiguity whatsoever regarding this *aya*. Therefore, those who imitate the wives of the Prophet and wear *hijab* are disobeying God's will. In *Islam ruh al-madaniyya* (Islam: The Spirit of Civilization) Shaykh Mustafa Ghalayini reminds his readers that veiling pre-dated Islam and that Muslims learned from other peoples with whom they mixed. He adds that '*hijab* as it is known today is prohibited by the Islamic *shari'a*. Any one who looks at *hijab* as it is worn by some women would find that it makes them more desirable than if they went out without *hijab*.' [25] A similar argument is produced by Zin al-Din based on interviews she conducted with women before and after wearing *hijab*.

Zin al-Din points out that Islam is not confined to a few urban Muslim women or to some known families in rural societies. Veiling was a custom of rich families as a symbol of status. She quotes Shaykh Abdul Qadir al-Maghribi who also saw in *hijab* an aristocratic habit to distinguish the women of rich and prestigious families from other women. She concludes that *hijab* as it is known today is prohibited by the Islamic *shari'a*.[26]

In the fourth part of the book Zin al-Din discusses the answers, objections, and reactions that she received from such important Muslim authorities as Shaykh Sa'id al-Baghdadi, Shaykh Muhammad Ibrahim al-Qayati al-Azhari from the school of Azhar University in Cairo, Shaykh Muhammad Rahim al-Tarabulsi and Shaykh Mustafa al-Ghalayini. It appears that the heated arguments that followed the publication of her first book only made her stronger in her defence of women's rights. She dedicated her first book to her father, her second book to all women: 'Because you have the spirit of the mother and because I believe that reform in the East is built on the basis of your freedom and your struggle for what is right. May you have an overflow of God's light.'

Nazira Zin al-Din had her supporters. Writer Amin al-Rihani, head of the Syrian government Taj al-Din al-Husni, and Education Minister Muhammad Kurd Ali[27] sent her letters of support. The French Consul in Beirut wrote to her that he ordered parts of her book to be translated so that he could study it. She was the talk of Cairo, Alexandria, Damascus, Aleppo, and Baghdad. The Lebanese emigrants in Argentina, the United States, and Brazil sent her letters and wrote in their local newspapers in her support.

The book was reviewed in major journals and newspapers in Damascus, Beirut, Cairo, New York, Buenos Aires, São Paulo, Baghdad, Aleppo and she received letters from men of religion, heads of state and governments, and from editors and publishers all over the world.

At least three Muslim scholars agreed with Zin al-Din's arguments and raised similar concerns about the necessity of sifting Islamic legislation from rumors and falsifications which later became part of Islamic practices. Shaykh Muhammad al-Ghazali in his book *Sunna Between Fiqh and Hadith*[28] argues that women can assume any post they are qualified to assume except that of the caliph and this, he insists, is the rule of true Islam. He declares that those who claim that women's reform is conditioned by wearing the veil are lying to God and his Prophet. None of the four Imams has said that seeing a woman's face is an offence. In total harmony with Zin al-Din's arguments Shaykh Muhammad al-Ghazali expresses the opinion that the contemptuous view of women has been passed on from the first *jahiliya* (the Pre-Islamic period) to the Islamic society. He uses the same argument, citing the same *aya* as cited by Mustafa Ghalayini[29] in order to prove that Muslim women do not have to cover their faces and hands. Al-Ghazali's argument is that Islam has made it compulsory on women not to cover their faces during *haj* and *salat* (prayer) the two important pillars of Islam. How then could Islam ask women to cover their faces at ordinary times?[30] Through his detailed study of the time of the Prophet Muhammad he reaches the conclusion that it was a time when *sufur* was prevalent.[31] He stresses that 'looking down at women is a crime in Islam, and that true Islam rejects the customs of nations which impose constraints on women or belittle their rights and duties.'[32] Hence, according to al-Ghazali, our customs and habits should be scrutinized in order to leave only what is closely connected with the Islamic *shari'a* and our adherence to these rules should be in proportion to their harmony with the Qur'anic text.

Like Zin al-Din, al-Ghazali is a believer and is confident that all traditions that function to keep women ignorant and prevent them from functioning in public are the remnants of *jahiliya* and that following them is contrary to the spirit of Islam. God said in the Glorious Qur'an: 'The Believers, men and women, are protectors, One of another; they enjoin What is just, and forbid What is evil: they observe Regular prayers, practice Regular charity, and

obey God and His Apostle. On them will God pour His mercy:
for God Is Exalted in power, Wise.' (*Sura Tauba, Aya* 71) Like Zin
al-Din, Shaykh Ghazali insists on a basic Muslim right to compare
different interpretations and different versions of Islamic sayings
and to choose the more reasonable and the more useful to follow.
The easier to adopt for Islam is the religion of *yusur* (flexibility)
and not of *usur* (intransigence). As a Muslim scholar, he rejected
the undermining of women's will in marriage and was not against
her initiating marriage if her situation required it. Efficient and
knowledgeable women should be able to assume any post they
like except that of the caliph. Women can consult and give their
opinion and the weight of their opinion is in proportion to its
validity and correctness. He says 'we don't yearn to make women
heads of state or government, but we yearn for one thing, a head
of state or government should be the most efficient *person* in the
nation.'[33] Commenting on all these wrong attitudes to women al-
Ghazali says that during the time of the Prophet women were
equals at home, in the mosques and on the battlefield. Today true
Islam is being destroyed in the name of Islam.

Another Muslim scholar, Abd al-Halim Abu Shiqa, who wrote
a scholarly study of women in Islam entitled *Tahrir al-mara'a fi 'asr
al-risalah*: (The Emancipation of Women during the Time of the
Prophet)[34] agrees with Zin al-Din and al-Ghazali about the discrepancy between the status of women during the time of the
Prophet Muhammad and the status of women today. He says:

> Through my study of the time of the Prophet I found texts and sayings
> of the Prophet which show women acting in all kinds of professions in
> total difference to what we see, understand and interpret today. This
> great discrepancy explained to me why so many women got away from
> (Islam) because it simply deprived them of the rights of life; that is why
> I felt it my duty to offer the women from the habits and rules of *jahiliyya*
> which are mistakenly thought to be Islamic.[35]

He agreed with Zin al-Din and al-Ghazali that Islamists have
made up sayings which they attributed to the Prophet such as
'women are lacking in both intellect and religion' and in many
cases they brought sayings which are not reliable at all and promoted them among Muslims until they became part of the Islamic
culture.

Like Zin al-Din and al-Ghazali, Abu Shiqa finds that in many
countries very weak and unreliable sayings are invented to support

customs and traditions which are then considered to be part of the *shari'a*. Like Zin al-Din, he argues that the text of the Qur'an proves that both men and women are from the same self and quotes the same *aya* that Zin al-Din quotes: 'O mankind! reverence Your Guardian Lord, Who created you From a single Person, Created, of like nature, His mate, and from them twain Scattered (like seeds) countless men and women; Reverence God, through Whom Ye demand your mutual (rights), and (reverence) the wombs (That bore you): for God Ever watches over you.' (*Sura Nisa', Aya* 1) He Argues that it is the Islamic duty of women to participate in public life and in spreading good: 'The Believers, men and women, are protectors, One of another: they enjoin what is just, and forbid what is evil.' (*Sura Tauba, Aya* 71) It is the same *aya* quoted by Imam Muhammad al-Ghazali to prove the same point.

As for those who prevent women from going out to work, Abu Shiqa answers: 'if women are prevented from going out to work, what is the meaning of the following *aya*: 'Do not desire what God had granted to others; For men a share of what they earn and for women a share of what they earn' (*Sura Nisa', Aya* 32). He also agrees with Zin al-Din and Ghazali that *hijab* was for the wives of the Prophet and that it was against Islam for women to imitate the wives of the Prophet. If women were to be totally covered, why did God ask both men and women to lower their gaze. (*Sura al-Nur, Aya*(s); 30–1) In most of his arguments he cites the same verses cited by Zin al-Din and shows a similar understanding of them. There is no difference at all between Zin al-Din, al-Ghazali and Dr Abdol Halim Abu Shiqa.

Shaykh Muhammad Husayn Fadl Allah, in his book *Ta'amulat Islamiyya hawl al-mara'* (Islamic Speculations About Women),[36] also agrees with these three Muslim scholars on most issues concerning women's *hijab*, freedom, work and political responsibilities. He stresses that Islam sees men and women as one in humanity and responsibility.[37] Islam neither absolves women from their responsibilities nor does it undermine their femininity. Quite the contrary: Islam stresses that women should feel and enjoy their beauty but without any display or attempts to provoke desire. This is precisely the understanding of Zin al-Din and al-Ghazali of *Aya* 59 of *Sura al-ahzab* that is taken by some Muslim scholars to mean the imposition of *hijab* on all Muslim women. It is almost certain that a comparative study of the works of these four Muslim scholars would yield fruitful results. It was Muhammad al-Ghazali who wrote an introduction to Abu Shiqa's book, *Tahrir al-mara' fi 'asr al-risalah*. In this introduction, al-Ghazali says: 'I wish this book had appeared centuries ago and exposed women's issues in Islamic society in such a mature way. Because Muslims have deviated from the instructions of their religion in dealing with women, dark rumors and fabricated *hadith* spread among them leaving Muslim women in deep ignorance, quite removed from religion and life ... This book takes Muslims back to the correct *sunna* of their prophet with no minus or plus.'[38]

While the views of the three Muslim men writing over half a century after Zin al-Din are given some space in Arabic papers and journals, Zin al-Din has not been referred to either by them or even by a woman scholar like Fatima Mernissi who addresses the same subject.[39] One wonders what would have happened to Zin al-Din had she published her books in the 1990s instead of the 1920s? Would she find any *shaykh* to answer her arguments or would she be silenced in one way or another? One cannot help drawing comparisons with Taslima Nasrin, whose statements on Islam are not yet properly quoted, nor is it precisely known what she actually said. Yet some Islamists have called on Muslims to kill her. There is no *aya* in the Qur'an that allows any Muslim, not even the Prophet Muhammad himself, to subscribe to killing another person simply because he or she has expressed views that contradict the views of a certain Muslim scholar, school, or group. I can only agree with what Lisa Beyer wrote in her article 'Life Behind the Veil': 'if the wives of Muhammad lived in parts of the contemporary Islamic world, they might be paying a high price for their independence.'[40]

Notes

1. Qadariyya Husayn, *Shahirat al-nisa' fi'l-'alam al-Islamiyya* (Famous Women in the Muslim World). Translated from Turkish by Abdol Aziz Amin al-Khanji (Cairo: Matba'at al-Sa'adeh, 1924), p. 33.

2. Muhammad Shahrur, *al-Kitab wa'l-Qur'an* (The Book and the Qur'an) (Damascus: al-Ahali publishers, 1992), p 594.

3. Husayn, *op. cit.*, p. 74.

4. Abdol Sir Afifi, *al-Mara'a al-arabiyya fi jahiliyatiha wa Islamiha* (Arab Woman in her Jahiliya and Islam), (Cairo: Matba'at al-Ma'arif, 1933), p. 138.

5. *Ibid.*, p. 139.

6. *Ibid.*, p. 142.

7. Fatima al-Batoul Mersa, 'Muslim Women in Arab History,' *al-Ahram*, Cairo, 15 April 1989, p. 5.

8. Hussein, *op. cit.*, p. 179.

9. *Ibid.*, pp. 179–80.

10. See Afifi, *op. cit.*, part two, p. 147.

11. *Ibid.*, pp. 147–9.

12. *Ibid.*, pp. 153–4.

13. *al-Fatat wa'l-shiukh*, printed by Nazira Zin al-Din's father Sa'id Bik Zin al-Din (Beirut, 1929), p. 75.

14. Nazira Zin al-Din, *al-Sufur wa'l-hijab* (Beirut: Quzma Publications, 1928), p. 37.

15. *Ibid.*, p. 37.

16. *Ibid.*, p. 21.

17. *Ibid.*, p, 69.

18. *Ibid.*, p. 27.

19. See *ibid.*, pp. 42–8.

20. *Ibid.*, p. 125.

21. *Ibid.*, p. 125.

22. *Ibid.*, p. 135.

23. See *ibid.*, pp. 191–2.

24. *Ibid.*, p. 226.

25. Shaykh Mustafa al-Ghalayini, *Islam ruh al-madaniyya* (Islam: The Spirit of Civilization) (Beirut: al-Maktabah al-Asriyya, 1960), p. 253.

26. *Ibid.*, pp. 255–56.

27. Zin al-Din, *al-Fatat wa'l-shiukh*, *op. cit.*, part 3, pp. w-6.

28. Shaykh Muhammad al-Ghazali, *Sunna Between Fiqh and Hadith* (Cairo: Dar al-Shuruq, 1989, 7th edition, 1990).

29. Ghalayini, *op. cit.*, p. 254.

30. al-Ghazali, *op. cit.*, p. 44.

31. *Ibid.*, p. 49.

32. *Ibid.*, p. 52.

33. *Ibid.*, p. 56.

34. Abd al-Halim Abu Shiqa, *Tahrir al-mara' fi 'asr al-risalah* (Kuwait: Dar al-Qalam, 1990).

35. *Ibid.*, p. 5.

36. Shaykh Muhammad Husayn Fadl Allah, *Ta'amulat Islamiyya hawl al mara'* (Beirut: Dar al-Milak, 1992).

37. *Ibid.*, p. 25.

38. Abu Shiqa, *op. cit.*, p. 5.

39. *al-Harim al-siyassi; al Nabi wa'l-nisa'* (Political Harim; The Prophet and Women) Translated by Abd al-Hadi Abbas (Damascus: Dar al-Hasad, 1990).

40. *Time*, Fall 1990, p. 37.

6

Networking for Change: The Role of Women's Groups in Initiating Dialogue on Women's Issues[1]

Farida Shaheed

Women's lives are situated in a complex web of influences that derive from personal and political developments, cultural and structural environments, and local, national, and international concerns. At any given time, this web of influences determines for the individual woman what is probable, possible, or out of bounds. It is in the light of their knowledge and experience of these multiple factors that women have devised their strategies for survival. Women's mobilization therefore depends both on the resources available to them and on their ability to analyze and understand these factors. Women's groups can facilitate mobilization by demystifying the factors that constrain women's potential and by providing support mechanisms for change. Here we will examine the contextual constraints that have shaped women's strategies for survival and well-being in the Muslim world and the relevance of networking as a strategy for accelerating change.

First, it should be said that the essential components of patriarchal structures in a Muslim society are the same as elsewhere, and women's subordination occurs at multiple levels: in the structures of family and kinship, in state policies and programmes, in the discourse of dictatorial and populist ideologies, and in the politics and policies of the new world order.

Second, the impression that the Muslim world is homogeneous is a myth deliberately nurtured by vested interests. While some similarities may stretch across cultures, classes, sects, religious schools, and continents of the Muslim world, the diversities are at least as striking. Interaction between women from different Muslim societies indicates that their experience ranges 'from being strictly closeted, isolated and voiceless within four walls, subjected to public floggings and condemned to death for presumed adultery (which is considered a crime against the state) and forcibly given in marriage as a child, to situations where women have a far greater degree of freedom of movement and interaction, enjoy the right to work and to participate in public affairs, and also exercise a far greater control over their own lives.'[2]

This is hardly surprising since the communities and states that make up the Muslim world have widely divergent cultures, social structures, and histories. Consequently, while it is frequently claimed that any given state, society or community is Islamic, it is in fact not Islamic (i.e., ordained by religious scriptures), only Muslim (i.e., comprised of people who adhere to Islam). This distinction is particularly important today when religious idiom is increasingly colouring the political discourse in so many Muslim communities in which ever more strident claims and counter-claims over who is the only true mantle-bearer of Islam compete for popular support and political power. These discourses posit uniformity and yet the actual diversities in structures, norms, and cultures visible in the Muslim world reflect the degree to which the assimilation of Islamic doctrine depends on a particular society's understanding of Islam on the one hand, and on how it grafts this understanding onto prevailing structures, systems, and practices on the other.

Third, women themselves are not an undifferentiated mass defined exclusively by gender. Within and across societies they are distinguishable (and often divided) by class, race, and ethnicity, factors which moderate women's interaction with each other and with the state and religion. Indeed, the diversity of Muslim societies and the differing realities of women within them have produced a plethora of feminist responses in the political arena that range from the exclusively secular to the exclusively theological, with many permutations in between. Despite all these diversities, what women in most Muslim societies share is that the cultural articulation of patriarchy (through structures, social mores, laws, and political power) is increasingly justified by reference to Islam and Islamic doctrine, a process facilitated by Islam's central role in the self-definition and cultural reality of Muslims at large.[3]

Here, it is important to understand that religions are neither unidimensional nor fixed in time. Attitudes and practices vary according to sect, ethnicity, and class, and can with time be deep-ened or modified, abandoned or continued, replaced or revived. Every religion also operates at different levels – as faith, as an embodiment of social customs, as a mobilizing force in the political arena. Finally, for many people what threads these together is the role of religion as a means both of self-identity and of identification and understanding of one's particular environment and the world at large. The environment itself is not static. Structural and material changes in the means and relations of production occur (in the twentieth century at an increasingly rapid pace), forcing people to engage in a continuous process of adaptation. In this, the understanding and analysis of change and the resultant adaptation is filtered through people's world view, in which religion plays a greater or lesser role. It is the ability of religions to reinterpret traditions continuously in the light of altered circumstances that allows them to survive.

In their attempts to redefine their lives, women confront the obstacle of a social code that is presented – and commonly internalized – as having religious sanction. In reality, the frequency with which customs unconnected and sometimes contradictory to religious doctrine are practiced by communities as supposedly religious, is visible proof that attitudes towards and practices flowing from religion are determined as much by collective memories, existing social structures, and power relations as by doctrines.[4] Most individuals do not, however, distinguish customs, practices, or attitudes from their faith and self-identification. To a large extent, therefore, improving everyday reality is conditional on women's ability to distinguish their religious faith from the social customs that have become its symbolical representations.

Of equal importance to women's strategies is the increasing use of religious idiom in the political arena. The political use of Islam is not new to the Muslim world; indeed its presence is strong enough for one feminist to conclude that 'not only have the sacred texts always been manipulated, but manipulation of them is a structural characteristic of the practice of power in Muslim societies.'[5] Whether Islam has been used by those in power or those seeking it, by right-wing elements or – and less frequently – by progressive forces, it has been invoked in a bid for political power: for consolidating support or legitimizing force.[6] Furthermore, in the second half of the twentieth century, the political use of Islam has almost inevitably militated against women's self-realization, undermining women's ability to assume control over their own lives by locating both the discourse and decision making in religious scholarship, an area that has long excluded women.

It is against this rather complex background that women in the Muslim world face the challenge of evolving strategies for survival and well-being. Challenges appear at two different levels: first, at the level of public discourse in national and international policies; second, in women's everyday experiences of gender and religion. At the level of discourse three issues need to be addressed: first, the premium placed on gender roles and family/personal laws; second, the myth of one monolithic world of Islam bolstered through political discourses and third, the isolation in which many women in the Muslim world have been obliged by circumstances to conduct their struggles. At the level of the everyday existence, there is a need to understand women's experiences of religion and gender in the light of their different locations in class, culture and political preferences, and, secondly, to review the tendency of many women's movements to focus on the public and political to the virtual exclusion of the personal, and to examine how this affects their ability to meet the challenge of altering women's everyday lives. At the levels of both public discourse and everyday existence, dichotomous choices need to be replaced by multiplicity and by an acceptance of diversity. Equally, at every level, issues of development and human rights must be integrated and acknowledged as two sides of the same coin.

The Public Discourse on Islam

In much of the Muslim world the politico-religious discourse at both the national and international levels has been characterized by an unfortunate emphasis on gender roles as the determining criteria of an identity which is distinguishable from that of 'the other,' most frequently the West but also other peoples and cultures in the South. This emphasis is not limited to verbal assertions in public discourses or to social norms, but is concretized in the selectivity with which Muslim jurisprudence or *shari'a* is applied.

In most Muslim-majority countries the legislation governing commerce, revenues/taxes, administrative matters, public service and other public sectors such as banking, the military, and political structures, has little to do with Islam and yet provokes little debate. The laws applied in these fields are either legacies of the colonial period or have been adopted from elsewhere. In sharp contrast, the official laws governing personal and family matters are almost universally premised on Muslim jurisprudence and justified by reference to Islamic injunctions. Throughout much of the world, therefore, the Muslim identity of a community appears to hinge almost exclusively on the regulation of family and personal matters.[7] The emphasis on gender as a cornerstone of cultural identity is neither new nor limited to the Muslim world, where it can at least be traced back to experiences of colonization or dependency on the West.

The prioritization of gender in cultural self-definitions has been studied both inside and outside the Muslim world. In the former, Leila Ahmed, for example, shows how the portrayal of women's oppression in colonized societies by colonizers was used 'in the rhetoric of colonialism, to render morally justifiable its project of undermining or eradicating the cultures of colonized people.'[8] In the latter, Lata Mani analyzes the public discourse that took place in colonized India on the controversial practice of *sati* (the burning alive of a wife with her dead husband) found amongst some Hindu communities and finds that women became the 'currency ... in a complex set of exchanges in which several competing projects intersect[ed].'[9] The parameters of the discourse set by the colonizers were not challenged by nationalist forces, who responded either by defending all 'traditions' in their confrontation with the colonizers or by initiating reform for women from within the traditional-religious framework as a means of proving themselves worthy of membership in the club of 'modern' administrators and governors. All those who participated in the debate transformed women into a symbolic embodiment of tradition. Women became the ground on which tradition was debated and reformulated, at the same time that the definition of tradition saw a 'colonial privileging of scripture.'[10] This privileging continues today, actively promoted by elements who, in their pursuit of political power, articulate demands in a religious idiom. The frequently undifferentiated image of the Muslim world projected in the non-Muslim world (frequently as unmanageable fanatics) facilitates this privileging.[11]

Laws governing personal and family matters are of critical importance for women because they play a major role in determining the boundaries within which most women can hope to define a socially acceptable individual identity for themselves. Because in the Muslim world personal/family laws are almost invariably classified as Muslim and justified with reference to Islamic doctrine or culture, the identity/space defined for women in any particular

context is automatically elevated to the status of a generic definition of 'the Muslim woman.' A person who challenges any aspect
of law relating to family or personal matters is therefore deemed
to be refuting, or at the very least challenging, the very definition
of a Muslim woman accepted in a particular setting.

Equating any questioning of existing Muslim laws (which per-
force have been drafted by fallible human beings) with a rejection
of Islamic injunctions is a very potent formula for maintaining the
status quo, since it threatens challengers with ostracism. (The same
argument is used to maintain ethnic or national control.) The fear
of being pushed beyond the collectivity of one's nation, religion,
and ethnic group, of being cast out and losing one's identity,
militates against initiating positive action for change. Under these
circumstances, questioning, rejecting, or reformulating 'Muslim'
laws is indeed a major undertaking and one that women – isolated
as they are and collectively the least powerful social group not just
in terms of socio-political and economic structures but also in the
vital fields of culture, jurisprudence, and Islamic scholarship – are
ill-equipped to face.

It is important to situate national discourses, and the attempts
by politico-religious groups to appropriate definitions of gender
and to monopolize the religious discourse within this, squarely in
the context of a struggle for political power and to avoid viewing
these as part of a religious debate (as is too frequently the case).
The domination of the religious idiom in the public political
discourse is often facilitated by a crisis of national identity and the
failure of non-religiously defined political groups to present a
viable alternative.[12] In Pakistan, for instance, a qualitative change
in the use of religious discourse in the 1970s resulted when opposition to the ruling party brought together a motley collection of
political parties, including 'mainstream' and 'secular' parties, who
allowed their demands to be articulated in religious idiom, preparing the ground on which General Zia ul-Haq was to erect his
'Islamization' campaign.

Under Zia (1979–88) the religious discourse was used by a
politically illegitimate martial law regime possibly as a means of
containing intra-state conflict, but definitely as a cloak for imposing
ever more repressive and undemocratic measures and preempting
opposition to these. While the use of religion did nothing to resolve
regional discontent, it was more successful in immobilizing opposition[13] and, in the process, gave currency to religiosity as a key to

accessing state power. As a by-product it increased sectarianism and related violence as different groups vied with each other for the mantle of religious leadership, and promoted intolerance as politicians entered the game of proving their 'Islamic credentials.'[14]

Finally, as stated earlier, the existence of one monolithic world of Islam is a myth deliberately propagated by politically powerful elements for their own benefit. This myth explodes in the face of the conflicts dotting the Muslim world on the issue of whose Islam is to be adopted at the community, state or international level. It is also belied at other levels: firstly by the sometimes radically different laws in the world formally classified as Muslim by different cultural groups; secondly by differences in what is considered 'Muslim' and what is not by different communities, and thirdly by the uneven application of even those rules accepted as Muslim within communities.[15] Each of these variations is indicative of influences extraneous to religious faith in determining reality and definitions of 'Muslim-ness.'

In the case of women, perhaps the most striking illustration of the practical implications of different definitions is the case of female circumcision – or female genital mutilation – that originates and is most widespread in parts of Africa but is shocking to the rest of the non-Shafi'i Muslim world.[16] On the other hand, women from Arab communities are shocked by the widespread practice amongst Muslim communities of South Asia of the bride bringing a dowry with her at the time of marriage. In Pakistan the uneven application of Muslim laws is visible in, for instance, the lack of protection under statutory law of women's religious right to choose a spouse,[17] and the absence of punitive actions for not giving women their due share of inheritance. This points to the existence of dual legal systems within a society: a formal, codified legal system and a parallel system in which customary laws and practices commingle. Further subdivisions are possible. Countries may have two formal codes, the one religious and the other civil (such as in India, the Philippines, and Senegal). Two (or more) versions of customary laws may be discernible: one derived from socio-historical circumstances, the other from Islam. Such parallel systems relate disproportionately to matters concerning personal and family law (in contrast, any suggestion that multi-religious states should allow each community to regulate its own affairs in matters of export–import or military service would be dismissed out of hand). Parallel legal systems are of vital importance to women precisely because the maximum combined impact is felt in family and personal matters.

Nor, by any means, is codified law the sole mechanism a society has to impose external controls on individuals. Violence or the threat of violence by individuals or groups is one example of non-legal (or actually illegal) methods of exercising control. The most efficient method of control, however, is perhaps through the laws an individual internalizes in the process of socialization. Because they require little recourse to overt external enforcement, these unwritten laws are often greater obstacles to women's autonomy than formal legislation. Few Muslim countries have passed laws excluding women from specific occupations or specialized technical schools, limiting their physical mobility or prescribing a particular dress code, or restricting their political participation. Nevertheless in all these areas women's lives are circumscribed by internalized social codes. While it is clear that the law may allow these rules to exist by omission, in some areas informal, internalized 'laws' may actually be in conflict with statute law. In Pakistan, for example, the law rejects the concept of *hilala* which prescribes that, before a divorced couple can remarry each other, the wife must first marry (and divorce) another man. The Muslim Family Laws Ordinance (1961) of Pakistan states that this only applies after the same couple have married and divorced each other three times. Nevertheless *hilala* is practiced in some parts of the country.

Finally, when different coexisting legal systems offer a variety of procedures and options for dealing with the same issue, almost inevitably, and irrespective of the source of law, it is the one that is most disadvantageous for women that is, in fact, implemented. In South Asia, for example, Muslim women were deprived of their religiously sanctioned right to own and inherit property through the imposition of British colonial laws. Clearly non-Muslim, the colonial law was subsequently amended (by the Muslim Personal [Shari'a] Application Acts 1935–43) to incorporate Islamic doctrine granting women inheritance rights. Despite the unquestionably non-Islamic source of the original law, and the history of social activism needed for reform, women continued to be deprived of inheritance in the newly independent Islamic Republic of Pakistan by reference to 'local customs.' Similarly, while the formal state law in Pakistan rejects the oral repudiation of a wife as constituting a legitimate divorce, this practice is widespread, socially accepted and justified by reference to Islamic doctrine. [18] In contrast to the above two instances, where customary practices take precedence over formal law, is the case of adultery. Traditionally, communities in the province of Punjab responded to cases of adultery by forced marriages, social ostracism, public humiliation, or a combination of these. Following the introduction by the martial law regime in 1979 of a supposedly Islamic law covering all manner of extramarital intercourse – this law discriminates against women and provides for harsher punishments that violate human rights (imprisonment, flogging, fines and, under certain circumstances, stoning to death) – customs have been abandoned in favour of the formal law.[19]

Obviously, then, laws are not immutable but shaped by socio-economic and political developments; they are imposed by those in power and involve a constantly changing selection of customs, traditions, religious codes, and external sources (for example, the colonial codes). If research indicates that imperatives other than religious correctness govern the practices of Muslims, in which a major determining factor is the perpetuation of a patriarchal society, the interweaving of traditional customs, mores, and beliefs with religion obscures the sources of both the law and ethnically defined or geographically specific frameworks outlining the parameters of a Muslim woman's identity.

The seeming helplessness of a majority of women in the Muslim world to mobilize effectively against and overcome adverse laws and customs is not just the result of women's economic and political powerlessness. Two other factors contribute to keeping women immobile: one is a lack of knowledge concerning statutory laws in their own countries and those of other Muslim communities, as well as the sources of these; the other is the interlocking of customs, religion, and law in such a manner as to render it impossible for the average Muslim woman to conceive of being able to retain her Muslim identity if she rejects certain laws or customs (for example, female genital mutilation in Sudan, Somalia, Senegal, and parts of Nigeria, Egypt, and elsewhere). Together these factors promote an erroneous belief amongst women (also amongst men, but we are concerned here with women) that the only existence possible for a Muslim woman who wishes to maintain her identity – however that may be defined – is the one delineated for her in her own national context. Presented as products of self-evident consensus, cultural identities are in fact socially constructed concepts that reflect patterns of dominance and opposition found within a society. They are exploited by those in power (or those aspiring to such power) to their own advantage.

Since women invariably hold little power, they and other less powerful elements of society tend to be the recipients of cultural dictates and public discourses rather than those who formulate them. This often restricts the options available to women in terms of strategies for change and survival, but does not immobilize them. Indeed, as Fatima Mernissi notes, if the discourse calls upon women to veil themselves, not to work, or to behave in a particular manner, the call itself bears testimony and is a response to the reality of (some) women not veiling, going to work, or behaving differently – in other words, to women's success in redefining traditional notions of gender in their favor to a degree that provokes a response.[20] While women have successfully changed their lives, until recently many have struggled and survived in isolation. In contrast, politico-religious groups have been able to conveniently cite so-called Islamic laws already being applied in various Muslim countries in support of their own demands for more stringent, essentially undemocratic, or discriminatory 'Islamic' laws.

The National Discourse and Everyday Realities in Pakistan

Between 1977 and 1988, the politically and socially conservative discourse adopted by the military regime (the so-called Islamization campaign of Zia ul-Haq) the laws passed by ordinances and the measures instituted provoked the quickest and sharpest reaction from urban professional working women who daily encountered the impact of the conservative discourse (as something new) in their homes, through the state-owned television that blamed working women for the (real and visibly rampant) corruption in society and the disintegration of values in the family; in the streets, going to or returning from work; and in their work environments, where every man seemed to have been granted a state license to pass judgment on women's dress and therefore – by a quantum leap – moral ethics. In the cities non-working elite women, too, were shocked out of their complacency when the government adopted the discourse of the politico-religious parties that, until then, had been disparaged as anti-modern and therefore of no importance. Feeling themselves to be the direct targets of the discourse (if not all the measures), women from the upper middle and middle class formed the main force of a vociferous opposition to state policies.

This group consisted of precisely those women who had most radically redefined the contours of their personal lives, substantially increasing their space in terms of mobility, education, and employment, first during the nationalist movements and then in the early decades of independence. Unfortunately, the altered circumstances of this privileged group did little to change the horizons of the majority of women outside their class and metropolitan locations. In a society such as Pakistan, segregated not just by gender but also by class, social contact and interaction across classes is limited. Consequently, the changed reality of many women's lives was only marginally visible in public spaces and, where it did appear, class identity shielded women embodying this change in their appearance or behavior from overt criticism. This is not to imply that women achieved these rights without a struggle, or that they did not face public harassment, nor am I suggesting other classes of women experienced no change. But the achievements of one class of women did not automatically result in equivalent achievements for women of other classes and, equally, the changes experienced by women of other classes were far less dramatic. For the majority of Pakistan's women the new acceptability of female education was probably the most important innovation that independence brought, not least because attending schools requires children to leave the household compound (the level of mobility increasing in proportion to the educational level) and allows interaction with others outside the immediate family circle, and both these outcomes broaden experience.

The lack of public mobilization of women, other than those professionally employed, on women's issues in the period 1979–88 needs to be examined. The discourse and debate on women – shaped by the rhetoric of the religious right – remained almost exclusively urban. Nor, in the main, was it aimed at the majority of poor women, whether rural or urban, whose transgressions of patriarchal norms, where these occur, do not seem to be perceived as threatening the status quo. There is no doubt that this decade was the most retrogressive for Pakistan's women, marked by state-sponsored legislation, directives, and campaigns seeking to reduce women's rights, to curtail their access to economic resources, and to restrict both their mobility and visibility. Yet, ironically enough, in this same decade the largest number of women were recruited into the formal labor market and the number of women in the informal sector also grew;[21] female applicants for higher education increased, as did the number of technical training institutes for women; and, in urban areas, even as dress codes became more uniform, an unprecedented number and new class of women started appearing in public places of leisure such as parks and restaurants.

A study, 'Women, Religion and Social Change,' conducted towards the end of the Zia era in 1988, provided interesting insights on how women experienced such contradictory influences, the extent to which the official discourse penetrated women's daily lives, and how this interfaced with women's experiences of religion.[22] In the context of women's strategies for survival, the most significant were the centrality and paramount role of the family; the reality of religion in women's lives through prayers, rituals, and practice; and the cognitive disconnection between the two.

While the family is the focal point for women's identity, social interaction, and support, it is also the seat of patriarchal control. Women recognize and easily describe the operational structures of control and authority within the family as determined by age and gender, enumerating the various restrictions imposed upon them and the resultant problems – controlled and limited mobility, being told what to wear or not, where to go or not, and so on. Although class, ethnic and religious identities do modify the quality of control exercised,[23] for the vast majority of women the family is where definitions of gender are most immediately experienced, and therefore need to be challenged. This is easier said than done, since it requires women to balance the projected benefits of rebellion against the certainty of disrupting their primary source of support, and facing the possibility of complete ostracism, or even death.[24] To initiate change women would, at the very least, need alternative reference points and access to systems of support.

The severe limitation imposed on women's physical mobility, however, isolates them in a small social circle centered on the family, minimizing interaction with others, and limiting their access to experiences of alternative definitions of self. The narrower their point of comparison is, the greater the likelihood will be of the existing cycle being reproduced without change. Respondents who had moved with their families from rural or small-town backgrounds (with their own cultures) to larger cities explained that this relocation to a new environment catalyzed a new awareness in themselves. Their families, who represented the norm in the previous setting, now seemed conservative by comparison to others, and their own lives as women appeared more strictly controlled than that of their new peer group. The newly expanded framework of their experience allowed them to make this comparison while exposure to the concrete reality of alternative possibilities inspired in these women (particularly the young) a desire to change the circumstances of their own lives. This supports the contention of those who maintain that while controlling women through identity has multiple ramifications – in which religion, nationality, ethnicity and class all come into play – 'depriving [women] of even dreaming of a different reality is one of the most debilitating forms of oppression [they] face.'[25] It is the vision of a different reality that propels the reformulation of the present one, and it is in their ability to open the doors to a multiplicity of possible alternatives that women's national and international networks can make their most important contribution.

Dreaming of alternative lives and potential change is difficult in the heavily male-dominated society of Pakistan where female role models are rare. Women's identification of the people they admire vividly illustrates the bleakness of a male-dominated landscape in which few women can become public or private figures of admiration. Both history and religion emerge as areas inhabited primarily by men, and even people women know and admire personally are more likely to be men than women. In the study female friends appeared as significant role models only in the upper class – where women have far greater opportunities to change the parameters of their lives. Women politicians, on the other hand, and particularly Benazir Bhutto (who contested elections and became prime minister during the study), inspired the poor more than the rich. Clearly, women are obliged to live their lives and conceive their hopes for the future within very limited horizons and, were it not for those rare women who become important political figures, women as a group would be virtually non-existent as people who inspire respect and admiration.

In sharp contrast to that strain of feminist analysis – both within and outside Pakistan – that sees religion as a major source of women's oppression, women themselves do not view everyday experiences of religion as either oppressive or a factor of constraint. Nor did they perceive the structures operating in the family, or relationships within these, as deriving from religious tenets.[26]

The extent to which religion is internalized can be gauged from the failure of women in the study to mention any religious activities when describing their daily routines. The integration of religion into women's routine appeared far more dramatically in response to direct questions on religious practices, indicating that rituals and practices – as much as household responsibilities, child care, agriculture or care for livestock, studies, or a job – shape and structure a woman's day in Pakistan, irrespective of whether she is a Christian, Hindu, Parsee, or Muslim, or whether she lives in a rural or urban setting, is poor or rich.

Women who expressed a sense of helplessness, unfulfilled desires, and stunted growth at the end of Zia's decade of 'Islamization' identified traditional culture (which includes, but is not limited to, religion), society, and male control as the root cause. They complained of the lack of freedom to decide matters for themselves, the lack of self-confidence (and permission) to travel and be mobile, the inability to earn, of the ties of children and other restraints that bind them. In other words, women complained about the restricted repertoires of permissible experiences for women in their context, without relating this to religion in any way. In a class-based society, the disadvantages of being female were most acutely and immediately felt by the poor, who are additionally disadvantaged in so many other respects, including a narrow range of experience. With education and less severely controlled lives, women expand their reference points and are better able to shape their own lives. In a sense, religion, in conjunction with cultural traditions, colors the context in which women live, but the actual contours of this life, the avenues that are open and the barriers imposed – the road map, as it were, to living – are seen as being socially determined and male-imposed, with elasticity increasing with class and according to ethnic identity.

The Feminist Response

One of the distinguishing factors of religion is its capacity to provide self-affirmation at the personal psychological level as well as at the level of the social collectivity. Through its rituals, practices, and structure, religion allows an immediate sense of participation and belonging unavailable to vast numbers of women in other aspects of their lives.[27] Neither daily nor episodic religious

events are seen by most women as intrusive in their lives; if anything they are welcomed. It is important to note that the participatory nature of religion is neither limited to nor dependent on its
function of social bonding. If periodic religious events provide a
vehicle for reaffirming membership in a community, the individual,
in and by herself, is the pivot of daily prayers. The participatory
nature of religion tends to be overlooked by the feminist discourse
and, at least in the context of Pakistan, is not provided for in
feminist activism. Even ignoring the psychological healing that
religion may provide women, and focusing just on social aspects,
in the absence of alternatives it is unlikely that women will willingly abandon precisely those structures that provide them with
solace and support.[28]

One of the most striking aspects of the study, 'Women, Religion
and Social Change', was that in the course of several sittings in
which women were encouraged to speak of their daily lives and
experiences of time, space, body, and womanhood, hardly any
woman referred to the political discourse so prominent in the
mass media of the time and the focus of activist women's groups,
much less to the laws, directives, and policies passed during that
period. In contrast, women's public response to the conservative
political discourse led by middle-class professionals focused almost
exclusively on these issues. Despite its narrow base, the emerging
women's movement in Pakistan had remarkable success in some
areas: it put women on the national agenda, mobilized resistance
against discriminatory laws and directives, delayed the enactment
of certain laws (and contributed to important amendments in
proposed legislation),[29] and catalyzed new women's advocacy
groups, which in turn are making their mark. On the other hand,
it did not develop into a mass movement mobilizing women across
class boundaries and the urban–rural divide.

One reason for this undoubtedly relates to the personal background of the activists. Women who had most radically altered
the parameters of gender definition for themselves figured promin-
ently amongst the activists. Most shared the privileges of their
class, so that, by comparison to women of other classes, gender-
based discrimination was felt more acutely. These were also
women who, having gained the most, had the most to lose, and
(correctly in my opinion) viewed themselves as the principal target
of the discourse. Moreover, they had the resources and support
systems needed to defy the constraints imposed by a martial law

environment. Groups of women who had benefited less (or not at all) from redefinitions of gender norms in the previous fifty years may have felt less threatened by the new discourse and directives (though poor women were most directly, and adversely, affected by new criminal legislation). Certainly they had fewer support systems and resources with which to resist the new trend.[30]

A second set of reasons relates to the type of activism that emerged in response to state-sponsored moves. Not only was it largely reactive in nature and addressed to policy makers at the state level, but its agenda was dictated by those leading the discourse from the other side. To a large extent, the movement simply reacted to changes in legislation and directives in a struggle to safeguard women's existing legal rights and to highlight the injustices caused by new directives and laws. The law, of course, is important, and given the drastic nature of laws proposed and passed and the resulting atmosphere, urgently needed to be countered. Considering the bewildering pace of the agenda set by the state and the religious right (sometimes in unison, sometimes alternately)[31] it is understandable that the energies of women's advocacy groups were consumed by the imperatives of responding. Unfortunately, the formal law is far removed from most women's lives and a recent survey revealed that statute law is rarely applied in family matters because communities tend to ignore it in favour of traditions.[32] Apart from legal or administrative matters, women's groups mobilized around the extremely relevant issue of violence against women. But the nature of public campaigns is such that they tend to highlight extreme cases of violence that, even when they horrify, women may not see (or want to see) as affecting them at a personal level. While women activists have raised the far more common issue of domestic violence, groups have not, as yet, come to grips with the issue in a manner that would modify the experiences of women subjected to it.

Having focused either on the law or on exceptional cases as a priority, women activists in Pakistan are still grappling with the challenge of developing effective campaign strategies on issues that confront the vast majority of women on a daily basis, such as the lack of mobility that controls access to health and educational facilities and employment opportunities, or women's exclusion from decision making in their families generally, and particularly on the basic issue of choosing a spouse. Yet these are some of the everyday constraints dictated by the social construction of the

female gender that women themselves identify as basic determinants of the quality of their lives.

It is unfortunate that while a basic premise of feminist analysis
is that the oppression of women derives from the political being
personal and vice versa, women's movements have concentrated,
to such a large extent, on devising structures and strategies for
addressing the political. In Pakistan, women's groups have as yet
to initiate collective support mechanisms for dealing with personal
oppression even for their own class of women.[33]

Precisely because the control of women is exercised through
the intrinsic linkages that bind the political and personal, catalyz-
ing change is facilitated by a leadership rooted in its own environment. The stronger the class divisions of a society are, the
sharper will be the divisions between women from different classes
and the greater the distances that separate them. In the absence
of face-to-face interactions, the vast disparities in experiences,
parameters and textures of life experienced by different groups of
women limit the potential of women from one particular class –
especially those having most successfully altered their lives – to
function as a daily reference point for others. Under these circumstances, middle-class urban groups are better equipped to raise
consciousness and lobby with governments and special interest
groups (such as trade unions and political parties) than to mobilize
women and initiate change at the community level, particularly
when the communities in question are themselves fragmented.

Professional middle-class activists are better placed to address
issues at the public and policy-making levels. Indeed, had women
not actively and vociferously opposed both the religious discourse
and the policies adopted under Zia (the former continuing after
his death and the latter still on the statutes), the situation for
Pakistani women would have been even bleaker than it appears
today. By virtue of both class advantage and personal circumstances such groups are often amongst the first to mobilize on
women's issues. By their action and discourse these groups can
and do catalyze ideas and the formation of other groups. By their
very existence urban middle-class women's groups provide proof
of women's active commitment to changing their own lives and
suggest possible strategies for doing so. At the same time urban-
based professional women must consciously seek linkages with
groups whose frame of reference may be different from their own
– that is, network actively and systematically. To some extent this

is already happening in Pakistan where links have been forged between urban women's groups and grassroots organizations such as Sindhiani Tehrik, with a predominantly rural and small-town base and tens of thousands of members.[34]

Conclusion

If women's relationship with religion sometimes appears to be generally inward-looking rather than located at the intersection between religion and politics, it would be a mistake to presume, therefore, that the political discourse leaves women unaffected. The monopolization of the religious discourse by politico-religious groups in pursuit of political power has seriously negative repercussions for women because it erodes both the scope for spirituality and autonomous interpretations. In a world where meanings have increasingly become dichotomous, instead of reflecting the plurality that normally exists, women whose faith is a living reality are being presented with the choice of either abandoning their faith altogether or conforming to the dictates of the political agendas of groups that have chosen a religious discourse.[35] This is equally true with respect to ethnic, cultural, or national identity, where definitions are decided for and imposed on women. To break through these imposed definitions women (and men, but especially women) need to have access to (or to invent) reference points and parameters for identity and self other than those defined and promoted by the dominant male groups, whether politico-religious or secular.

At the conceptual level, women must be enabled to distinguish between the various strands of religion, custom, and culture woven into an identity that is presented to women as an indivisible whole. They require the tools with which they can challenge both the doctrinaire, legalistic version of religion and the ethnic and religious chauvinism currently ascendant in the political arena without necessarily being obliged to renounce either their religion or their ethnic identity. It is in this context that networks can play a vital role.

Women must start assuming the right to define for themselves the parameters of their own identity and stop accepting unconditionally and without question what is presented to them as the 'correct' religion, the 'correct' culture, or the 'correct' national identity. By linking women and women's groups within and across

Muslim communities, increasing their knowledge about both their common and diverse situations, and strengthening their struggles by creating the means and channels needed to support their efforts internationally from within and outside the Muslim world, networks can assist women affected by Muslim laws to analyze and reformulate the identity imposed on them and by so doing to assume greater control over their lives. This summarizes the self-defined terms of reference of the international network, Women Living Under Muslim Laws (WLUML), set up in 1986 with the aim of breaking the isolation of women by providing information, solidarity, and support. The formulation of the network's name is an acknowledgement of both the complexity and diversity of women's realities in the Muslim world. A less obvious concern that went into the choice of name is that women affected by Muslim laws may not be Muslim, either by virtue of having a different religion or by virtue of having chosen another marker of political or personal identity. The emphasis in the name and in the group is therefore on the women themselves and their situations, and not on the specific politico-religious option they may exercise. As a network, WLUML extends to women living in countries where Islam is the state religion as well as to those from Muslim communities ruled by religious minority laws; to women in secular states where a rapidly expanding political presence of Islam increasingly provokes a demand for minority religious law as well as to women in migrant Muslim communities in Europe, the Americas, and Australasia; it also includes non-Muslim women who may have Muslim laws applied to them directly or through their children.

There are many other women's networks that include women from the Muslim world. Some have a specialized focus (such as the Global Network for Reproductive Rights, or the International Women's Rights Watch focused on CEDAW), others are concerned with building international solidarity (ISIS-Women's International Cross Cultural Exchange, ISIS International, Sisterhood Is Global, to mention a few). Still others have a regional focus, such as the Women, Law and Development Forums. One interesting networking initiative has recently emerged in the Maghreb, where activists from Tunisia, Morocco, and Algeria have formed a network by the name of 'Collectif '95' organized to resist a state-sponsored initiative (presented in Kuwait in 1993) to impose a uniform family law in all Arab states. Fearing the implications of legislation that would further reduce women's rights in the family, activists networked to preempt this by producing a counter-draft proposal for a uniform code of the family based on gender equality. As suggested by its name, Collectif '95 is also strategizing for change through the World Conference on Women in Beijing in 1995.

One of the greatest advantages networks have over organizations is their fluidity. They provide a vehicle for individuals and organizations to share information, analyses, and strategies without trying either to homogenize the diversity of concerned people or to control their autonomy in matters of political or personal choices. People can learn from the sharing of experiences and information and decide for themselves what appears most relevant in their own contexts. For example, all groups in Collectif '95 are developing their own strategies for lobbying with their national governments on the collectively formulated proposal.

Networks are also a viable alternative to the 'either/or' discourses of dominant groups. Maintaining that feminism can only be defined in secular terms or that women can only operate in the religious framework both give credibility to the opportunistic dichotomy of choice defined by politico-religious parties and other identity-based political groups. Neither seems to respond adequately to the needs of women as a whole. The task of redefining gender simultaneously entails a redefinition of all the other markers of identity important to an individual. For some, it may be class, for others religion or culture, for still others profession. There is no logical reason to assume that each marker is equally important at all times for all women. Avoiding the dichotomous logic of dominant male discourse, networks provide a channel through which women can learn of different alternatives and be free to make their own autonomous choices. They also provide an alternative reference point for women (as seen earlier, a particular need of women in the Muslim world) and provide legitimacy for change.

Finally, the fact that patriarchal controls operate through the personal and not just the political is a serious challenge for feminist groups whose structures and styles are still largely derived from those of political movements that have always been centered on the public to the virtual exclusion of people's private spaces. Religion, too, operates at both levels, and can therefore be seen to pose a similar challenge. One of the problems facing feminist groups is that definitions of the female gender shared by women across class and ethnic divides are those of limitation and oppression. This distinguishes gender identity from identities of community (ethnic or religious) that allow women to share in myths of greatness and strength, and not just oppression. A community's promise (whether spoken or not) independently to look after its own is beyond the scope of women's groups, whose promises for improved conditions usually depend for implementation on state structures that in much of the Muslim world have not been able to deliver on promises made. By itself, networking may not be able to develop a shared identity of strength for women, but it does at least give them access to some success stories of women mobilizing for change.

Another challenge for feminists groups is evolving strategies for meaningful change in the realm of the personal, and not just the political. One strategy would be for women's groups to stop separating rights issues from developmental ones. Accelerating women's access to education, health facilities, and employment opportunities automatically broadens mobility and expands access to information. Coupled with support systems, these measures can help loosen the ties of patriarchal control over women at the level of the everyday. There is some indication that, at an informal level, this is starting to happen in Pakistan.[36] Efforts will have to be systematized and a conscious strategy evolved to accelerate this process.

Finally, advocacy initiatives must be pursued at the national policy level and the discourse of the politico-religious groups must be consistently and vocally opposed at all levels. Local initiatives need to be strengthened through linkages at the national and international levels, and strategies must be evolved to address, effectively respond to, and modify the contextual constraints within which women are obliged to live their lives. No single women's group can adequately assume such diverse roles. However, a multitude of autonomous groups effectively networking may achieve the critical mass needed to transform women's struggles for survival into workable strategies for bringing about a gender-equitable society, whether in the Muslim world or elsewhere.

Notes

1. This paper draws extensively on the collective experiences and analysis of women involved in the network Women Living Under Muslim

Laws, and I would like to acknowledge them all here. Parts of the analysis have been incorporated into an earlier paper, Farida Shaheed, 'Controlled or Autonomous: Identity and the Experience of the Network Women Living Under Muslim Laws,' *Signs*, 19, 4 (Summer 1994), pp. 997–1019.

2. Women Living Under Muslim Laws, *Plan of Action (Aramon)*, 1986.

3. My reflections on this topic are presented in an earlier paper, Farida Shaheed, 'The Cultural Articulation of Patriarchy: Legal Systems, Islam and Women in Pakistan,' *South Asia Bulletin*, 6,1 (Spring 1986), pp. 38–44.

4. This is borne out by the empirical findings of the country projects of the Women and Law in the Muslim World Programme initiated by the international network, Women Living Under Muslim Laws, in 1992. The 21 country projects initiated (out of 26 planned) are all at different stages of implementation. Research has been completed in Pakistan, Bangladesh and Sri Lanka; partial information is also available from several other countries.

5. Fatima Mernissi, *The Veil and the Male Elite: A Feminist Interpretation of Women's Rights in Islam* (New York: Addison Wesley, 1992), pp. 8–9.

6. Though the statement was made with reference to the specific context of Pakistan, it is generally applicable to other parts of the Muslim world. Khawar Mumtaz and Farida Shaheed, *Women of Pakistan: Two Steps Forward, One Step Back?* (London: Zed Books and Lahore: Vanguard Books, 1987), p. 1.

7. It would be interesting to carry out a study to see how much public discourse focuses on the need to 'Islamize' these other sectors compared with the amount of energy time and space devoted to women's appropriate dress codes, family laws, etc. I am convinced that the contrast would be extreme.

8. Leila Ahmed, *Women and Gender in Islam* (New Haven and London: Yale University Press, 1992), p. 151.

9. Lata Mani, 'Contentious Traditions: The Debate on Sati in Colonial India,' in Kukum Sangari and Sudesh Vaid (eds), *Recasting Women: Essays in Colonial History* (New Delhi: Kali for Women, 1989), pp. 88–126.

10. *Ibid.*, pp. 88–126.

11. For discussions on the image of 'fundamentalists' and its impact on people's self-perceptions, see Fatima Mernissi, *The Fundamentalist Obsession with Women: A Current Articulation of Class Conflict in Modern Muslim Societies* (Pakistan: Simorgh, 1987); Homa Hoodfar, 'The Veil in Their Minds and On Our Heads: The Persistence of Colonial Images of Muslim Women,' *Feminist Research Resource*, 1994, 22, 3/4, pp. 5–18; Rana Kabbani, *Europe's Myths of the Orient* (Bloomington: Indiana University Press, 1986); and Ahmed, *op. cit.*

12. The majority of women in the Muslim world live in nations where, prior to independence, numerous cultural-structural entities ordering life coexisted either in harmony or in competition with each other for

legitimacy and supremacy. Diversities, however, were in contradiction to both the logic of nation states and the modernization ethic. Delegitimized in the era of the nation state, diversity was either ignored or suppressed in the course of nationalist struggles. See Shahida Lateef, *Muslim Women in India: Political and Private Realities: 1890s–1990s* (New Delhi: Kali for Women, 1990). States like Pakistan became self-gerant on the basis of a nationality hastily cobbled together and premised on a unity that was either imagined or contrived – in either case, short-lived. Following independence, attempts by those in power to promote markers of identity designed to homogenize people into an undifferentiated 'citizenry', whose principle collective point of reference would be the state, have failed. If anything, the response to unequal economic and social development and blatant injustices has been a strengthening of sub-state bonds of community and authority and a 're-tribalization of society.' See Abbas Rashid and Farida Shaheed, 'Pakistan: Ethno-politics and Contending Elites,' manuscript prepared as part of the UNRISD project on Ethnic Conflict and Development, 1993. The continued fragmentation of society is perhaps best exemplified by the parallel systems of law and governance that continue to flourish in Pakistan where, on the ground, the operational law is rarely that of the state, particularly in family and gender matters. See also Deniz Kandiyoti, 'Women and Islam: What are the Missing Terms?', *Women Living Under Muslim Laws Dossier* (Grabels: December 1988 – May 1989), pp. 5–9.

13. Abbas Rashid, 'Pakistan: The Ideological Dimension,' in Mohammad Asghar Khan (ed.), *Islam, Politics and the State: The Pakistan Experience* (London: Zed Books, 1985).

14. Abbas Rashid and Farida Shaheed, 'Ethnic and Sectarian Violence in Pakistan', paper presented at the seminar 'Violence in Society,' Goethe Institute, Karachi, Pakistan, October 1992.

15. For example, a recent internal correspondence of the Women Living Under Muslim Laws network (Dakar, 10 January 1995) reported the position taken in Senegal that exhumation was un-Islamic. This would mean that the Muslims in Pakistan, and presumably many other places where exhumation is allowed and has been justified also through religious argumentation, would be un-Islamic. Similarly, while the state of Pakistan has declared the Ahmedi sub-sect to be non-Muslims, they continue to form part of the *ummah* in other communities. On the other hand, the Bohra sub-sect accepted in Pakistan and throughout South Asia as Muslims are not considered Muslims in South East Asia (discussions of the WLUML Women and Law Programme Working Meeting, December 1994, Lahore). The experience of the WLUML network shows that there are innumerable such discrepancies, pointing to the role of factors other than scriptures, doctrines and religious concerns in determining definitions of Islam.

16. In 658 AD the selection of the fourth caliph occasioned a split in the Muslim world into Sunnites (the followers of the Prophet's tradition) and Shi'ites (those who accept only the traditions of the Prophet's family). Both follow specific texts of *fiqh* (religious knowledge) as sources of the *shari'a*. Additionally, Sunni Islam has four major schools of law, developed on the basis of interpretation of theology and law during the first century of the introduction of Islam: Hanafi, Maliki, Shafi'i, and Hanbali. The Hanafis are located in Turkey, Sudan, Egypt, Syria, and Central and South Asia; the Malikis are dominant in North and West Africa; the Shafi'i school is found in Indonesia, Malaysia, Lower Egypt, and parts of the Arabian Peninsula, Central Asia, and East Africa; and the Hanbalis are mostly in Saudi Arabia. On the question of women's rights, status, and role, the four schools agree in principle. The differences between them relate to details of legal procedures. See Khawar Mumtaz, 'The Changing Status of Women in Muslim Societies, Special Report: Anthropology,' *1993 Britannica Book of the Year* (Chicago: Encyclopedia Britannica, 1993).

17. Pakistan's laws are based on the Hanafi school of jurisprudence that specifies this right. Under other schools of thought (e.g., Maliki, Shafi'i), women are denied this right which rests with the woman's male guardian, or *wali*.

18. Another vivid illustration from Pakistan of the exercise of the worst option for women is that poor Christians have adopted polygyny from the predominantly Muslim environment, but in contrast, the Christian community has so far failed to liberalize grounds for divorce, beyond bigamy, change of religion, and adultery.

19. For details and discussion on the Enforcement of Zina Section of the Hudood Ordinances, 1979, and the issues involved, see Mumtaz and Shaheed, *op. cit.*, and Asma Jahangir and Hina Jilani, *The Hudood Ordinances. A Divine Sanction?* (Lahore: Rhotas Books, 1990). The death penalty applies only in the case of a voluntary confession before a competent court (a retraction at any point before the execution annuls the confession) or the eyewitness evidence of four Muslim male adults of good repute.

20. Mernissi, *The Fundamentalist Obsession with Women: A Current Articulation of Class Conflict in Modern Muslim Societies, op. cit.*, p. 8.

21. Pakistan Institute of Labour Education and Research and Shirkat Gah, 'Female Participation in the Formal Labour Force,' unpublished report of 1993 study.

22. This regional study encompassing Sri Lanka, India and Pakistan was carried out under the aegis of the International Centre for Ethnic Studies (Colombo). The study had several aspects including life histories and a household survey of over 400 women. In Pakistan the research was carried out by Shirkat Gah Women's Resource Centre. The eight communities selected for the survey were: Sunni, Shi'a, and Christian families in Lahore; a Punjabi village; Mohajirs (Urdu-speaking migrants from

India), Pakhtuns, Parsees and Sindhis in Karachi; and a Sindhi village. Having decided not to ask questions related to income, the study roughly divided communities into upper, middle and poor income groups on the basis of informants' classifications. These classifications were uneven, since upper-class Christians, for example, would normally be considered middle-class by researchers, while the Parsee lower-income group enjoys a national middle-class standard.

23. Upper-class urban women enjoy greater freedoms than less-advantaged groups; of the different religious communities studied, Parsees had the least rigid structures; and so on.

24. Newspaper reports, appearing almost daily, of women mutilated or killed by their brothers, fathers or other male relatives for presumed illicit sexual relations bear testimony to the severity of the family's control over women. Exercising free will in marriage can also provoke violent reactions. Oppression in the family is vividly portrayed in women's accounts of their lives and in their fiction. See, for example, Margot Badran and Miriam Cooke, *Opening the Gates: A Century of Arab Feminist Writing* (Bloomington and Indianapolis: Indiana University Press, 1990).

25. Women Living Under Muslim Laws, *op. cit.*, p. 7.

26. Exceptionally, a few older women attributed the husband's authority over his wife to his position of 'god on earth' (*majazi khuda*). This now increasingly rare belief is, however, derived from custom rather than religious doctrine and, indeed, is antithetical to Islam.

27. Durre Samina Ahmed, 'Modernist Rationality, Religious Fundamentalism and the Struggle for Pakistan,' paper for a conference on the 8th Five Year Plan, Islamabad, July 1991.

28. I would like to acknowledge the insights provided by Durre Ahmed, who amongst many other things is an academician and practicing psychologist based in Lahore, in our discussions of women's experiences of and relationship to religion.

29. The Law of Evidence (Qanun-e Shahadat) and the Qisas and Diyat Ordinance are examples. For details see Mumtaz and Shaheed, *op. cit.*, and Shahla Zia, 'Some Experiences of the Women's Movement: Strategies for Success,' paper written for the Women and Law Pakistan Country Project, Lahore, 1994.

30. During the peak of the Women's Action Forum's activism in the martial law period, a lower-middle class woman in professional employment explained that she was unable to participate in a public demonstration because, unlike upper-middle and middle-class women who, if beaten up by the police, would on returning home be applauded and encouraged by their families, women in her position would not only not receive any sympathy but could expect a thrashing for involvement in such activism. Another working-class woman accurately described her fears that arrest might result in rape for women of her class, and pointed

out that the more privileged women would at least not confront this particular problem.

31. See Mumtaz and Shaheed, *op. cit.*, for an account of the Zia period and women's response to it.

32. The Women and Law Country Project Pakistan, carried out by Shirkat Gah in the context of the WLUML Women and Law in the Muslim World Programme, has documented this and is bringing out a handbook on customary practices, the regional diversities in practices and a comparison with the statutory provisions. A summary of this information is already available in the form of a comparative chart.

33. Very recently, an initiative in this direction has been established by a new women's group, Bedari, in Islamabad.

34. Sindhiani Tehrik started off as the women's wing of the Sindh Awami Tehrik, a Sindhi nationalist political party. Many of the issues the Sindhiani Tehrik takes up are related to the province's political agenda (e.g., against the repatriation of Biharis from Bangladesh, opposition to the construction of large dams that would reduce the water flow to Sindh, etc.); however, its links with women's groups have strengthened its focus on women's issues.

35. I am not questioning the sincerity of belief amongst members of politico-religious groups (indeed I have no reason to presume a lack of conviction). I am merely emphasizing that theirs is a political agenda rather than a religious one, in that it would have minimal life outside the political framework.

36. Farida Shaheed, Sohail Warraich and Asma Zia, *Women in Politics: Participation and Representation in Pakistan*, Special Bulletin (Lahore: Shirkat Gah-Women Living Under Muslim Laws, 1994).

7

Rhetorical Strategies and Official Policies on Women's Rights: The Merits and Drawbacks of the New World Hypocrisy

Ann Elizabeth Mayer

In the US since the 1970s people have complained that it was much easier to fight racial discrimination in the old days, when Americans were open and unashamed about their racist attitudes and these were embodied in laws that clearly discriminated on the basis of race. Today, aside from rare unreconstructed racists, it is virtually unthinkable for anyone in a position of authority to state openly that discrimination against persons of any race is justifiable. One might expect that people who campaigned for racial equality would rejoice that the notion of race-based discrimination has become unacceptable, but the complaint now is that racism survives in more subtle and complex forms and that the new hypocrisy is much more difficult to grapple with than open racism. It is harder to combat practices and policies motivated by discrimination but ostensibly neutral in terms of race or even ostensibly beneficial to non-whites.

This essay suggests that, with regard to campaigns on behalf of equal rights for women, we now face similar frustrations due to the new world hypocrisy on questions of women's rights. Spokespersons who are prepared to admit publicly that they consider women inferior or that they favor discrimination against women are becoming increasingly rare. Instead, rhetorical strategies that proclaim support for women's equality are pursuing policies that are inimical to women's rights. The result is what might be called 'the new world hypocrisy.'

Appeals to domestic and/or religious laws to justify non-compliance with the international norm of full equality for women are becoming a significant problem. Generally, a breach of an international obligation cannot be defended by saying that the state is observing the requirements of its own domestic law.[1]

Muslim countries justify deviating from the principle of full equality for women by claiming that their domestic laws are not manmade but divinely ordained; they assert, therefore, that denying equality to women under their domestic laws lies outside the normal prohibition against the use of internal rules to evade international responsibility. In this essay the use of Islamic rationales for discrimination will be shown to be part of an international pattern of hypocrisy on women's rights issues, in which governmental spokespersons who use similar strategies to justify deviations from international human rights law nonetheless insist, against all evidence to the contrary, that they accept the principle of women's equality.

The rhetoric in reservations made by several Muslim countries when ratifying the Convention on the Elimination of All Forms of Discrimination Against Women (CEDAW) will be dissected in what follows.[2] However, because there is a tendency to treat the problems of accommodating women's equality in Muslim milieus as if they were unique, examples involving the US and the Vatican will be compared to demonstrate that resistance to the international norm of women's equality and double talk about women's rights are not limited to Islam. The US can invoke its Constitution and the Vatican can invoke natural law and Church tradition just as Muslim countries invoke Islamic law. In all three cases, however, the common strategy is to appeal to the laws of Nature, which have made women different from men. The rhetorical strategies attempt in all cases to establish that the speakers' opposition to the principle of women's equality as established in international law is based on higher laws that the speakers are powerless to alter.

Muslim Countries and CEDAW

Many countries that have ratified or acceded to the CEDAW treaty have entered reservations. Indeed, as has been pointed out in a recent article, more reservations 'with the potential to modify or exclude most, if not all, of the terms of the treaty' have been entered to CEDAW than to any other convention.[3] It is acceptable under international law to make reservations to a treaty, but a state is not supposed to make reservations that are incompatible with the purpose of the treaty. Rather than doing so, a state should simply decline to become a party to the treaty. In the case of Muslim countries, vague 'Islamic' reservations have been entered to CEDAW that appear to be incompatible with its purpose.[4] However, the governments involved seek to convince the world that their reservations are not incompatible with the goal of achieving equality for women.

The objection made by Egypt in 1981 to Article 16 of CEDAW at the time of its ratification merits examination. Article 16 provides for the equality of men and women in all matters relating to marriage and family relations during marriage and upon its dissolution. Egypt sought to justify its reservation to this article by a longer than usual explanation. (Letters have been added in brackets to Egypt's explanation to facilitate identifying passages that will be analyzed subsequently.) Egypt asserted that it had to adhere to provisions of the Islamic *shari'a*:

> [a] whereby women are accorded rights equivalent to those of their spouses so as to ensure a just balance between them. [b] This is out of respect for the sacrosanct nature of the firm religious beliefs which govern marital relations in Egypt and which may not be called in question and in view of the fact that [c] one of the most important bases of these relations is an equivalency of rights and duties so as to ensure complementarity which guarantees true equality between the spouses. [d] This is because the provisions of the Islamic Sharia lay down that the husband shall pay bridal money to the wife and maintain her fully out of his own funds and [e] shall also make a payment to her upon divorce, [f] whereas the wife retains full rights over her property and is not obliged to spend anything on her keep. [g] The Sharia therefore restricts the wife's rights to divorce by making it contingent on a judge's ruling, whereas no such restriction is laid down in the case of the husband.[5]

A few aspects of the hypocrisy and twisted logic in this statement deserve special attention. Egypt equated its laws governing personal status with 'firm religious beliefs' that are sacrosanct and cannot be questioned. However, a distinction can readily be made between Divine Law itself and Egypt's own laws. The latter are obviously subject to alteration at the wish of the government, having changed considerably since the beginning of this century and having been altered in 1979, at the time the CEDAW text was being finalized, and twice in 1985.

Contrary to Egypt's assertion, the *shari'a* rules in Egypt's personal status laws are sharply at odds with the principles of male–female equality. Its *shari'a*-based rules uphold the traditional patriarchal family unit, in which the husband is the master and the provider and the wife is a dependent subject to his control. Thus, as in other patriarchal systems, the 'balance' in the rights of the spouses is sharply tilted in the husband's favor. The section following [a] speaks as if it were self-evident that the difference in treatment of men and women in Egyptian personal status law is 'just.' In fact, the justice of the patriarchal scheme they embody has been vigorously contested. As is well known to the government, Egyptian feminists do not accept that these laws are just; they have challenged these laws and called for their reform, and debates over whether and how these laws should be reformed have raged in public for years.[6] Similarly, the claim that these laws guarantee 'true equality' in the section after [c] is debatable, since, certainly, nothing like actual equality is being afforded. To agree one has to assume that women are naturally suited for roles as dependants and homemakers, and men suited for the roles of masters and providers, so that the discriminatory treatment mandated by Egyptian law makes women as equal as they should be. This entails accepting ideas directly at odds with Article 5 of CEDAW, which calls for elimination of practices and prejudices based on the idea of the inferiority or the superiority of either sex or stereotyped roles for men and women.

The section following [b] speaks of *shari'a* law on women as if it offers a single, settled, and definitive model of family law that was obviously binding on all Muslims and cannot be called into question. This is not true. Since the early centuries of Islam the Qur'anic verses and the *hadith* affecting women's rights in the family have been subject to a wide range of diverging interpretations by Islamic jurists, with the interpretations of Sunnis and Shi'is particularly at variance. As great as the variety of interpretations has been in the past, it is even greater today. Many contemporary Muslims find the juristic interpretations made in the pre-modern period inadequate and reject them as no longer binding. Over the last decades a growing feminist literature has added a fresh layer of interpretations and new insights that go well beyond the liberal reformist interpretations introduced in the late nineteenth century. At the same time, fundamentalist ideologues are reinterpreting the Islamic sources in ways that affirm their vision of the way Islamic precepts should apply to the problems of modern life. There is enormous interpretative diversity on the question of what the Islamic sources mandate in terms of status for women.

This diversity is reflected to some extent in the diversity in personal status laws in contemporary Muslim countries. Some essentially embody medieval juristic interpretations; others have selectively modified and updated aspects of old *shari'a* rules. Turkey has gone so far as to discard Islamic law altogether. Egypt has personal status laws that embody an in-between position, comprising some modest reforms to the pre-modern *shari'a*. The Egyptian personal status law reforms have been criticized by Egyptian feminists and by conservatives, albeit from different perspectives. There is no national consensus that Egypt's personal status law, as reformed, embodies the perfect restatement of *shari'a* principles. The fact that the government has made a number of changes to its personal laws, is itself an indication that it does not in reality consider *shari'a* law immutable. In addition, Egypt does not accept the binding force of *shari'a* law in other domains. If Egypt really followed the principle that it had to retain *shari'a* laws because they were religiously mandated, one would expect Egyptian law to follow *shari'a* across the board; but Egypt long ago discarded Islamic law in favor of French-inspired law except in personal status matters. This is in fact one of the grievances that Islamic fundamentalists invoke in their challenges to the religious legitimacy of the government. In these circumstances, it was strange for Egyptian spokespersons to talk as if Egypt were inextricably bound to follow Islamic norms. Sections [d] and [f] misrepresent the nature of the exchange involved in a *shari'a* marriage – the truth is that the husband's financial obligations *vis-à-vis* his wife correlate exactly with his superior rights and his legal prerogative to demand sexual submission and obedience from her. That is, the man's dower payment and support obligations are the basis of the inequality of the spouses and the wife's inferior position. Moreover, in section [f] there is no acknowledgment that, regardless of the theory that the wife is not obliged to support the family, under present economic conditions in Egypt, wives generally do find that they also have to work outside the home and to contribute their earnings to the family – though this has not been reflected in an adjustment in the husband's superior rights. Indeed, even where the wife is the sole breadwinner in the family, the husband retains his superior legal rights, which proves that no principle of balance and complementarity in rights and obligations is actually in effect. That is, Egypt was deliberately obscuring the discriminatory character of its laws. What happens upon divorce is also inaccurately represented. Contrary to the claim following section [e], as Egyptian law now stands, the husband does not always have to pay the wife when they divorce; sometimes he owes no payment and sometimes the wife pays.

The statement in section [g] speaks as if it were self-evident that the husband, who theoretically bears the financial obligation of paying the bride price and maintaining his wife and his family, should have an unrestrained right to divorce, whereas the wife, theoretically his dependant, has to establish grounds before a judge in order to obtain a divorce. However, one could easily turn this proposition on its head and say that the wife, who is presumably generally the financially more vulnerable partner and who often will get a very paltry payment upon divorce, is the one who is most exposed to hardship and most likely to see her livelihood suffer upon divorce. That being the case, any restraints on ending the marriage should, in the interests of equity, apply at least as strongly to a divorce sought by the husband as they do to a divorce sought by the wife.

What Egypt asserted in this disingenuous explanation of its CEDAW reservation was in essence that, although *shari'a* rules did not accord men and women identical treatment, they essentially achieved the male–female equality mandated by CEDAW, albeit by a different route. Of course, this necessitated misrepresenting elements of Egypt's law and steering the discussion away from issues where Egyptian law too obviously violated the principle of male–female equality. Polygamy and inheritance law (according to which women are given one half the share of a male inheriting in the same capacity) were not mentioned. This deceit and evasiveness proves that Egypt had no real confidence in the sufficiency of its *shari'a* justifications for denying women equality. If Egypt had such confidence, it would not have needed to misrepresent the features of *shari'a* law that discriminated against women but would have simply stopped after saying that Egypt followed a divinely inspired law and therefore did not care whether or not its laws were in conformity with CEDAW. Of course, doing this would have meant acknowledging that Egyptian laws conflicted with the international human rights norm of equality, which Egypt was not disposed to do. It seems that appeals to the *shari'a* were merely tools in Egypt's efforts to confuse observers and mute international criticism.

Rhetorical strategies like Egypt's do succeed in muddying the

waters and confusing observers who are concerned to respect
religious differences. See, for example, the reaction of one author
to the way *shari'a* law was presented in the Egyptian reservation:

> To the extent that the Sharia may give women advantages over men
> in marriage, perhaps for the sake of redressing or compensating advant-
> ages enjoyed by men in certain regards, it is not in conflict with the
> aim of the Women's Convention.[7]

The author seems to believe that Egyptian laws might actually
aim to effect a 'just balance' in the rights of the spouses and that
Egypt might have been raising a legitimate question, whether
CEDAW aimed at equal rights for women or identical rights.
Egypt had succeeded in making her wonder if equal rights regarding the discharge of different domestic tasks of equal value might
be claimed to satisfy CEDAW. The author still had doubts; she
realized that a reservation like Egypt's might possibly reflect a
patriarchal model of society that preserved sex role stereotyping
in violation of the purpose of CEDAW – but, confused by the
assertions in the Egyptian reservation, she was not sure whether
it was a reservation of this kind.[8] She understood Egypt to be
presenting the *shari'a* in a light more sympathetic to women's
equality than other Muslim states were doing in their reservations
– the reservation entered by Bangladesh, for example, simply
stated that the provisions of CEDAW Article 16 were objectionable
because they were in conflict with *shari'a* law.[9]

This author referred to Theodor Meron, a respected expert on
international law, who has also expressed concern that aspects of
CEDAW are incompatible with respect for principles of religious
freedom in the Declaration on the Elimination of All Forms of
Intolerance and of Discrimination Based on Religion or Belief.[10]
Meron places claims based on principles of religious freedom in
several areas above CEDAW principles, assuming that equal rights
for women were less important than freedom of religion, although
nothing in the two international instruments suggests that one is
to outrank the other. For example, he seems unsympathetic to the
Article 5 provision of CEDAW requiring states to take appropriate
measures to modify 'social and cultural patterns of conduct of
men and women, with a view to achieving the elimination of
prejudices and customary and all other practices which are based
on the idea of the inferiority or the superiority of either of the
sexes or on stereotyped roles for men and women.' He dismisses

the importance of prohibiting religiously inspired discriminatory practices within the family, asserting that 'religious practices within the family which have relatively less significance for women's ability to function as full human beings in society might be permitted even though those practices perpetuate stereotyped roles ... .'[11]

Meron is willing to accommodate such stereotyping, asserting that:

> To require the elimination of sex-role stereotyping in the teaching of religious doctrine would constitute coercion to alter religious practice or belief, in violation of Art. 1 (2) of the Declaration, to the extent that such stereotyping is a genuine doctrinal feature of the religion.[12]

Meron apparently does not take into account that the views of women regarding how their religion should affect their rights might be as appropriate a point of departure as a 'genuine doctrinal feature of the religion.' Of course, in almost all cases a 'genuine doctrinal feature' would be one developed by men. Attitudes like Meron's prepare the ground for according a respectful hearing to representatives of Muslim countries when they claim that it is fidelity to their religion that stands in the way of following CEDAW principles. However, Meron's discussion of CEDAW deserves to be distinguished from the positions articulated by representatives of countries like Egypt in that at least he candidly acknowledges that his privileging of the principle of religious freedom results in accepting discrimination against women in violation of CEDAW. Egypt, in contrast, resorted to deliberate obfuscation in refusing to concede that its laws discriminate against women, even where they sharply diverge from CEDAW norms of equality by relegating women to a subordinate status.

Morocco emulated Egypt in the reservations it entered upon acceding to CEDAW in June of 1993. Morocco is eager to advertise in the West its progressive policies and the advances that Moroccan women have made, and it wanted to enhance its image by ratifying CEDAW – but, naturally, only subject to major reservations. Morocco said that it would apply provisions of Article 2 to the extent that they did not conflict with the *shari'a*, without specifying what that would involve. With regard to Article 16 provisions, and especially the one on the equality of men and women in respect of rights and responsibilities on entry into and at dissolution of marriage, Morocco explained its reservations as follows:

Equality of this kind is considered incompatible with the Islamic Shariah, which guarantees to each of the spouses the rights and responsibilities within a framework of equilibrium and complementarity in order to preserve the sacred bond of matrimony.

The provisions of the Islamic Shariah oblige the husband to provide a nuptial gift upon marriage and to support his family, while the wife is not required by law to support the family.

Furthermore, at dissolution of marriage, the husband is obliged to pay maintenance. In contrast, the wife enjoys complete freedom of disposition of her property during the marriage and upon its dissolution without supervision by the husband, the husband having no jurisdiction over his wife's property.

For these reasons, the Islamic Shariah confers to the right of divorce [sic] on a woman only by decision of a Shariah judge.

Like Egypt, Morocco was not prepared to acknowledge that an intent to allow discrimination lay behind its reservation. Like Egypt, Morocco ignored the changed economic realities that required women to contribute their wealth and earnings to keep the family going and that resulted in households where women were the sole breadwinners – without any corresponding adjustment in their rights. It admitted that certain provisions of the Moroccan personal status code accorded women 'rights that differ from the rights conferred on men' but insisted that these rules could not be 'infringed upon or abrogated because they derive primarily from the Islamic Shariah, which strives, among its other objections [sic], to strike a balance between the spouses in order to preserve the coherence of family life.'[13] Like Egypt, Morocco did not deal with areas where the discriminatory character of *shari'a* rules was undeniable. For example, the Maliki version of the *shari'a* followed in Morocco permitted a woman's guardian to consent to marriage on her behalf, thereby allowing him to contract her to a husband whom she did not want to marry. Morocco avoided mentioning the rule that a woman's consent to her own marriage was not required because a rule like this all too clearly revealed women's subjugated status. According to Morocco's rhetorical strategy, the disparities in the treatment of men and women were to be explained solely in terms of a concern to effect a perfect equilibrium. Patriarchal controls over women that were entrenched in Moroccan custom and law were not to be acknowledged.

The Moroccan reservations indicated that the duty to abide by *shari'a* law stood in the way of adhering to international human rights law, as if it were beyond the capacity of the state to modify *shari'a* law. However, Morocco, only a few months after making these reservations, changed the *mudawwana*, its *shari'a*-based code of personal status law, to make reforms that, although modest, broke with *shari'a* tradition. For example, after the reforms, a guardian could no longer contract a marriage on a woman's behalf without her consent. Also, the husband could no longer unilaterally decide whether his household would be polygamous: the first wife was given the right to terminate her marriage if he married a second time. In addition, the husband forfeited his right to unilateral extrajudicial repudiation; he could only obtain a divorce before a judge after an arbitration proceeding before a conciliation commission.[14]

After the 1993 Moroccan personal status reforms, Najat Razi, the president of the Association Marocaine des Droits des Femmes, clearly expressed her dissatisfaction with the level of equality women had achieved, saying: 'Discrimination is maintained, and the Mudawwana is still in part contrary to the international conventions.'[15] Her formulation is revealing. Men supportive of the Mudawwana see – or pretend to see – a harmonious equilibrium in traditional *shari'a* precepts; the Moroccan feminist view is that, even as modified, the personal status law remains discriminatory and unacceptable under international standards.

Not only did the 1993 modifications in Morocco's personal status law show that *shari'a* rules in Morocco were not above change, but the direction of the changes in the rules on polygamy and divorce showed that the supposedly perfect balance in the rights and duties of the spouses in *shari'a* law was no longer judged acceptable, even by Morocco's conservative, male-dominated government. It was noteworthy that the *shari'a* rules on divorce requiring women but not men to obtain a judge's ruling to divorce, which Morocco in June of 1993 had presented as part of the perfect *shari'a* balance, were among the rules altered only a few months later. Moreover, these changes in the Moroccan divorce law showed that a Muslim country sharing Egypt's rationale for making its reservations to CEDAW could conceive of the husband's right to divorce in Islamic law as being subject to a kind of regulation that, according to the Egyptian view, was inappropriate in the light of the husband's financial obligations to his wife under the *shari'a*.

Morocco also followed Egypt in failing to acknowledge the

cleavage between traditionalists and feminists on the question of women's rights. Anyone who knew the positions of Morocco's vigorous feminists was aware that the positions being articulated by Moroccan representatives at the UN did not represent their views. Moroccan feminists acted as though their right to claim the benefit of universal human rights norms supporting women's equality was a given. This feminist perspective is one that any sincere advocate of human rights would endorse, since modern human rights law assumes that denials of human rights under domestic law violate international law, which is the controlling standard, and that all states have the duty to bring their domestic legislation into conformity with international human rights law. For Morocco's feminists, adopting CEDAW principles and adhering to international law seem to have been primarily conceived in secular terms, as a challenge to male vested interests in maintaining the patriarchal and discriminatory norms of Moroccan law. Some showed little interest in quibbling over whether rules of Islamic law would be violated by CEDAW, while others showed a disposition to deny that authentic Islamic teachings were incompatible with women's equality.[16]

The contingency of local interpretations of Islamic requirements is strikingly illustrated in the Tunisian case. The status of women in Tunisia is relatively good and Tunisian personal status law is the most advanced in all the Arab countries. Polygamy was ended in 1956, and divorce is available to men and women on an equal footing. Adoption, unequivocally barred in *shari'a* law, was legalized, and inheritance law has been reformed. That is, *shari'a* principles that Egypt and Morocco invoked as immutable were overridden by Tunisian legislation in the 1950s. Nonetheless, Tunisian personal status law remains by self-designation 'Islamic,' and Tunisia invoked Islam, albeit indirectly, in 1985 when entering its reservation to CEDAW Article 2.[17] Since Tunisia still retains some discriminatory features of *shari'a* law in its code of personal status, the implication seemed to be that the *shari'a* principles that had been retained in Tunisian law were immutable. But after entering its 'Islamic' reservation to CEDAW, Tunisia then proceeded in 1993 to enact new reforms to some of the remaining *shari'a*-based rules in its personal status laws, not eliminating all discriminatory features, but making some additional progressive reforms.

In what sense, then, can it be said that *shari'a* law is an impediment to the reform of domestic laws to make them conform to

the principles in CEDAW? The various national formulas of *shari'a*
law obviously only constitute an obstacle to legal reforms for as
long as the men in power choose to retain them as the law of the
land. Whenever governments decide that changes are in order,
shari'a rules give way to government-sponsored initiatives, even if
the latter conflict with Islamic precepts.

Kuwait made several reservations to CEDAW, only one of which
related to Islam. It refused to give women the right to vote or to
transmit their nationality to their children and said that it was not
accepting the CEDAW dispute resolution mechanism. Kuwait also
claimed that, Islam being its state religion, it could not accept
CEDAW provisions on equal rights for men and women in matters
of guardianship or adoption of children. That is, its version of
what was objectionable from an Islamic standpoint had little in
common with the Egyptian or Moroccan versions.

Kuwait added further confusion when it signed CEDAW in
February of 1994 but entered reservations that were substantially
different from those of other Arab Muslim countries. Kuwait objected to the provisions that gave women political rights (women
in Kuwait are not allowed to vote), women's right to give their
nationality to their children, and equal rights for both spouses in
child custody decisions.[18] Only the last was related to provisions
in *shari'a* law. That is, Kuwait's reservations did not follow a
particularly Islamic pattern, even though Kuwaitis are overwhelmingly Muslim and Kuwait's personal status law is theoretically
based on *shari'a* law. Seen in relation to the laws in other Muslim
countries, the reservation on women's voting rights seems particularly odd, since even a self-proclaimed Islamic state like Iran allows
women to vote. On the matter of passing on nationality, Kuwait
and Tunisia differed, too, for in 1993 Tunisia had changed its law
to allow Tunisian nationality (a Western concept unknown to the
shari'a) to be passed on by the mother under certain conditions.[19]

Obviously, there is no consistent 'Islamic' pattern in these
reservations. According to Dr Badriya al-Awadi, a prominent
Kuwaiti academic and a supporter of women's rights, Kuwaiti
women were being denied the equality guaranteed by both the
Qur'an and the constitution.[20] In this feminist view, the discrimination behind the reservations violated principles set forth in the
prime Islamic source. She characterized the Kuwaiti government's
policy of signing CEDAW while denying women their political
rights as hypocritical.[21] On 14 April 1994, a conference in Kuwait

of women from Arab countries called for recognition of the political rights of Kuwaiti women and for the Kuwaiti government to review its reservations to CEDAW.[22] However, perspectives like this, which represent the views of Muslim feminists, are too rarely considered in international fora when cultural defenses to human rights are under discussion.

Sweden, one of the few countries where progress towards full equality for women is relatively well advanced, was one of several countries that reacted to reservations such as those Egypt entered with justifiable skepticism.[23] Sweden stated in objecting:

> the reason why reservations incompatible with the object and purpose of a treaty are not acceptable is precisely that otherwise they would render a basic international obligation of a contractual nature meaningless. Incompatible reservations, made in respect of the Convention on the elimination of all forms of discrimination against women, do not only cast doubts on the commitment of the reserving state to the object and purpose of this Convention, but moreover, contribute to undermine the basis of international contractual law.[24]

However, few countries followed Sweden's lead in skeptically appraising the supposedly Islamic rationales offered for deviating from CEDAW principles. Most allowed reservations like Egypt's to be entered without scrutiny or objection. This general toleration of religious rationales for denying women rights guaranteed by CEDAW reinforces the impression that Egypt's position was not really out of line with the approaches of many other countries, whether they were Muslim or not. Misuse of reservations is not discouraged by any provision in the text of CEDAW and this has prevented other states from rejecting reservations that they find unacceptable. In this respect CEDAW differs from the race discrimination convention, which does include a provision allowing a vote by two-thirds of the parties to declare a state's reservation unacceptable on the grounds of incompatibility with the object of the convention. The disparity suggests that the international community as a whole takes the need to prevent racial discrimination much more seriously than the need to prevent sex discrimination, giving real teeth to the convention on the former and only lip service to the goals of CEDAW. Indeed, a feminist critique of how the present system of international law incorporates male biases makes the toleration of reservations to CEDAW seem the inevitable consequence of systemic sexism.[25]

The variation in approaches taken by Muslim countries to law reform brings to mind the Norwegian government's objections to Libya's reservation to CEDAW. Libya also argued that it could not accept principles in conflict with personal status laws derived from the *shari'a*. Norway, another of the rare nations where women's rights are relatively well advanced, observed that personal status laws that were supposedly dictated by the *shari'a* were in fact 'subject to interpretation, modification, and selective application in different states adhering to islamic [sic] principles.' Norway noted that reservations based on *shari'a* law in these circumstances 'may create doubts about the commitments of the reserving state to the object and purpose of the Convention.'[26]

Political shifts can also determine a country's stance on whether 'Islam' stands in the way of approving CEDAW. For example, Iran and Pakistan, which both had played constructive roles in the preparation of CEDAW, suddenly shifted their positions after the clerical takeover following Iran's Islamic Revolution and the inauguration of the Islamization program carried out under Zia's dictatorship in Pakistan. The election of Benazir Bhutto as Prime Minister after Zia's death seemed to signal another switch in Pakistan's orientation, but her first term was cut short. In her second term, which began in October 1993, it seemed that she might be adopting a more energetic policy on behalf of women's rights.[27] Despite clear evidence that Muslim countries' stances on women's rights are politically determined, it is all too infrequent for official UN delegations to try to penetrate the mystificatory invocations of 'Islam' that are exploited to deflect scrutiny of discrimination against women.

If one scrutinizes the Islamic arguments that have been used by Muslim countries to rationalize the mundane political forces behind their declared policies on women's rights, they usually react angrily. They obviously do not want exposure of the reality behind their hypocritical statements that their laws achieve 'true equality' and perfect balance in their treatment of women. In 1987 the UN Committee on the Elimination of Discrimination Against Women recommended a study of how women were faring under Islamic law based on findings that Islamic law robbed women of equality. It was logical to seek to examine Islamic law in this context, since governments had been officially invoking Islamic law in their reservations to CEDAW as the reason why they could not endorse all parts of the Convention. However, Muslim countries, including

Iran, Senegal, Morocco, Oman, Sudan, and Bangladesh, objected, asserting that the proposal was insulting to the world's Muslims.[28]

The 'Islamic' reservations of countries like Egypt and Morocco and the condemnations of plans to study these reservations involved untenable positions, amounting to Muslim countries telling the world that:

1. Islamic law was immutable, when they changed their Islamic laws at will;
2. there was a single normative Islamic model, when personal status laws varied dramatically from one Muslim country to another and changed over time within one country;
3. their women could not have the equality mandated by CEDAW because of Islam, but that women in their societies were equal under Islamic law;
4. they were entitled to insist in international fora that their religious obligations to honor the *shari'a* justified their reservations to CEDAW, but the subject of how women were treated under the *shari'a* could not be examined in these same international fora.

The Vienna Declaration and Programme of Action from the June 1993 World Conference on Human Rights took a position on the problems of CEDAW reservations that shows that the legitimacy of the Islamic reservations to CEDAW is an issue that will not go away. In paragraph 39 it stated:

> Ways and means of addressing the particularly large number of reservations to the Conventions should be encouraged. Inter alia, the Committee on the Elimination of Discrimination against Women should continue its review of reservations that are contrary to the object and purpose of the Convention or which are otherwise incompatible with international treaty law.

Unfortunately, the declaration and program did not squarely address the question of the use of religious rationales for denying rights provided under CEDAW. In an ambiguous formulation, paragraph 38 called for 'the eradication of any conflicts which may arise between the rights of women and the harmful effects of certain traditional or customary practices, cultural prejudices and religious extremism.' The use of the term 'religious extremism' instead of 'religion' let Muslim countries off the hook. Of course, countries like Egypt, Iraq, Kuwait, Libya, Morocco and Tunisia, which invoked Islam as the reason for their CEDAW reservations, would not admit that in denying women full equality they were following policies dictated by religious extremism. The issue was whether domestic laws denying women rights provided under CEDAW could be justified by using religious rationales. Beyond that, the issue was whether religious rationales devised by them and preferred by men as justifications for retaining laws in conflict with CEDAW deserved to be accorded unquestioning deference by the international community.

The US and CEDAW

Consideration of the US case shows how these Middle Eastern and North African examples are simply part of a larger pattern of official spokespersons hypocritically assuring the world that, yes, they agree that women should be equal and, no, their laws are not discriminatory – but they cannot accept the CEDAW principles guaranteeing women full equality. Although the US signed CEDAW while President Carter was still in office, there was resistance to ratification for twelve years under Republican presidents, which was not surprising in light of the policies of the Reagan and Bush administrations toward women's rights.

The way American conservatives opposed to CEDAW conceive of the CEDAW model of male–female equality in relation to the rights afforded women under US law is like the way Muslim governments see CEDAW in relation to their domestic laws. Conservatives opposed to the proposed Equal Rights Amendment (ERA) to the US Constitution, which was designed to eliminate discrimination against women, often referred to 'laws of Nature.' Thus, the ERA was attacked by opponents like Senator Sam Ervin, a conservative Southern Democrat who charged that it made men and women into identical legal beings with the same rights and subject to the same responsibilities.[29] That is, it made men and women more equal than Nature intended them to be.

Americans who believe that the laws of Nature mandate unequal rights for men and women may think that domestic US standards establish the definitive model of male–female equality and the optimum level of protection for women's rights. Therefore, they conclude that any equality provisions that go beyond these – like those in CEDAW – must be wrong-headed. For example,

Bruce Fein, writing in the arch-conservative *Washington Times*, asserted that CEDAW was objectionable because it would prohibit 'non-invidious, gender distinctions.'[30] He apparently assumed that the notion of women having the same rights as men was misguided and that discriminatory features retained in US law were 'non-invidious, gender distinctions,' that is, benign distinctions that appropriately recognized the actual differences between males and females.[31] Fein's thinking seems to have been influenced by the prejudicial notions about the inferiority of women and stereotyped views of gender roles that pervade US culture.[32] These stereotypes can have the result of making familiar patterns of discrimination and inequality seem somehow just and natural, in much the same way as patriarchal biases in Muslim countries induce men to think it is natural for them to enjoy superior legal rights.

One of the things that led Bruce Fein and others to object to CEDAW is that ratifying CEDAW could, depending on one's point of view, require amending rights provisions in the US Constitution and/or would violate the complicated system of Federalism established in the Constitution, which requires the national government to defer to state laws regarding the family.[33] The idea that the US Constitution could be judged by international standards is not accepted in US law, where the Constitution reigns as the supreme law – above all other laws, including international law and treaties ratified by the US. Thus, the reporter for a prestigious commission appointed by the US President to study the constitutionality of US ratification of human rights treaties affirmed that the US might constitutionally 'ratify or adhere to any human rights convention that does not contravene a specific constitutional prohibition ... .'[34]

Like the *shari'a*, the US Constitution is resistant to change. The world's oldest constitution still in use, it is a revered symbol of the nation, a relic from the eighteenth century that is carefully preserved in the National Archives. It has a status that is close to sacred. It is so untouchable that its original version is still untampered with, even though it is replete with archaic features, containing references to the slave trade, admonitions to the states not to confer titles of nobility, prohibitions of laws working 'corruption of the blood,' etc. The rights provisions are few and lacking in most of the protections set forth in modern human rights law. Of course, since the proposed ERA was rejected, the US Constitution provides no guarantee of any rights for women, except in the Nineteenth Amendment, which prohibits the use of sex to deny the right to vote. Nonetheless, Americans, who are very tradition-bound, prefer to uphold their Constitution with all its archaisms intact rather than to write a new constitution that would meet the standards of modern constitutionalism and protect human rights according to international norms.[35] The result of this disinclination to update is that, as of 1994, Americans have a constitution that lags far behind its counterparts in places like Europe and Canada. Moreover, the rights afforded to Americans in the Bill of Rights are far inferior to the extensive rights enjoyed by Russians and South Africans under their new constitutions. It seems fair to speculate that there may be women cardinals in the halls of the Vatican and a woman Prime Minister in Riyadh before the US Constitution is modified in ways that accord American women the rights set forth in CEDAW and other international instruments.

Over the protests of conservatives, the ERA was submitted for ratification by the states in 1972. Conservative religious groups were in the forefront of the campaign against the ERA, which finally led to its defeat in 1982.[36] In its extremism, the invective used by US religious leaders to condemn women's demands for equal rights could rival the condemnations of feminism by the most retrograde Islamic leaders. When, after the defeat of the ERA, the state of Iowa considered adopting a similar amendment to its constitution, it was denounced by Pat Robertson, a right-wing television evangelist and unsuccessful presidential candidate. Robertson claimed that the Iowa ERA was part of a feminist agenda that he described as 'a socialist, anti-family political movement that encourages women to leave their husbands, kill their children, practice witchcraft, destroy capitalism and become lesbians.'[37]

Preoccupied with the 1972–82 campaign for the ERA, few Americans paid much attention to the failure of the Reagan administration to support the ratification of CEDAW. For a Republican administration like Ronald Reagan's, which condemned the ERA, the far more ambitious principles of CEDAW were anathema. Of course, the US resistance to ratification of CEDAW was not unique; it has been generally reluctant to ratify international human rights conventions, which has led to unseemly delays in the US becoming a party even to conventions like the International Convention on Civil and Political Rights, which contains the so-called 'first generation rights' that the US supports, but which was not ratified till 1992.

Despite the defeat of the ERA and the US failure to ratify CEDAW, one would be hard pressed to find an American official prepared to acknowledge in an international forum that US law was discriminatory or that US women did not have equal rights. On the contrary, in international venues the US tends to portray its rights record in a highly favorable light and to act as if problems of women's rights were confined to exotic places like Africa and Asia. Of course, the American officials offering these portrayals are most often men.

Under Reagan the US position effectively amounted to claiming that:

1. No, American women could not have constitutionally guaranteed equal rights – except for the right to vote, and
2. No, American women could not have the rights protections afforded by CEDAW, and
3. Yes, American women were fully equal with men.

Just as shifts in politics have affected the positions of Muslim countries on CEDAW, shifts in American politics affect official US positions on whether CEDAW should be ratified and on whether the US Constitution presents an obstacle to ratifying CEDAW. Democrats have tended to favor ratifying international human rights treaties, and President Kennedy even asserted that US law was already in conformity with international human rights law, so that ratifying the conventions entailed no conflicts with the US Constitution.[38] With the election of a Democratic President in 1992, the executive branch did an about-face on the merits of ratifying CEDAW; under Clinton the US is now officially committed to achieving ratification. (The Democratic administration of Bill Clinton seems to have decided that CEDAW can be ratified even without an equal rights amendment being added to the US Constitution.) However, as of 1994 the US Senate had still not given its consent, leaving CEDAW unratified.

In 1992 Republicans paid a political price for their opposition to women's rights. Many analysts would agree that the Democratic victory in the last presidential election occurred not only because the faltering economy worried voters but because Republicans had shown such lack of sympathy for the cause of women's rights and had made a close alliance with conservative religious groups opposed to women's equality. In this regard, many voters seem to have been alienated by the speeches made by arch-conservative foes of women's rights at the Republican Convention in August of 1992. The organizers mistakenly allowed right-wing zealots access to the podium during prime viewing time, when they could be seen by millions. The zealots included Patrick Buchanan, a conservative Catholic and a pugnacious defender of Vatican positions who had unsuccessfully competed to win the Republican presidential nomination in 1992. He castigated Hillary Rodham Clinton for her 'radical feminism' and announced that there was a 'religious war' going on in the country, a 'cultural war' for the soul of America.[39] The kind of frank attack on women's rights mounted by Buchanan and his ilk seems to have backfired badly.[40]

The Republican loss in 1992 probably reinforced the awareness of opponents of women's rights that in a democracy it is necessary to adopt the double talk of the new world hypocrisy. One can expect that, henceforth, experienced mainstream Republican operatives will not allow speakers so lacking in subtlety to expose their real agendas regarding women's rights. More refined hypocrisy will be the order of the day, as Republicans come to terms with the reality that there is broad popular support for a level of rights for women that they philosophically oppose. The Clinton administration, which has been faltering and has been bearing the brunt of well-organized attacks by conservatives, may not manage to hold on to power for a second term. If the Republicans recapture the White House in 1996, sophisticated attacks on CEDAW, accompanied by much double-talk designed to deny that Republicans are opposed to equality for women, will be resumed.

The Vatican Position on the 1994 Population Conference

As disappointing as the US record was, there were other players on the international scene with even more reactionary stances. One does not need to waste time wondering what reservations the Vatican entered when ratifying CEDAW, because, of course, the Vatican would never consider ratifying such a document, even with copious reservations. To learn the Vatican's reaction to the growing consensus supporting women's equality, one has to look at statements that it makes on other issues, such as its position on the 1994 Cairo population conference. Proof that it was not only Muslim governments that were hypocritical with regard to women's rights came in June of 1994, when the Vatican revealed its strong opposition to the feminist influence at the upcoming population conference. Because of this feminist influence, which in the opinion of the Church was harmful, there were measures on the conference agenda concerning safe abortions and women's right to control their fertility, which were supported by the Clinton administration. Such measures reflected what the Vatican chose to call 'cultural imperialism.' As is well known, the Church currently opposes all but 'natural' birth control and condemns abortion, whereas feminists tend to believe that a woman's control over her body and the procreative process is essential for her to enjoy full rights. The Vatican did not accept this. As one report had it:

> The Vatican disputes the suggestion by conference organizers that some proposals would elevate the standing of women. Vatican officials say the church prefers to promote its own concept of women as deserving equality and special respect, but within the context of church tradition.[41]

Church tradition was invoked by the Vatican as if it were sacrosanct. However, despite Vatican efforts to associate Church teachings with natural law, authoritative moral norms ingrained in the conscience of humankind and ascertainable by the use of reason, it was obvious that Church teachings were tied to history and politics. Morality as set forth in natural law should be immutable, but the Church tradition on abortion has changed over time, its present position dating back only to the nineteenth century.

It had long been obvious that the exclusively male Church hierarchy was not in sympathy with feminism or with women's demands for equality. Nonetheless, the Church felt obliged to insist that, in opposing the Cairo conference agenda, it was not questioning women's equality with men, just as it had insisted in May of 1994 that its policy banning women from the priesthood could not be construed as discrimination against women.

The Vatican, like the defenders of discriminatory *shari'a* laws in Middle Eastern countries, must have been feeling threatened by the growing international consensus that discriminating against women was wrong. Faced with this consensus, it realized that articulating candidly its views on women's rights threatened to delegitimize Vatican positions. The Church was therefore forced to resort to double-talk and to assert that its discriminatory rules were not discriminatory and that its opposition to equality for women was motivated by its belief that women deserved equality.

Where the Catholic Church is concerned, the same male biases and stereotyping of women have come into play as one sees in Muslim countries and among US opponents of women's rights – all connected to supposed inalterable differences between men and women that were decreed by Mother Nature. After the controversy about the Vatican stance opposing the population conference exploded, the Pope sought to defend the Vatican against charges that it disregarded women's rights by insisting on women's difference from men, maintaining that women achieved perfection, affirmation and 'relative autonomy' when they were 'equal to men but different' in the world and in the Catholic Church. He asserted that they would fail to achieve true freedom by trying to be like men, claiming: 'Perfection for women does not mean being like men, a masculinization to the point that they lose their own qualities as women.' Of course, this objection deliberately missed the point. Pope John Paul II was probably aware that women in demanding the same rights as men were not asking to be transformed into men and divested of their characteristics as women. Rather than seeking to masculinize themselves, women were asking for non-discriminatory treatment in laws that would nonetheless take into account in appropriate ways the realities that women got pregnant and bore children. The Pope revealed that he was actually taking issue with the women's movement by obliquely implying that militant feminists were intemperate and unreasonable, arguing: 'Diversity does not necessarily mean implacable opposition,' and saying that the movement should be based on the concept of equal dignity of the human person, both male and female.[42] In insisting on men and women's equality in 'dignity' – equality in 'dignity' being significantly different from equality in 'rights' – he adopted a strategy that Muslim conservatives opposed to women's equality have utilized.[43] With these assertions, the Pope not only revealed that he relied on sex stereotyping but that he was determined to obfuscate the Vatican's position on women's rights. Like Muslim countries and like the US government, the Vatican wanted to go on record as being officially in favor of women's equality. However, the Pope inadvertently disclosed that his ideas about women coincided with the premise that lay behind the Egyptian statement regarding Egypt's reservation to CEDAW, that 'true equality' for women entailed rights and obligations that differed from those enjoyed by men.

As noted, in its campaign against the feminist agenda at the population conference the Church spoke as if the measures on abortion and women's rights reflected 'cultural imperialism' – suggesting that the US was attempting to impose on others ideas that were peculiar to US culture. Muslim feminists in the Middle East, used to hearing similar charges about American cultural imperialism being behind demands for greater freedom for women, will understand the motives for making such charges – to delegitimize indigenous voices clamoring for women's rights in non-Western societies. In fact, what the Vatican really deprecated and did not want to see influencing others was the American tendency to question and criticize the Vatican's discriminatory policies.[44] Joan Dunlop, president of the International Women's Health Coalition, a private group working with women in developing countries, had justification for charging: 'The Vatican's inflammatory language is a smoke screen; they are threatened by women having a say in their own lives.'[45]

Conclusion

Just as women from around the world forged new bonds of solidarity at the 1993 Vienna human rights conference, so the opponents of women's rights from different cultural and religious backgrounds are discovering how much their programs have in common – and are forming alliances to forestall further progress towards equal rights for women. Disappointed that it had lost its Republican allies in the White House with the 1992 Democratic victory, the Vatican turned to Islamic clerics and representatives of Muslim countries like Iran who were opposed to the emphasis that the Cairo population conference was placing on women's rights and women's autonomy.[46] The famous Islamic university of al-Azhar in Cairo, and the representatives of Libya, Morocco, and Iran, quickly aligned themselves with the Vatican. Al-Azhar denounced the program of the Cairo conference as contrary to basic precepts of Islam and called for the program to be reworded to eliminate statements in conflict with Islamic law.[47]

The Vatican had a great deal in common with the spokespersons for Muslim countries that were resisting CEDAW principles of equality for women, but an alliance that cut across an otherwise vast religious gulf by itself necessitated additional doubletalk, since neither side would admit that antipathy to women's equality was the shared motivating factor behind their alliance.

One sample of the new hypocritical rhetoric can be found in the language in a letter to the *New York Times* in defense of the Vatican–Muslim alliance, proposing that it was grounded not 'on religious values, but on a respectful approach to the dignity of the human person.'[48] In this defense of the Vatican's position, appeals to a specific religious tradition have been dropped and replaced by a generic appeal to respect for an abstract concept of human 'dignity.' The actual harm done to women by denying them contraceptive freedom and the negative impact of uncontrolled fertility were deliberately suppressed. In the long run, we should expect more of this, as the foes of women's rights move to internationalize their positions.

Conservatives are also mobilizing women's support to counter feminism. Opponents of women's rights have found it useful to have their campaigns fronted by women who are prepared to attack feminist projects. The participation of women dilutes the impression otherwise created that men are seeking to deny rights to women.[49] For example, a recent article has pointed out how what might be called 'the religious right' in Pakistan has organized women to fight feminist ideas in attempts to discredit Pakistan's feminist groups like the impressive Women's Action Forum (WAF).[50] That men opposed to women's equality employ women for their goals does not, of course, mean that women who oppose feminism always act under the aegis of men, or that they do not have their own reasons for opposing equal rights for women.[51]

Other links could be forged, as well, that could create a formidable international coalition of interests opposed to women's equality. Women opposed to CEDAW might also decide to join forces across cultural and religious frontiers. It would not be surprising if Muslim women like Zaynab al-Ghazali, an Egyptian fundamentalist activist, should forge an alliance with Christian fundamentalist women and other US women who were anti-ERA and who would be appalled at the notion of an international version of ERA principles.

The new world hypocrisy on women's rights has drawbacks; it requires feminists to change tactics. Spokesmen from countries like Iran and Saudi Arabia who are prepared to endorse blatant, *de jure* discrimination against women are becoming quaint anachronisms. Soon they will be replaced by more sophisticated spokespersons like the ones now familiar in the US, who will no longer openly acknowledge that they oppose equality for women.

Instead, their rhetorical strategies will include insisting that equality, properly understood, precludes – or at least does not require – adopting principles like those in CEDAW. To rationalize their official policies in conflict with CEDAW, they may appeal to laws of a supposed higher authority – like *shari'a* law, the US Constitution, Church tradition, or Nature. We have to clarify issues that the enemies of women's equality are seeking to muddy by claiming to support women's equality but then twisting and distorting the concept of 'equality' to serve agendas designed to deprive women of rights. We now have the time-consuming and difficult task of exposing the new world hypocrisy by dissecting what these programs really entail. We need to focus attention on the reality of continuing disparities in rights for women and men and the practical consequences that these have for women's lives. We need to educate women not only to understand their rights under CEDAW, but to distinguish these from the pseudo-rights being put forward by groups with anti-feminist agendas.

So long as Muslim countries continue to appeal to 'Islam' to justify opposing CEDAW, the contingent, man-made nature of the rules depriving women of equal rights must be highlighted, and the international community must be disabused of the myth that there exists a monolithic and retrograde Islam that precludes according equal rights to women. Official assertions that the current *shari'a*-based rules achieve the CEDAW goal of equality for women, albeit by a different route, need to be challenged. However, if such challenges work, Muslim countries are likely simply to adjust their tactics and seek to deflect consideration of the discrimination facing women by invoking overarching abstractions like their supposed concern for 'human dignity.'

To look on the brighter side, one can at least say that all this signifies the degree to which the principle of equality for women has gained normative force around the globe – so that even the enemies of women's rights are forced to pay lip service to it. The days of arguing for the general proposition that discrimination against women is wrong will soon be behind us. That battle has essentially been won.

We need to exploit the growing international consensus and solidarity among women on these issues, at the same time preparing ourselves to combat the international solidarity that is being forged among groups that oppose equal rights for women. Despite the progress we have made, the way ahead is not going to be smooth or easy. In fact, I predict that, when we look back, it will often be with nostalgia for the good old bad old days, when the fight was for recognition of the simple proposition that discrimination against women was wrong. It is much easier to articulate and to communicate this truth, which with benefit of hindsight seems self-evident, than to fight the new world hypocrisy.

Notes

1. Malcolm N. Shaw, *International Law* 2nd edn (Cambridge: Grotius, 1986), p. 100.

2. It would be interesting, of course, to peruse the reasons for non-ratification of CEDAW as well, if these were ever presented in a set of statements of governmental positions comparable to the collection we have of official reasons for CEDAW reservations.

3. Belinda Clark, 'The Vienna Convention Reservations Regime and the Convention on Discrimination Against Women,' *American Journal of International Law* 85 (1991), p. 317.

4. I have indicated in another essay why I am not persuaded that the international community must accept these without further scrutiny. See my chapter, 'Cultural Particularism as a Bar to Women's Rights. Reflections on the Middle Eastern Experience,' in Julie Peters and Andrea Wolper (eds), *Women's Rights, Human Rights. International Feminist Perspectives* (New York: Routledge, 1994).

5. Lars Adam Rehof, *Guide to the Travaux Preparatoires of the United Nations Convention on the Elimination of All Forms of Discrimination against Women* (Boston: Martinus Nijhoff, 1993), p. 257.

6. See Fawzi Najjar, 'Egypt's Laws of Personal Status,' *Arab Studies Quarterly* 10 (1988), pp. 319–44.

7. Rebecca Cook, 'Reservations to the Convention on the Elimination of All Forms of Discrimination Against Women,' *Virginia Journal of International Law* 30 (1990), p. 704.

8. *Ibid.*, pp. 704–5.

9. *Ibid.*, p. 703.

10. See Theodor Meron, *Human Rights Law-Making in the United Nations. A Critique of Instruments and Process* (Oxford: Clarendon Press, 1986), pp. 62–6, 153–60.

11. *Ibid.*, p. 159.

12. *Ibid.*, pp. 159–60.

13. From the 'Declaration and Reservations made by the Government of Morocco upon Accession,' 23 June 1993, in Annex II, 'Reservations made upon ratification from 1 August 1992 to 1 August 1993'.

14. 'Les femmes accueillent avec prudence la réforme de leur statut,' *Le Monde*, 22 October 1993 (author's translation).

15. *Ibid.*

16. The works of Fatima Mernissi are interesting in this regard. See her *The Veil and the Male Elite: A Feminist Interpretation of Women's Rights in Islam* (Reading, Mass.: Addison-Wesley, 1991) and *Islam and Democracy. Fear of the Modern World* (Reading, Mass.: Addison-Wesley, 1992).

17. Tunisia referred to Article 1 in the Tunisian Constitution, making Islam the state religion, as the obstacle.

18. 'Legislation Must Be Enacted to End Sex Discrimination: Women Activists; First Article of the Election Law Criticized,' Moneyclips, 19 April 1994, available in LEXIS, NEXIS Library, ALLWLD File.

19. The reformed Tunisian code of nationality in Article 12 provides: 'Devient Tunisien, sous réserve de réclamer cette qualité par déclaration dans le délai d'un an précédant sa majorité, l'enfant né à l'étranger d'une mère tunisienne et d'un père étranger.'

20. 'Kuwait's Voteless Women Hail South African Poll,' Reuters World Service, 27 April 1994, available in LEXIS, NEXIS Library, ALLWLD File.

21. 'Legislation Must Be Enacted,' *op. cit.*

22. 'Women Demand "Natural Rights",' Moneyclips, 14 April 1994, available in LEXIS, NEXIS Library, ALLWLD File.

23. The relatively more advanced status of women in Sweden was not coincidental. A recent study has shown that reservations to CEDAW, as well as failures to ratify CEDAW, correlate with relatively low rates of literacy, school enrollment, economic participation, and involvement in the political process on the part of women in the countries involved. On the other hand, ratification correlates with relatively high rates in these categories. See 'International Standards of Equality and Religious Freedom: Implications for the Status of Women,' in Valentine Moghadam (ed.), *Identity Politics & Women. Cultural Reassertions and Feminism in International Perspective* (Boulder: Westview, 1994), pp. 434–7.

24. Rehof, *op. cit.*, p. 281.

25. See Hilary Charlesworth, Christine Chinkin, and Shelley Wright, 'Feminist Approaches to International Law,' *American Journal of International Law* 85 (1991), pp. 613–45.

26. Rehof, *op. cit.*, p. 280.

27. See, for example, 'Benazir Vows to Protect Women's Rights,' *Xinhua News Agency*, 15 June 1994, available in LEXIS, NEXIS Library, ALLWLD File.

28. 'Women: UN Rejects Proposed Study of Women's Status under Islam,' Inter Press Service, 26 May 1987, available in LEXIS, ALLWLD File. Even countries like Iran that have not ratified CEDAW do not want the actual status of women under the laws in Muslim countries examined, because they likewise deny that they discriminate and use similar equivocal formulas about how women are treated under their laws. See, for example, the comments of President Rafsanjani, who insisted in a news conference

that 'We define women in society as complete human beings possessing personalities that are equal to those of men. Naturally, because of the physical and spiritual disposition of women – you cannot deny the physical difference – there are instances when we take into consideration certain conditions regarding women or men and these are mostly to the benefit rather than detriment of women.' See 'Iran; Rafsanjani's News Conference: Economy, Foreign Relations, Role of Women,' BBC SWB, 4 February 1993, available in LEXIS, NEXIS Library, BBC File. Of course, Iranian feminists do not agree that Iran's discriminatory laws are 'mostly to the benefit' of women.

29. Renee Feinberg, *The Equal Rights Amendment. An Annotated Bibliography of the Issues 1976–1985* (New York: Greenwood Press, 1986), p. 3.

30. See comments by Bruce Fein in Sarah Zearfoss, 'The Convention for the Elimination of All Forms of Discrimination Against Women: Radical, Reasonable, or Reactionary?' *Michigan Journal of International Law*, 12 (1991), p. 905.

31. For example, although US women can serve in the military, they are excluded from a variety of positions, including many roles in combat.

32. For a discussion of these, see Fein and Zearfoss, *op. cit.*, pp. 911–12.

33. For a general discussion see Malvina Halberstam and Elizabeth Defeis, *Women's Legal Rights: International Covenants an Alternative to ERA?* (Dobbs Ferry: Transnational Publishers, 1987), pp. 50–63.

34. *Ibid.*, p. 61.

35. In a meeting of mostly liberal intellectuals gathered in 1986 to compose 'a meaningful contemporary Constitution' the participants backed down from challenging the Constitution, despite all its archaic features. However, Betty Friedan did at least say that there should be an equal rights amendment. See 'Constitution Gets Liberal Thumbs Up,' *New York Times*, 5 October 1986.

36. Among other things, the ERA was portrayed as anti-family, threatening to morality and traditional values. See Feinberg, *op. cit.*, p. 17. For the reasons for the defeat, see generally Mary Frances Berry, *Why ERA Failed. Politics, Women's Rights, and the Amending Process of the Constitution* (Bloomington: Indiana University Press, 1986).

37. 'The Democrats as the Devil's Disciples,' *New York Times*, 30 August 1992.

38. Halberstam and Defeis, *op. cit.*, p. 173.

39. 'God-fearing Republicans give Democrats hell,' *Toronto Star*, 22 August 1992, available in LEXIS, NEXIS Library, ALLWLD File.

40. 'Cultural Warriors Misfiring: Jurek Martin Finds the Bush Campaign Lagging in the Polls Again,' *The Financial Times*, 27 August 1992, available in LEXIS, NEXIS Library, ALLWLD File. Even conservative George Will was disgusted by the tactics of the Bush campaign with 'its riff-raff of liars and aspiring ayatollahs.' *Ibid.*

41. 'Vatican Fights Plan to Bolster Women's Role,' *New York Times*, 15 June 1994, available in LEXIS, NEXIS Library, ALLWLD File.

42. 'Pope Says Women Should not Try to Be Like Men,' Reuters, 22 June 1994, available in LEXIS, NEXIS Library, ALLWLD File.

43. See Ann Elizabeth Mayer, 'Universal versus Islamic Human Rights: A Clash of Cultures or a Clash with a Construct?' *Michigan Journal of International Law* 15 (1994), pp. 330–1.

44. For example, in the face of the Pope's assertion that women had to be excluded from the priesthood, a survey showed that 60 per cent of American Catholics thought they should be ordained. 'Faith to Face: The Pope's Fallibility in Quashing Debate,' *The Guardian*, 11 June 1994, available in LEXIS, NEXIS Library, ALLWLD File.

45. 'Vatican Fights Plan,' *op. cit.*

46. *Ibid.* See also the full-page advertisement condemning the 'cultural imperialism' of the US policy on the population conference that was published in the *New York Times* on 15 August 1994. Prominent American Catholics were joined by Jewish leaders and representatives of two Islamic organizations in signing their names to the advertisement, which presented the US position as one hostile to the family and insensitive to religious values.

47. 'Muslims Echo Pope's Rejection of UN Population Document,' *The Washington Post*, 12 August 1994, available in LEXIS, NEXIS Library, ALLWLD File.

48. See letter from Tona Varela in letters to the editor section, *New York Times*, 27 June 1994.

49. Susan Faludi's recent book, *Backlash. The Undeclared War Against American Women* (New York: Crown, 1991), presents an important assessment of how the opponents of women's rights in the US have managed to coopt women as they waged their campaign against feminism.

50. See Khawar Mumtaz, 'Fundamentalism and Women in Pakistan,' in Moghadam, *op. cit.*, pp. 237–8.

51. For an introduction to the complex subject of women joining in the efforts to fight women's rights in the American context, and a valuable bibliography of the relevant literature, see Roberta Klatch, 'Women of the New Right in the United States: Family, Feminism and Politics,' in Moghadam, *op. cit.*, pp. 367–90.

TWO

Women and Violence – Selected Cases

8

The Ambiguity of *Shari'a* and the Politics of 'Rights' in Saudi Arabia

Eleanor Abdella Doumato

In January 1993 the government of Canada granted refugee status to a Saudi Arabian national on the grounds of gender-related persecution. Advocates for the young woman had argued success-fully that her basic human rights to life, liberty and security of the person were threatened because of her refusal to accept the restric-tions that apply to women in Saudi Arabia. She could not work, study, or dress as she pleased, she claimed, and her freedom of movement in and out of the country was restricted. Furthermore, the persecution was the result not only of government policy but of public attitudes toward non-conforming women, as she had been 'subjected to violence on numerous occasions simply for walking down the street alone without covering her face.'[1]

In the arena of international opinion, the question of human rights in the Kingdom of Saudi Arabia has focused largely on restrictions placed on women in spite of well-documented informa-tion regarding arbitrary arrest, detention, and torture among the general population and denial of religious freedom to all but Sunni Muslims. The reason for this emphasis on women is that gender-based inequalities in citizenship rights and human rights are policies instituted and enforced by the state as representing the will of the people, the values of religion, and the common good. In Saudi Arabia, what are viewed as inequalities as measured against United Nations standards are viewed both by policy-making agencies and by public opinion as the proper Islamic balance of rights and responsibilities between men and women. Unlike human rights violations that governments carry out in secret and seek to deny, restrictions on women are apparent to the most casual observer and are promulgated openly as a matter of civic pride.

The recent experience of human rights activism in Saudi Arabia has shown that issues underlying human rights for women are inseparable from the problem of human rights violations in society at large. As this paper will show, these issues are mired in the ambiguity of Islamic rhetoric, which promotes 'rights' for 'everyone' when in fact there is no consensus as to what constitutes a right or who is entitled to exercise that right. Instead, the definition of 'rights' in the language of Islamic rhetoric is elastic, depending upon the speaker, and rights are dispensed not as something due to an individual but as something to be allocated according to religious, ethnic, national, tribal, or gender identity. For women, human rights are caught in the additional bind of a political culture that links government legitimacy to Islam and women's role to cultural authenticity, so that women's rights are hostage to shifting political currents and struggles over who is allowed to define national culture. The experience of human rights activists since the 1990–1 Gulf crisis illustrates the ambiguity of human rights in the rhetoric of Islam, and illuminates the challenges facing advocates for women's rights in the current political climate of Saudi Arabia.

The Arena of Contention: *'Shari'a* Rights'

In May 1993 an organization was formed which its founders called, in English, the Committee for the Defense of Legitimate Rights (CDLR) and, in Arabic, Committee for the Defense of Shari'a Rights.[2] At its founding, it was hailed by some as the first true, indigenous human rights organization in Saudi Arabia. In its charter, the founders stated that their purpose was to support the protection of rights affirmed in the Islamic *shari'a*. 'All men are brothers in Islam,' the charter says, and 'it is an obligation upon Muslims to support the oppressed, eliminate injustices, and defend the rights prescribed by the shari'a for man.'[3] The committee had been founded in reaction to political repression and broad-based dissatisfaction with the Saudi regime.

The government greeted the committee with unbridled hostility. Four of those who signed the charter were dismissed by the government from university teaching positions. Another two, who are lawyers, had their law offices closed by government order. Muhammad al-Mas'ari, a US-trained theoretical physicist, spokesman for the committee and son of one of the signatories to the charter, Abdallah ibn Sulayman al-Mas'ari, was arrested and detained without a statement of charges.[4] Subsequently imprisoned for six months, al-Mas'ari now operates his committee out of London, speaking on behalf of a coalition of politically liberal and religiously conservative voices who have in common their opposition to the policies and authoritarian practices of the Saudi ruling family.

The experience of the committee in its attempt to operate inside the kingdom is more than a story about arbitrary arrest and suppression of civil liberties. It is also a story about the ambiguity of the rhetoric of human rights in Islam, and the way Islamic rhetoric can be manipulated to obfuscate what people actually mean when they talk about 'rights.' The day after the formation of the committee, those who signed the charter were denounced by the most influential body of religious scholars in the kingdom, the Council of Senior Muslim Scholars, which is financed by the government and is expected to provide Islamic sanction for government policy. The denunciation was issued by the head of the council, Shaikh Abd al-Aziz ibn Baz, the most eminent religious figure in the country, and was given wide publicity on the front pages of the Saudi press. The council called the committee 'illegitimate' and 'superfluous' because the kingdom is already ruled by the *shari'a*, and therefore the rights of everyone are already protected by law.[5] In effect the council was using the *shari'a* as an argument to suppress the committee, just as the committee had used the *shari'a* to justify its coming into existence.

The *Shari'a* as Defender of Group Rights: A Salafi View

In statements issued from London in 1994, subsequent to the committee's original manifesto, the CDLR clarified its objectives. Among these was the intent 'to elucidate and assert the concept of human rights in Islam and eliminate the distortions created by the Saudi regime's erroneous practices and severe abuses and massive violations of human rights.'[6] The CDLR also stated that it had adopted the idea that human rights were universal and included 'the rights of individuals, groups, and society,' and that it undertook 'to defend them all.' The organization would also observe, however, 'the Islamic code of ethics', value 'its activities', and comply 'fully with the guidelines of the Qur'an and the sunna.'[7]

The ambiguity of the language of rights in Islam used by the committee was not lost on liberal, Shi'a, or other minority Saudis who might have been expected to be the natural allies of a human rights organization. Despite the committee's lofty goals, some dismissed it out of hand, and it was greeted with deep skepticism, if not apprehension, by Shi'i Muslims.

The reason for this skepticism is that some members of the committee may be considered Salafi, or 'purists,' associated with the post-Gulf War revival of the Wahhabi movement. The Wahhabi interpretation of Islam was the ideology underpinning the Saudi conquest of the peninsula in the 1920s and the prevailing ideology in Najd, the central part of Arabia throughout the nineteenth and early twentieth century. The Wahhabi interpretation of Islam calls for a literal understanding of Qur'an and *hadith*, and conformity in the behavior of the Muslim community of believers according to standards determined by Wahhabi *ulama*. In Najd, correct behavior for women is predicated on face veiling and separation from unrelated men. The Wahhabis especially disapprove of ritual practices that demonstrate reverence for saints and martyrs on the grounds that these acts are polytheistic, since the act of praying to a saint attributes powers to a holy person that should be attributed only to God. The Wahhabis consequently disapprove of the Shi'a in particular because of their reverence for the descendants of the Prophet through his son-in-law Ali, and for their Ashura ceremonies in commemoration of the martyrs of Shi'a tradition.

One of the men who signed the charter of the committee for legitimate rights is Abdallah ibn Abd al-Rahman al-Jabrin, an Islamic scholar who follows the Wahhabi tradition, and who was in 1992 a member of the Council of Senior Ulama. In his view, 'legitimate rights' are not rights to be applied to everyone. Instead, rights are to be allocated according to religious persuasion; they are for male Muslims who have correct beliefs, such as themselves, and not for wrong-believing Muslims, such as the Shi'a. Prior to signing the declaration of the Committee for the Defense of Legitimate Rights, al-Jabrin had issued a statement declaring that Shi'a citizens of the kingdom were apostates, which is tantamount to declaring that the half-million Shi'a in the country deserve the death penalty.[8] In al-Jabrin's view, the Shi'a are not only to be excluded from the 'brotherhood of Islam,' they should be drummed out of citizenship in the Saudi Islamic state.[9] This attitude toward Shi'a is not a marginal view. Shaikh ibn Baz, as head of the Council of Senior Ulama and thus head of the official clergy supporting the Al Saud regime, has issued similar *fatwas*, referring to Shi'a as polytheists and apostates.[10] The government did not react to al-Jabrin's *fatwa*,[11] or to a letter of Shaykh Nasir ibn Sulayman al-Mar in May 1993 urging suppression of Shi'ite rituals and their economic and social isolation so that Shi'a can no longer 'contaminate' Wahhabi society.[12] This suggests either that the rulers recognize that antipathy toward the Shi'a has substantial resonance among their hard-core Wahhabi constituency, or that allowing this kind of fear mongering offers the benefit of intimidating Shi'a and liberal critics of the regime by waving before them the specter of an alternative to Saudi rule which is far less palatable than the present regime.

Gender on the Scale of Rights

Human rights activism since the Gulf War has also raised public discussion on interpretations of the rights of women as a group according to the *shari'a*. As with the debate over rights for Shi'a, the rights of women in the *shari'a* are subject to shifting interpretations, and the range of interpretations can be clearly seen in the events that followed the women's driving demonstration that occurred on 6 November 1990, during the American military build-up after Saddam Hussein's invasion of Kuwait. The demonstrators had articulated a feminist interpretation of rights accorded to women in the *shari'a* in a letter sent to Prince Salman, governor of Riyadh, before driving cars as a group to express their desire for an end to the ban on women driving. The letter refuted moral arguments against allowing women to drive, and noted that allowing it would remove the economic burden of having to hire a chauffeur and would facilitate their participation in the development of the country, which, they argued, was compatible with Islam:

> Your Royal Highness, an objective evaluation of our demand will reveal that ultimately, we have not demanded something ruled out by our religion and its tolerant teachings. On the contrary, our demand is corroborated by religion. The tradition of our Prophet Muhammad, may God's blessing be upon Him, the four Caliphs and the early believers and their dependence on the efforts of women are evidence confirming the greatness and comprehensive nature of Islam in acknowledging the rights of everyone. The Prophet, may God's peace and blessing be upon him, said, 'Take half of your religion from this red-haired woman.'[13]

This argument was acceptable to many liberal thinkers, including some university students, and even to some conservatives, including Dr Muhammad al-Mas'ari, the religiously conservative physics professor who was to become the exiled spokesman for the Committee for the Defense of Legitimate Rights. The weight of public opinion, however, was not in favor of women's right to drive.

The Supreme Council of Scholars rendered a judgement on the driving demonstration which gave precedence to the protection accorded women in Islam over the equality accorded women by virtue of the example from the life of the Prophet's wives, declaring women should never be allowed to drive because driving exposes their dignity to harm, and is therefore un-Islamic. This interpretation of women's rights from the establishment clergy was echoed within the ranks of the less-educated religious police, some of whom regarded the women's attempt to drive as beyond the bounds of morality. By the act of exposing themselves behind the wheel of a car, by their failure to completely cover themselves with *hijab*, these women were, in the eyes of religious police, 'sluts who advocate vice and corruption on earth.'[14]

In the university, where some of the demonstrators were teachers, considerable anger was expressed toward the women. One was attacked by a student who burst into her office, pulled her hair, and knocked a verse from the Qur'an off the wall.[15] One of those who were most critical of the demonstrators was Abdullah ibn Hamad al-Towayjri, a religious scholar and one of the original signatories to the charter of the Committee for the Defense of Legitimate Rights who wanted the demonstrators jailed. For many, the boldness of their demand to drive had become the emblem of submission to Western values, and the *hijab* and homemaking the symbol of cultural resistance to the overwhelming Western influences in the country: subsequently, one children's television program taught a song to impress upon children that to be a proper Saudi woman means not driving a car.[16] At the same time, Salafi mosque preachers in Riyadh were demanding a total ban on women taking jobs in Saudi Arabia. The government also gained political capital out of the event: in punishing the demonstrators by suspending them from their jobs and confiscating their passports, the regime seized an opportunity to display its willingness to take a stand for 'Islam' and 'tradition.'

The following February, the issue of women as the conduit of Western influences again arose when scores of university professors and religious scholars, including the head of the Council of Senior Scholars, Ibn Baz, signed a petition to the king requesting reforms in government administration,[17] but also asking for reforms that would more firmly institutionalize Islam throughout society and government. 'This state is noted for declaring its adoption of the *shari'a*,' the petition began, 'and scholars and experts have continued to give advice to their rulers regarding the advice imparted to them by God.'[18] The signatories asked for 'the formation of a consultative council to decide internal and external issues on the basis of the *shari'a*;' for all laws and regulations 'of political, economic, administrative or other nature' to be reconciled with principles of the *shari'a*, 'and legislation not conforming to *shari'a* to be repealed.' They asked for jurisdiction of the *shari'a* courts to be extended to cover all legal disputes, including commercial and civil matters, and for the lifting of restrictions on Islamic banks.[19] As for individual rights, these were desirable, but what they were was left hanging in the limbo of *shari'a* ambiguity: 'The rights of individuals and society must be guaranteed,' the petition said, and 'every restriction on people's rights and their will must be removed, to ensure the enjoyment of human dignity, *within acceptable religious safeguards*' (emphasis mine).[20]

The petition also asked for control over the media whose function should be 'to educate, serve Islam and express the morals of society.'[21] In a subsequent letter sent to the king, the petitioners explained that they wanted the 'Saudi media to be committed to Islam in all that it publishes ... and to fight destructive currents, atheistic tendencies...and attempts to divert the Muslims from their creed ...' The letter then got down to the real fault that the religious leaders found with the media, which was the portrayal of women in ways that encourage liberal sexuality. 'How do series loaded with sexual hints and temptations fit in with this policy?' the letter asked. 'How do the songs which go with music and their low words about love fit in with this policy ... films which excite the instincts and which show women in scandalous sexual scenes which tempt and carry destructive thoughts and deviant behavior?'[22] For the religiously conservative, then, 'religious safeguards' that circumscribe the exercise of 'rights' are necessary to protect the culture, and since women who are chaste and invisible are the very emblem of culture, control over even the image of women is a necessary safeguard to cultural preservation.

Shari'a as Defender of Individual Rights: a 'Secularist' View

A petition sent to the king in December 1990 directly challenged the conservative monopoly on defining *shari'a* and, indirectly, their monopoly on defining women's rights. In this petition, 43 public figures from the business, literary and scholarly community also accepted the importance of *shari'a* as the guide for society, but set forth a rationale for employing *shari'a* as a vehicle to open up society rather than to impose boundaries. The rationale was premised on the recognition that only the Qur'an and *hadith* are infallible sources of divine law to be obeyed, but that everything else, such as judicial commentaries and Qur'anic exegesis, is subject to human interpretation, and therefore no one should be allowed to claim an exclusive right to determine *shari'a* rules. The petition asked for a systematic framework for *fatwa* so that 'scholarly opinions may be freely examined and questioned without any limits.'[23]

Building on this method of 'secularizing' *shari'a*, the petitioners were able to make discrete statements about human rights, without the kind of qualifying conditions attached to the principles of human rights in the religious petition. For example, the petition called for a 'commitment to total equality among all citizens in all aspects of their life, without distinction based on ethnic, tribal, sectarian or social origins,' and stated that 'the principle of protecting citizens against interference in their lives except *by a court order* must be firmly established.'[24]

The secular petition also expressed concern about the media, recognizing (as the religious petition did) that they had a duty to 'preach good over evil,' but its authors wanted a 'precise law reflecting the most advanced legislation in other countries.' Unlike the religious petition, which called for unlimited overseeing of the media to determine what is or is not Islamic, the secular petition asked that the media themselves be given the freedom to make decisions without fear of arbitrary censorship and punishment.

Whereas the religious petition avoided mentioning rights for women, the secular petition asked for the establishment of the principle that women may work outside their homes: 'Although we believe that nurturing the new generation is the highest duty of Muslim women, we nevertheless believe that there are numerous fields of public life where women can be allowed to participate –

within the scope of the *shari'a* – thus honoring them and acknowledging their role in building society.'[25] Stating a commitment to women's right to work was brave on the part of the secularists, but it is significant that even to enter into any discussion about rights, they had to first acknowledge marriage and motherhood as the primary Islamic goals for women and to acknowledge that there were 'Islamic' limitations on women's work outside the home.

The New Basic Law: Ambiguity Codified

The contents of the two petitions presented unacceptable alternatives for the Saudi regime. The secular petition was impossible (even if the regime was attracted to its liberal philosophy), if only because the regime's own religious establishment backed the religious petition.[26] In addition, conservative voices in opposition to Saudi policies and to the inundation of the country by Western culture had grown in volume, and society as a whole had become more conservative. The regime would therefore be particularly vulnerable to accusations of abrogating its claim to rule by *shari'a*, its main claim to legitimacy. Nor could the regime embrace the demand to codify the *shari'a* and apply it to the spectrum of government operations without divesting itself of power in favor of the *ulama* and turning the country away from the Western-oriented development agenda that has guided Saudi policy for the last 25 years.

King Fahd's solution, coming after years of promising and then failing to deliver a written codification of laws, was a new Basic Law issued by royal order on 1 March 1992.[27] The emphasis on *shari'a* in the Basic Law puts in writing some of the ambiguities regarding rights and legal authority that existed before. Article 1 reiterates the long-established principle that the constitution of Saudi Arabia is God's Holy Book and His Prophet's Tradition (that is, the Qur'an and the *hadith*). The religious basis of Saudi rule is again confirmed in article 7, which states that the Qur'an and *hadith* 'are the source of authority of the government,' and that 'they are the arbiters of this law and all other laws.'[28]

As the basis of the Saudi system of government, the *shari'a* is ambiguous not only because it is uncodified in written statutes, but because it is subject to the interpretation of the Council of Senior Ulama. The members of the council theoretically remain the ultimate source of interpreting the laws of the kingdom, but the 18 members of the council serve at the king's pleasure and are appointed by him. The head of the council has ministerial rank but is not a member of the Council of Ministers, which acts as the executive and legislative governing body. In order to acquire the force of law, the decisions of the Council of Senior Ulama have to be approved by the king or the king and the Council of Ministers.[29] Thus, not only is the meaning of *shari'a* subject to interpretation, but its application is not consistent.

Jurisdiction of *shari'a* courts is exclusive and *shari'a* rules are consistent only in family law and in criminal matters of a non-political nature.[30] Jurisdiction is also usual when it comes to rules about social behavior and women. In practice, royal decrees, secular commercial codes and administrative procedures function outside the jurisdiction of *shari'a* law. However, the fact that the *shari'a* is not all-encompassing from a juridical point of view does not detract from its importance and the problem of its ambiguity for the individual: the areas in which *shari'a* does apply and the cultural world view it shapes affects people in their day-to-day life, in their work, in their education, in their recreation, and in their personal life.

The Consultative Council introduced in the new Basic Law is only an advisory body with no legislative power, and the new law consolidates powers in the hands of the king. As for human rights, article 26 of the Basic Law says that 'the state shall protect human rights according to the shari'a,'[31] but without codifying the protections offered in the *shari'a*, the new law is at best equivocal.[32] It does not, for example, ban torture or inhumane punishment, which is allowed under the Saudi penal system. It does not ban discrimination on the basis of religion, so that the currently practised discrimination against Shi'a in employment, education, government service, and religious practice, as well as discrimination against non-Muslim foreigners, may continue. It does not protect the right of assembly or association, so that political organization, political activity and labor unions remain illegal, and even such benign organizations as women's charities operate under government scrutiny. Free speech is not protected, but on the contrary suppressed, and editors publish in peril of arbitrary arrest.

The Basic Law also fails to provide for due process in the penal system. A person may be apprehended by the Shurta (Public Security Police), or al-Mabahith al-'Amma (General Investigations) for security offenses, or the *mutawwa'in* (patrolmen for the

Committee for the Propagation of Virtue and the Prevention of Vice) for a morals violation, without a clear statement of charges – which could be as minor as a traffic violation, a woman's walking alone at night, carrying religious literature, or an unmarried couple's dining in a restaurant – and be detained without any obligation on the part of the arresting authority to inform the arrested person's family or allow him to retain counsel. The new law calls for the right to privacy and the sanctity of the home, but with the caveat that searches may be conducted 'according to law.'[33] The applicable 'law' is unclear, and private homes continue to be subject to arbitrary police searches.

The Basic Law promises significant economic and social rights to Saudi citizens, including the right to receive the benefits of the social welfare system, employment for everyone, access to public education and health care. Nowhere, however, does the Basic Law specifically address women's rights. Their access to jobs is severely limited by the regulation that they may work only in places that are completely sex-segregated; they do not have the same educational opportunities as men have, and their access to health care is constrained by their inability to drive a car. It becomes apparent that without specific constitutional protection for human rights, the promise of protection based on the *shari'a* in the new Basic Law of Government remains nearly void of substance.

Ambiguity: A Help and a Hindrance to Women's Rights

From the standpoint of the rulers, the ambiguity of rights in the *shari'a* offers the flexibility needed to bend with the political wind, so that Islam can be evoked either to liberalize opportunities for women, or to levy new restrictions on them. Education for women, for example, was begun in 1960 by government fiat despite opposition, with the caveat that it would be 'within Islamic margins,' that is, only for the purpose of training women for tasks regarded as suitable, such as nursing, teaching, and motherhood. When higher education brought women into the professions, 'Islamic margins' were broadened until maintaining sex segregation could be considered the boundary of their ability to work. In response to rising conservative sentiment in the 1980s, however, Islamic margins were narrowed by government fiat and women's ability to manage businesses, travel abroad to study, eat in a restaurant, or select any course of study was limited. On the other hand, after the Iraqi invasion of Kuwait in 1990 and the Saudi government's decision to respond militarily, the regime recognized that civilian participation would be helpful in eliciting popular support for the war effort. The regime therefore obtained a *fatwa* from the Council of Senior Ulama approving the training of women as civil defense workers, and, had the efforts of the 2,000 women who subsequently entered civil defense training been required, their participation would have represented an unprecedented intrusion of women into male public space and a departure from established definitions of 'Islamic margins.'

The unfortunate side of ambiguity, then, is that there is no steady rudder to guide government policy, and women's rights are a permanent hostage to the vicissitudes of public sentiment or pressure from interest groups. A case in point is the United Nations Population and Development Conference held in Cairo in September 1994, when the Council of Senior Ulama succeeded in forcing the Saudi government to withdraw its participation.[34] As the Vatican and American Christian fundamentalists did, the *ulama* objected to facilitating the use of contraceptives and the availability of abortion, which the government, they noted, would be obliged to pay for. They also objected to the conference's recommendation to raise the minimum age for marriage, its advocacy of co-education as a means of achieving equality between the sexes, and its advocacy of confidentiality for young people receiving reproductive health care and information.[35]

At the top of the list of the objections was the conference's call for 'freedom and equality between men and women and the total elimination of differences between them.'[36] According to the council, equality between men and women is against God's law, the *shari'a*, and the law of nature dictated by women's physiology. By promoting equality and by advocating that women – married and unmarried – have the means to control their own reproduction, the conference was in their view advocating 'licentiousness, immorality and the spread of vice.' The agenda of the conference, the *ulama's* statement read, was an 'insult' to the values of Muslims. It was 'a vicious attack' against Muslim society by seeking to transform it from one where 'chastity and purity prevail,' to one like those which are afflicted with 'perversion' and where 'illicit sexual relations' are the norm.[37] The hostility of the *ulama*, then, had to do not just with the use of reproductive technologies, but with the implications of their use for male dominance over women and for the immorality implicit in unrestrained female sexuality. The hostility was above all a reaction to the conference's advocacy of sexual equality.

Even though the regime took immediate steps to alter the composition of the Council of Senior Ulama to render it more amenable to its will, it heeded the council's demand that it boycott the conference, indicating either that it thought public sentiment supported the council's interpretation, or that equality for women was not an issue worth confrontation with the regime's supporters among the religious hierarchy. In either event, the episode also indicated that in order to press a liberal agenda for women the regime needed, but did not have, an established moral and religious standard upon which to argue convincingly that Islam has other things to say about women.

The Constituency for Women's Rights

The rise in conservative sentiment and the vulnerability of the regime to internal criticism suggest that the flexibility offered in the *shari'a* is unlikely to work to the benefit of women in the immediate future. At the same time, direct advocacy on behalf of their rights according to international standards, such as that advocated in the Convention to Eliminate All Forms of Discrimination Against Women, is not going to provide a solution. The difficulties inherent in this approach can be seen in the experience of Shi'i human rights organizations that operated outside the kingdom after the Gulf War.

One of these was based in London and published a journal called *al-Jazirah al-Arabiyya*, and the other in Washington, DC, which published a newsletter in English called *Arabia Monitor*. Their main objective was to obtain the release of Shi'i men and women who had been arbitrarily arrested and tortured, and were being held incommunicado in Saudi jails, but the publications claimed a wider human-rights agenda. They called for a constitution with a clear statement of individual rights, including the rights of women in equality with men. They championed the women who were punished after the driving demonstration in 1990. They wrote with sympathy about the arrest of women for not being properly dressed or for being in the company of an unrelated man. Their publications included articles by women on their problems in the kingdom as women and as political dissidents,[38] and as prisoners in Saudi jails.[39]

In July 1993, these Shi'i organizations reached an accord with the Saudi government and stopped publishing. The Saudi regime was faced with criticism from many quarters, including Salafi within its own ranks, a militant right that was said to be armed, and Shi'i activists asking to be treated equally with other Saudi citizens. With the publicizing in the United States and Britain of human-rights abuses, the regime was facing embarrassment abroad as well as criticism at home. Rather than deal with opposition on two fronts, it was in the interest of the regime to compromise with the Shi'a, whose demands could be more easily satisfied than those of the Salafi. Consequently, the government and representatives of the Shi'i rights activists reached an agreement whereby all Shi'i political prisoners would be released, their passports returned so that they could leave the country, and discrimination against them in hiring and in education would be ended. In return, the Shi'a agreed to cease their publications abroad.[40]

The question of women's rights did not even arise in the negotiations between the Saudis and the Shi'a. In an interview, the publisher of one of the Shi'i journals was asked what happened to his call for women's rights. 'Women's rights,' he replied, 'are really a product of cultural understandings,' and he did not think that women's rights could really be addressed by the government until attitudes in society change. 'It is better to have an agreement right now that we can live with,' he said, 'and save the tricky issue of women until later.' For women, he said, 'there is nothing that can really be done except to carry on a dialogue with the important shaykhs in the kingdom and try to persuade them.'[41]

The waning of their enthusiasm for the cause of women's rights illustrates a fundamental difficulty in pursuing a women's rights agenda by direct confrontation: most people do not want it. Women's rights were not even worth mentioning in negotiations between the Shi'a and the regime because both sides recognized that most people do not want a women's rights agenda that is incompatible with 'cultural understandings,' one that calls for equality of opportunity for women in ways that are perceived to conflict with the *shari'a*, with 'family values,' or the authority of men.

In spite of the success of the Council of Senior Ulama in forcing a boycott of the UN Population Conference and the failure of the

Shi'i human rights organization to deliver a message on women's human rights, 'cultural understandings' are not fixed. In fact they are being challenged every day by the changing realities of daily life. One of these changing realities can be seen in the opportunities for women in employment, education and civic activities that have emerged in the last thirty years. Public education for girls was not available until 1960, almost ten years after it was available to boys, but by 1990 there were more girls than boys graduating from secondary schools, and girls as a group have excelled academically over boys. At the university level, the number of female graduates has been increasing at a faster rate than the number of male graduates, and in the humanities more female students are enrolled than males. In 1980 more than half of students studying abroad on government scholarships were women, an achievement that was reversed only as a result of government restrictions introduced in 1982 to prevented women travelling outside the country unchaperoned. By 1990, women constituted 7 per cent of the wage-earning workforce. Within the civil service, where women are employed in the sex-segregated public school system as teachers and administrators, women constitute a much higher percentage of the workforce. Women are also employed in banks, in the computer operations of utility companies, in television and radio programming, and in some ministries. They also work as clerical assistants, journalists, university professors, social workers, physicians, and nurses, and are active in women's charitable societies.

As a by-product of development, affluence, and social mobility, the extended family household in which the young wife becomes a subordinate of her mother-in-law has given way to the nuclear family household, where pressures to emulate the lifestyle of the older generation are mitigated by physical distance and privacy for husband and wife. In addition, women wage earners are having fewer children and getting married at a much later age than women without education or skills. The behavioral facts of life for women are therefore diverging from the cultural ideal of domesticated womanhood, and the perception of women as creatures of nature, trapped by their biology and ineducable because of limited intellectual capacity, is being undermined by the reality of women's achievements.[42]

In addition to the changing realities of women's daily lives, two other factors are causing society as a whole to examine its conceptualization of women. The first is the global mass media. Through video cassettes, satellite dishes, and foreign television programs, the global media have entered Saudi Arabia and cannot be shut out in spite of attempts to ban satellite dishes and censor what is viewed on videotapes and televisions in private homes. Today, watching television occupies a significant portion of the day for young Saudis,[43] and most of what they see comes from foreign programs, including programs from the United States, Britain and Canada, and especially from Egypt, which produces the most popular programs viewed on Saudi television.[44] Whether the media change behavior (as the signatories of the religious petition fear) is as yet an unanswered question, but the exposure to Western and Arab, non-Saudi lifestyles must certainly evoke self-examination among the viewing audience.[45]

Another factor challenging 'cultural understandings' is the literature that Saudi women writers have been producing for a number of years, seeking to raise questions about cultural issues concerning women and to change the way people think about them.[46] This literature, primarily essays, short stories, and poetry, appears in mainstream publications and is widely read by young people, especially university students. It is opening up a public discussion on matters once confined to religious authorities. As a medium of resistance and protest, it is successful, because literature can evade government censorship. Equally important, the reader willingly hears its message because it does not directly challenge the culture. Unlike open challenges such as the principles inscribed in CEDAW which oblige signatories to promote equality between men and women in ways that come into conflict not only with *shari'a* family law but with individual male identity,[47] the work of these women writers avoids assaulting established institutions such as the family, marriage, veiling, and sex segregation. Instead, ideas about change are presented from within these institutions. By presenting female characters as individuals instead of abstractions of a homogeneous category symbolizing 'woman' or 'culture,' by endowing female historical figures with positive attributes of respect, individuality, and strength, they undermine the dominant, religious, male-interpreted version of women's place in society. Most important, they are careful to insulate Islam from blame for social problems. By making a point of separating tradition from religion, they can criticize society with impunity. Women's literature cannot effect a sea change overnight, but it has stirred a cultural awakening from within, one not borrowed from the West, and one that does not openly challenge religious conservatives. What these women writers are doing, however slowly, is carving out a space where discussion can occur in the hope of creating new 'cultural understandings' about women and women's rights in Muslim society.[48]

Reconstructing Cultural Understandings: The Door to Reinterpreting *Shari'a*

The new realities and new ways of thinking about gender do not sit easily with contemporary male interpretations of the idealized, domesticated, Islamic woman as expressed in the *fatwas* of conservative scholars. Even so, the interpretations of conservative scholars such as Abd al-Aziz ibn Abdallah ibn Baz, Saudi Arabia's most eminent *shari'a* scholar, continue to exert political clout. These scholars, however, no longer possess a monopoly on the act of *ijtihad* (interpretation).

When the women's driving demonstration occurred, for example, the Council of Senior Ulama, ibn Baz presiding, ruled that driving is unacceptable in Islam because it is incompatible with the dignity of women and Islam requires the protection of women's dignity. Working within the late twentieth-century tradition of conceptualizing Qur'anic male 'guardianship' over women as 'protection' of women, the shaykh was thus able to transform the negative notion of male dominance into a positive ideal to be embraced as an attribute of Islamic society, and the effect is to transform rules on women from something burdensome to something desirable, even in the eyes of women themselves.

However, when the leaders of the demonstration sent their appeal for the right to drive to Prince Salman, they exercised their own version of *ijtihad*. Without challenging the concept of male 'guardianship,' they drew a parallel between themselves as participants in national development and the women of the Prophet's time who helped found the early Muslim community. Just as male scholars do, they drew on *hadith*, but chose to raise the example of the Prophet's wife Aisha to prove that the Prophet considered women to be competent, even exceptional, interpreters of religion. Even though the battle over the right to drive was lost, the women demonstrators succeeded in staking out a claim for themselves as *shari'a* interpreters. Moreover, the interpretation they offered was more compatible with present realities and the needs of working families than that offered by *ulama* whose opinions seem to operate in an idealized world where women's male 'protectors' are not saddled with the obligation of hiring drivers to transport commuting wives to work.

Over the last twenty years, official interpretations of women in the *shari'a* have continued to emphasize women's natural disabilities and the importance of male control over what women do. For example, a 1980 *fatwa* designed to reinforce the ban on women working in places where they will come into contact with men restated the moral dangers inherent in women's work outside the home, and went further to state that Islam requires women to stay home. Women's work, says the *fatwa*, is

> contrary to *shari'a* clauses which order women to stay at home and perform the jobs which concern them in their home where they are far from interaction with men. It is also contrary to plain, well-referenced legal evidence which prohibits a man from being alone with a non-related woman and from looking at her … .God said, 'Stay, ye women [sic] in your homes; do not exhibit (yourselves) as in the days of yore …[49]

The interpretation of the quoted Qur'anic verse to mean total home confinement may have been comforting in 1980 when government subsidies to male heads of households were generous and women were for the first time entering the job market in large numbers, in some cases in competition with men. In the times of financial stress of the 1990s, however, being told that a woman must not leave her home could only be heard by working families as out of touch with their financial needs and out of touch with the aspirations of daughters who are graduating from the university.

Today, in the context of women's academic success, interpretations of *shari'a* that have been used to validate commonplace pejorative attitudes about women may appear more ridiculous than learned. In 1980, for example, ibn Baz, then the Director of the Department of Islamic Research, issued an opinion in which he called for the punishment of a woman writer for mocking religion after she wrote an article complaining about women's child-like status in the kingdom, and saying that men claim women are 'lacking in both mind and religion' and believe that men are women's guardians.[50] In his opinion, ibn Baz wrote,

> It is known that it was God who made men 'guardians of women by what God has favored some (over others) and by what they spend of

their money.' It follows, then that attacking men's guardianship of women is an objection to God and an attack on His Book and on his prudent law... further, it was the Prophet who described women as lacking in mind and religion. He mentioned that a sign of a woman's lacking mind is that the testimony of two women equals that of one man. He mentioned also that a sign of her lacking religion is that she stays nights and days unable to pray (during her menstruation) and that she does not fast during Ramadhan when she is having her period.[51]

In ibn Baz's view, the guardianship of women by men is fixed in religion, and her mental and spiritual inferiority is confirmed in the laws of God and therefore cannot even be questioned. Nearly fifteen years after this episode occurred, however, the academic success of women has proved beyond question that women do have 'mind.' By the measure of grades and graduation rates, women as a group have even achieved academic superiority over men. If ibn Baz were today to attempt to rationalize the silencing of women by reason of women's diminished capacity, he would risk courting doubt about his own capacity to interpret God: anyone hearing this *fatwa* would have to conclude that either God was mistaken about the mental superiority of men, or God meant something else and his *shari'a* interpreter got it wrong.

Conclusion

Muslim society has a built-in mechanism for promoting the human rights of its people, and that is the holy law, the *shari'a*. It is a mechanism that can be used on behalf of human rights, not because it is fixed or God-given, but because it is in fact flexible, allowing for interpretation by men and women, and adaptable to changing needs and changing cultural understandings. The first challenge to human rights activists is to influence and inform cultural understandings, so that hearts and minds are opened to rethinking *shari'a* law.

Culture as an impediment to achieving equality among people and between men and women is not always so apparent as it is in Saudi Arabia. The case of 'Nada,' the Saudi refugee in Canada, points to a characteristic about the allocation of human rights for men and women that seems as true for Western countries as it is for countries of the Muslim Middle East. Nada came to public attention because the Canadian Immigration and Refugee Board

had at first refused to grant her refugee status. The initial recommendation on Nada's application had been that 'the claimant,
like all her compatriots, would do well to comply with the laws of
general application she criticizes and under all circumstances.'[52]
The board had made the same presumption about women's rights
upon which most rules that set different standards for women
than for men are predicated: there are cultural understandings
that presuppose a different standard of care and judgement in
determining how rights are allocated; rules about women are for
the best, and if women would just do what they're supposed to
do, they would have no problems. That a different standard is a
lower standard is not easily recognized.

Even those who deplore violations of human rights that occur
in ways that are easy to identify and understand are likely not to
acknowledge the essential paradox in having separate standards.
Edward Broadbent, president of the International Centre for
Human Rights and Democratic Development, who argued for the
recognition of women's rights as human rights to the Canadian
immigration board, put it this way: 'What does the very phrase
"human rights" mean to a woman in one of the many states in
the world that criminalize the activities described in the Universal
Declaration of Human Rights if they are done by women but not
by men?'[53]

In Muslim societies, different interest groups will couch human
rights in the rhetoric of Islam and mean different things, and they
will mean that rights are to be allocated to some people and not
to others according to identity category. In Saudi Arabia, the
Committee for the Defense of Legitimate Rights used the language
of Islam to legitimize their activism on behalf of human rights,
and the government scholars used the same language to delegitimize it. The car-driving demonstrators used the language of
Islam to legitimize their request to drive, while some *ulama* and
other women used the same language to castigate them for insulting Islam and family values.

Human rights and women's rights are both ambiguous in the
language of Islamic rhetoric, and women's rights are allocated
according to a different scale which is measured against the prerogatives of men: they are grounded in the right to be protected
by men and from men, in the right to stay home and raise children, to learn, and to preserve the dignity of the family and the
culture. The way to safeguard these rights is for women not to

trespass into men's public space: to remain within the family, not to drive or travel alone or without a man's permission, or manage a business alone, or work beside men, or study subjects that would lead to working alongside men, or appear publicly in 'immodest' dress.

The answer is hardly to try and impose international standards. Upon whom would they be imposed? This is not just a struggle against politically institutionalized inequality but against, as the Shi'i activist said, 'cultural understandings.' Women therefore cannot expect to piggy-back their struggle onto the wider social struggle for human rights and basic democratic freedoms. Should standards be imposed on governments? The pursuit of equality of rights is not going to be supported by government unless women can show that supporting women's rights is in the government's interests, or at least can do it no harm. Otherwise, why take the risk of provoking opposition in order to appease the interests of some women, especially when there is no apparent consensus even among women as to what women want? Furthermore, the Saudi regime, like the regimes in Iran and Sudan, finds that restrictions on women reaffirm their legitimacy and garners support. In some cases it is precisely the lack of rights for women that wins popularity for the regime.

The challenge to human rights activists is, therefore, to change cultural understandings that mold public opinion and inform those who interpret the *shari'a*. New ways of looking at history, at men and women as individuals, and at notions of human rights can provide religious people with the rationale and government with the political clout for progressive change to occur. It is the ambiguity in the language of rights in Islam that keeps the door open for the future and allows the *shari'a* to become the vehicle of actual change.

Notes

1. Letter from Edward Broadbent, president of the International Centre for Human Rights and Democratic Development, to the Honourable Bernard Valcourt, Minister of Employment and Immigration, dated 19 August 1992

2. 'I'lan ta'sis lajna al-difa' and 'an al-huquq al-Shari'a' in photocopied collection of *bayan* issued by the CDLR in Saudi Arabia, London, n.d.

3. Full text in *Arabia Monitor*, 2, 5 (May 1993), p. 6.

4. *Ibid.*, p. 3.

5. *al-Nadwa,* 13 May 1993, p. 1.

6. 'Introduction to the Committee for the Defense of Legitimate Rights,' in *CDLR Monitor,* London, 27 June 1994.

7. *Ibid.*

8. The text of al-Jabrin's *fatwa,* issued on 30 September 1990, is as follows: 'The slaughtering by a Shi'a is unlawful and so is the meat from his slaughter. The Shi'a are mostly polytheists since they always call on 'Ali in times of difficulty as well as in times of comfort ... .This is the greatest act of polytheism and apostasy from Islam for which they deserve to be killed ... .' Quoted from Amnesty International, *Saudi Arabia, Religious Intolerance: The Arrest, Detention and Torture of Christian Worshippers and Shi'a Muslims,* 14 September 1993, p. 16. Further comment and reaction from Shi'a in *Arabia Monitor* 2, 5 (May 1993), p. 3.

9. Executions ostensibly for apostasy or blasphemy do in fact occur in Saudi Arabia. See *Religious Intolerance, op. cit.*, pp. 16–17.

10. For example, *fatwa* number 20008 refers to Shi'a as polytheists, and says that it is not permitted for Shi'i men to marry Sunni women. *Ibid.*, p. 16.

11. Helga Graham, 'Saudis Break the Silence,' *London Review of Books* , 2 April 1993, p. 8.

12. *Arabia Monitor,* July, 1993, p. 12.

13. A reference to Aisha, the last wife of the Prophet. Photocopied document in author's possession.

14. 'From a Report by a Mutawwa,' English translation in possession of author.

15. Deborah Amos, *Lines in the Sand* (New York: Simon and Schuster, 1992), p. 128.

16. Eleanor Doumato, 'Gender, Monarchy and National Identity in Saudi Arabia,' *British Journal of Middle East Studies* 19, 1 (1992).

17. Middle East Watch, 'The "Religious" Petition,' *Empty Reforms, Saudi Arabia's New Basic Laws* (New York, 1982), pp. 61–2. In the petition, for example, the 400-plus signatories called for moral behavior on the part of Saudi government representatives in foreign countries; a curb of *wasta,* the granting of contracts and pay-offs to favored groups; fairness in the distribution of public funds, noting the waste of resources by the royal family while some sectors of society are deeply impoverished; an end to arbitrary detention and harassment by police. These requests were further explained in 'Clarification Document to King Fahd from Clergy,' *al-Sha'ab* (Egypt) 21 May 1991.

18. 'The Most Important Political Document in the History of the Kingdom of Saudi Arabia,' *al-Sha'ab* (Egypt) 21 May 1991.

19. 'The "Religious" Petition,' *Empty Reforms, op. cit.*, pp. 61–2.

20. *Ibid.*, p. 62.

21. *Ibid.*, p. 62.

22. 'Clarification Document to King Fahd from Clergy,' *al-Sha'ab* (Egypt) 21 May 1991.

23. 'The Secular Petition,' *Empty Reforms, op. cit.*, p. 59.

24. *Ibid.*, p. 60.

25. *Ibid.*, p. 60.

26. Shaikh Abd al-Aziz bin Baz was among the signatories, as were most of the religious establishment. *Ibid*, p. 61.

27. There were three laws issued: the Basic Law of Government, the Consultative Council Law and the Law of Provinces. *Ibid.*, p. 1.

28. *Ibid.*, pp. 9–10.

29. *Religious Intolerance, op. cit.*, p. 3.

30. Commercial, employment, and administrative matters are under the jurisdiction of specialized courts. *Ibid.*, p. 3.

31. *Empty Reforms, op. cit.*, p. 25.

32. The Basic Law states that individuals have the right to privacy and that it is illegal for the security authorities to arrest, spy on, or violate basic human rights of citizens. However, these rights are compromised in the 'Statue of Principles of Arrest, Temporary Confinement and Preventive Detention,' issued in November, 1993, article 1 of which states that 'Patrol forces and other public order officials shall have the right to detain any person in a situation giving rise to suspicion.' *Religious Intolerance, op. cit.*, p. 24.

33. *Empty Reforms, op. cit.*, pp. 25-42.

34. The council, under the leadership of ibn Baz, has normally functioned as an arm of the state, giving religious approval to policies already determined by the government. In the Gulf War, for example, ibn Baz held firm to an Islamic rationale for accepting American forces in the kingdom in the face of strong opposition, and, in 1991, the council castigated Islamic militant radicals who called for the deposition of the Saudi family. In December 1991, ibn Baz responded to militant attacks on the participation of women in higher education and their referring to members of the Women's Charitable Society as 'prostitutes' by a speech attacking these assertions as 'lies,' 'conspiracies against Islam and Muslims' and 'slander of innocent people's reputations.' See Youssef Ibrahim , 'The Saudis are Fearful Too as Islam's Militant Tide Rises,' *New York Times*, 31 December 1991.

35. *al-Nadwa*, 1 September 1994, p. 5.

36. *Ibid.*, pp. 1 and 5.

37. *Ibid.*, pp. 1 and 5.

38. *Arabia Monitor* was published between 1991 and 1993.

39. For example, Aliya Maki, *Diary of a Woman in Saudi Jails* (in Arabic) (London: al-Safa Press, 1989).

40. Youssef Ibrahim, 'Saudi Officials Reporting Accord with Shiite Foes,' *New York Times*, 29 October 1993, and interview by author with Ali al-Ahmed, co-publisher of *Arabia Monitor*, 3 November 1993.

41. Interview with Ali al-Ahmed, cited in note 40.

42. Statistical information on women in Saudi society is available in 'The Society and Its Environment,' in *Saudi Arabia, A Country Study*, Helen Metz, ed., Library of Congress, 1992.

43. In one survey of young viewers in the eastern, central and western sections of the Kingdom, television watching consumed between 3 and 4 hours a day for 45 per cent of respondents, while another 20 per cent watched as much as 6 hours. Another 9 per cent watched 7 hours or more. Adel Siraj Merdad, 'Foreign Television Programs and Their Sources: An Empirical Analysis of Media Usage and Perceptions of its Effects by Young Viewers in the Kingdom of Saudi Arabia,' unpublished doctoral dissertation, Wayne State University, 1993, p. 121.

44. *Ibid.*, pp. 44, 122.

45. One study gives anecdotal evidence to suggest that social behaviors in Jeddah and Dammam are changing. *Ibid.*, pp. 37–44. By contrast, a study of media influence conducted among students at King Saud University (in Riyadh, the most conservative region of the country) concluded that modernization was changing material life but changes in values and behavior were limited. This study also showed that changes were occurring unevenly, with the most conservative young people being the educated children of uneducated or low-income fathers. Suleiman Abdullah Al-Akeel, 'The Impact of Modernization on Saudi Society: A Case Study of Saudi Students' Attitudes,' unpublished doctoral dissertation, Mississippi State University, 1992.

46. This discussion of the writings of Saudi women is derived from the work of Saddeka Arebi, *Women and Words in Saudi Arabia, The Politics of Literary Discourse* (New York: Columbia University Press, 1994).

47. The Convention on the Elimination of All Forms of Discrimination Against Women was ratified by the UN General Assembly in 1979, and has not been signed or ratified by Saudi Arabia. CEDAW rests on the principle of rights being due to women as discrete individuals, which is incompatible with the Arabian social structure, where regulations and opportunities afforded women are predicated on the assumption of their dependence on men. Article 9 of CEDAW, for example, states that women must have equal rights to acquire, change or retain their nationality, and equal rights to the nationality of their children. In Saudi, men and women do not have equal rights to the nationality of their children, as men are considered to be the bearers of identity for the women over whom they have guardianship. Therefore, if a woman has married a non-Saudi, her children must petition for Saudi citizenship, while if the husband is Saudi and his wife not, the children are automatically citizens.

Article 10 of CEDAW calls for equal rights in education, including the same curricula, examinations, standards for teaching and equipment, and equal opportunity for scholarships and grants. However, in Saudi Arabia educational resources favor men because only men are considered to bear the responsibility for supporting the family. Men's campus facilities are larger and offer a broader range of courses, libraries for men are better equipped, and sports programs are available to men but not to women. Educational programs discourage women from studying subjects where employment would conflict with sex-segregation mores, and these same mores militate against co-education at any level. The availability of scholarships for women to study abroad is limited because of the need to be accompanied by a guardian.

Article 11 says that women must have the same employment opportunities available for men and equal pay for equal work. Saudi's labor law offers equal pay and extremely generous maternity benefits to women, but the ground rule for women's employment is that they do not work in places where they come into contact with unrelated men, which limits them primarily to education, medicine, and agencies that perform services for women; the rule eliminates work in shops, offices, and public facilities. Saudi women have the same legal capacity as men to contract, administer property, and appear in court as Article 15 requires, but women's testimony is considered of less worth than a man's, as prescribed in *shari'a*, and her insurable value (blood money) worth less than a man's. Article 16's call for equality in the dissolution of marriage and equal rights to guardianship conflict with *shari'a* family law, and the call for the right to freely enter into marriage and to choose one's spouse is at odds with custom. Furthermore, the call for 'equality during marriage' can be compromised by the inequality inherent in polygamous unions.

In Article 2, the convention obligates countries that ratify CEDAW to 'condemn discrimination against women in all its forms' and 'agree to abolish all existing laws, customs and regulations that discriminate against women.' Article 5 calls upon governments to modify social and cultural patterns to 'eliminate sex-role stereotypes and notions of the inferiority or superiority of either sex.' If implemented, these articles would, in essence, require a society such as that of Saudi Arabia to become something alien to what it is. (References to CEDAW are from International Women's Rights Action Watch, *The Convention on the Elimination of All Forms of Discrimination Against Women*, (University of Minnesota: The Women, Public Policy and Development Project of the Humphry Institute of Public Affairs, n.d.)

48. Selections of this literature produced by Saudi women can be found in Arebi, *op. cit.*

49. This *fatwa* was issued in 1980 by ibn Baz, then Director of the Department of Religious Research, Legal Judgements, Mission, and Guidance, in response to an announcement by the Bureau of Civil Service in the Eastern Province that women would be hired by the bureau as clerical workers. *Al-Da'wah* no. 764, 10/28/1400 AH 1980, quoted in Hamad Muhammad al-Baadi, 'Social Change, Education, and the Roles of

Women in Arabia,' unpublished doctoral dissertation, Stanford University, 1982, pp. 376–7.

50. *Ukaz*, 4/7/1396, 1976 quoted in al-Baadi, p. 132.

51. *Al-Da'wah* no. 747, 6/13/1400 AH, 1980, quoted in al-Baadi, p. 133.

52. Letter from Edward Broadbent, President, International Centre for Human Rights and Democratic Development, to Bernard Valcourt, Minister of Employment and Immigration, 19 August 1992.

53. *The Gazette* (Montreal), 11 March 1993.

9

The Politics of Dishonor:
Rape and Power in Pakistan

Shahla Haeri

> The desire to see you silent
> Billows up even from the grave.
> But the Speech is urgent
> When listening is a crime.
> Now I can see
> Expressions which daunted me
> Strike fear everywhere.

Kishwar Nahid[1]

The CIA (Crime Investigating Agency) treated me like a notorious criminal. Repeatedly they pulled my hair and slapped me on the face. They wanted me to make false sexual allegations against Asif Zardari (Benazir Bhutto's jailed husband), and wanted me to say that Benazir had given me [and the party's student wing] weapons to create chaos in Karachi, or that she had passed on national security tips to Rajive Ghandi. I refused it. They tortured me again. I was terrified and cried in my heart. A policewoman warned me about my interrogator's bad behavior. She said, 'You are not married. They make you married.'

Said Rahila Tiwana, a Pakistan People's Party (henceforth, PPP) student activist.[2]

I have lost my home, I know what my husband will do to me. I know that I am a *bayghairat* [without honor; losing one's self-respect] in the eyes of my *khandan* [family], which has disowned me. I have been sentenced for life for the crime of being raped, but this is not the end. I know that there is only humiliation in it for me now. Only God can grant me justice, but I must speak, so that maybe other women can be prevented from meeting a fate similar to mine.

Said Khurshid Begum, a poor washerwoman whose husband used to be a Pakistan People's Party supporter.[3]

I know that a lot of dirt is going to be flung at me. But I have decided
to take them on. And I hope I have the courage to see it through to
the end or I will kill myself.

Said Veena Hayat, a woman of the elite and a close friend of Benazir
Bhutto and her husband.[4]

In a rare moment in the history of Pakistani society a few raped
women decided to go public, and to shake their society out of its
long and complacent stupor.[5] Pakistani women have for centuries
buried in their hearts the rage and anguish of rape. In the interests
of family honor and for fear of ostracism, they were (and still are)
forced to keep quiet or face further humiliation and abandonment
by their families. Pakistani families customarily hide the 'shame'
of their women whose honor, *izzat*, has been 'looted'. The society
has actively discouraged public disclosures of rape, and until very
recently it preferred not to know. With courage and determination,
and a little help from their friends, these women broke this long-
standing taboo. This was the year 1991, a year after the ouster of
Prime Minister Benazir Bhutto by the then President Ghulam
Ishaq Khan.

What is culturally and historically specific about these rape cases
that set them apart from similar cases happening in Pakistan or in
other parts of the world? What gives them their uniquely Pakistani
flavor? My objective in this paper is to situate these particular
cases within the socio-political context of Pakistani society. I will
argue that what is unique to the rape of these three women is that
each one happened in the year following Benazir Bhutto's ouster
in 1990, and that one of the women was a personal friend of
Benazir Bhutto, while of the other two one was a supporter of and
one an activist in Bhutto's Pakistan People's Party. The rapes took
place in Karachi, the capital city of Sindh province from where the
Bhutto family hails. Theoretically, I will argue that 'political rape,'
is a modern improvisation on the theme of 'feudal' 'honor rape.'[6]
Symbolically, political rape in Pakistan draws on its feudal heritage
and it is in this sense that it manifests its cultural specificity. The
target of humiliation and shame is not necessarily a specific woman.
It is rather a political rival – an old enemy, on whom revenge is to
be taken. In its modern context, political rape has the tacit, and at
times explicit, legitimation of the state, just as honor rape has
continued to have cultural support and collective sanction.[7]

In the following pages, I will introduce each woman and her

case, followed by a brief discussion of the concepts of honor and political rape. My concern here is not so much with the details of these cases, as it is with identifying the ultimate target of the rape and the motivations behind it. I will briefly review the political situation in Pakistan, and consider some implications for human rights for women.

The Politics of Rape

On 7 December 1991 Pakistanis awoke to the public lamentations of an aged father, who, obviously in pain and weeping, revealed at a crowded press conference that his daughter, Veena Hayat, had been gang raped a fortnight before. This was an unprecedented act in Pakistan, particularly so for a man of his stature. He was Sardar Shaukat Hayat, a member of the landed aristocracy and the political elite, and an old colleague of Pakistan's foremost leader, Muhammad Ali Jinnah. No 'dishonoring' of women had been made public, let alone broadcast via the electronic and printed media. It had never happened before; at least not in this dramatic fashion and in such a public forum. He accused Irfanullah Marvat, the Karachi head of Pakistan's notorious CIA (Crime Investigating Agency),[8] the son-in-law of the then President Ghulam Ishaq Khan. Sardar Shaukat Hayat was quite clear about the motive behind his daughter's rape. She was punished, in his view, because she was a close friend of the opposition leader, Benazir Bhutto. He had no doubt that this act was the 'handiwork of the Sindh authorities.'[9]

At the time, Veena Hayat was a divorced woman who lived in a prosperous neighborhood of Karachi. She has two teenage sons. One of them was studying in the US at the time, and the other was at a friend's house. Her ordeal involved an evening raid by five masked men who gagged and tied her two servants, and then waited to ambush her when she arrived home. When Veena's car drew up they pulled her out of it, beat her up, and pulled her by her hair to the upper floor of her house where they humiliated and raped her. The masked men did not loot much, but stayed in her house for 12 hours, terrorizing, taunting, and torturing Veena and her domestic workers. Clearly, they were not ordinary *dacoits*,[10] or thieves, as was later claimed by the Sindh authorities. In the words of an observer, 'The Veena Hayat case had literally come to knock at the very gates of power.'[11]

Supported by the chief minister of the Sindh provincial government, Jam Sadique Ali, Marvat dismissed the allegations, countering that the PPP used their 'ladies' for political gain, hinting at a 'relationship between Veena and Asif Zardari (Benazir Bhutto's husband).'[12] Veena Hayat's case also polarized the complex and layered systems of justice in Pakistan. Her case was referred to the court, but she and her father refused to cooperate with the investigation, stating lack of trust in the judiciary's impartiality. Their apprehension was confirmed when the judge exonerated the head of the CIA (the President's son-in-law) of any wrongdoing. Falling back on a tribal honor system[13] instead Sardar Shaukat Hayat sought justice through his tribal *jirga* (consultative assembly), asking his brethren to restore his daughter's and his family's honor. Ironically, the head of the CIA himself, the man responsible for law and order, also seemed to trust tribal justice more. He too called on his own tribal *jirga* for support to counteract possible attacks by Sardar Hayat's fellow tribesmen. The political drama reached its peak when Sardar Shaukat Hayat, as if vindicated by their regression to 'tribal justice,' made a ritualized public appeal: 'We welcome his *jirga*. I hope his own community will take care of him. If there is a Marvat [the name of his tribe] code of honor, as I know it, they will.'[14]

There was an immediate outcry by the Pakistani women's and human rights organizations who organized demonstrations and teach-ins in major cities of Pakistan, including the capital city of Islamabad. There were numerous smaller gatherings and consciousness-raising events, including several hunger strikes in which Benazir Bhutto herself and some members of the opposition participated. The religious fundamentalist parties,[15] some of whom were part of the government coalition, remained mute. Only after much taunting by the outraged journalists, women, and human rights activists did the Jama'at-i Islami and a few other smaller parties condemn the act in a measured language, taking care not to antagonize the government or to appear to be jumping on the opposition's bandwagon.

Had it not been for the publicity surrounding Veena Hayat's case, perhaps the plight of Khurshid Begum would have gone unnoticed – except by a handful of women activists. Khurshid Begum was a poor washerwoman who, just a few days before Veena Hayat's ordeal, had also been raped, but her ordeal took place in police custody. Khurshid Begum's husband was a PPP supporter who was jailed for an unsubstantiated political allegation regarding the state's national security. Returning home on the night of 13 November 1991 from a visit to her husband, she was grabbed, she said in an interview, blindfolded, and thrown into a car 'like a bag of trash' by some policemen. She recalled opening her eyes to find herself in a dark room with a few tables, chairs and a picture of Muhammad Ali Jinnah.[16] She said that two uniformed women removed her blindfold, but they left the room quickly when 'a fat, drunk man with three stars' came in.[17] The fat man, said Khurshid Begum,

> was reeling and he laughed out loud upon seeing me. Then they closed the door and one man dragged me to the table by the hair. The fat policeman fell on top of me. I started screaming and struggling. I got up and ran around inside the room with one man hurtling me toward the other, grabbing me now by my hair, now by my breasts. My shirt tore from the middle. Then the fat man overpowered me, and in the presence of those two other beasts, satisfied himself of me. I felt like I was about to die.[18]

She too believed that the primary reason for her ordeal was political. 'I was victimized because my husband used to be a PPP supporter … . I don't work for the party. I wash clothes for people and feed my children … . Of course they attacked me for political reasons. The fat police officer said after he was through with me: "Ask Benazir to help you now."'[19]

Unlike Khurshid Begum, Veena Hayat was shielded by her family and given moral support. Veena hardly appeared in public and did not give many interviews. Khurshid Begum's family, on the other hand, distanced themselves from her and in her word wanted her 'blood.' Apparently ashamed of what had happened to Khurshid Begum, her brother-in-law summed up their family's collective sentiment when he told her to 'commit suicide.' 'I fear for my life,' lamented Khurshid Begum. 'The Baloch [her tribal ancestry], as you know, combine ignorance with pride. I don't know if even my husband would accept me once he is out of prison.'[20] Luckily for Khurshid Begum, she was given full moral, legal and material support by several Pakistani women's and human rights organizations.

Before Khurshid Begum and Veena Hayat yet another young woman suffered the fury of some political 'operators' in Karachi. Rahila Tiwana was a devoted 24-year-old political activist who belonged to the student wing of the Pakistan People's Party. I interviewed her several times in Karachi in May 1993, and had long discussions with her psychiatrist, Dr Haroon Ahmed, with Rahila's knowledge and consent.[21]

The beginning of the year 1991 coincided with her arrest, torture, and subsequent hospitalization in a psychiatric ward for over nine months. Rahila's father is a civil servant, living with his wife, his four daughters, of whom Rahila is the eldest, and one son in a comfortable state-owned house in a colony just outside Karachi. All her family members are devotees of Benazir Bhutto and activists on behalf of her party. Repeatedly she told me how much she loves Benazir and how worried she was for her leader's life because while she was in jail she heard her interrogators, including a cousin of the head of CIA, the same man accused by Veena Hayat, threatening to 'kill' Benazir Bhutto.

Before her arrest her house was searched, and she was arrested on the pretext that she had been given weapons and ammunition and had passed on secret messages to Indian agents. When she refused to cooperate with the Sindh authorities to fabricate charges of sexual misconduct and national security allegations against Benazir Bhutto and her husband, her interrogators turned savage. So severely was she beaten and tortured that at some point she lost consciousness.[22] Regaining her senses, she was horrified to find herself bloodied all over. She does not remember what happened to her. She does not think she was raped, though all her descriptions lead one to that conclusion. But whether she was actually raped or not her ordeal was horrendous enough to require her long rehabilitation in a psychiatric ward. Dr Haroon Ahmed shared with me the video tape of his conversation with Rahila, taken nine months after she was jailed and tortured. Rahila sobbed throughout her long interview; her face expressing the terror she had felt; her body shaking uncontrollably.

A Brief Historical and Political Background

Before moving onto an analysis of honor rape, I will briefly discuss the political and historical mediating structures, setting the context for an understanding of the dynamics of honor rape in Pakistan.

A former British colony, Pakistan is a young nation state, partitioned from India in 1947. Having gone though several bouts of military dictatorship its present form of government is democratic,[23] though besieged by vigorous fundamentalism and a well-entrenched feudal system. Added to the melange is Pakistan's complex ethnic and linguistic diversity.[24] The structural, cultural, and ideological interaction of these phenomena constitute the specificity of government in Pakistan, coloring the public's world view and expectations. As the religious backlash against modernism and modernity gains momentum, Pakistan, like many other Muslim nation states, seems to be sliding through the quagmire of crises of *identity* (ethnic and linguistic) and *legitimacy* (religious, secular).

With the sudden demise of General Zia ul-Haq in the summer of 1988, Pakistani politics have become ever more colorful, complex, and cunning. The pent-up political tensions, kept under tight control by General Zia's military regime, now burst furiously into the open, polarizing the nation along ethnic, religious, ideological, and political lines. These alliances, however, shift constantly, making any clear determination of who is where in Pakistan rather unreliable. Nonetheless, at the very basis of Pakistani socio-politics, one may identify a major divide between a deeply rooted aristo-cratic feudalism and corporate business, with the fundamentalists and the military throwing their support behind this or that alli-ance, as the political situation may demand. In real life the bound-aries of these realms are much more porous and permeable than this observation might imply but it nonetheless provides a useful analytic perspective.

Within this framework, one may identify Benazir Bhutto as representing the interests of the feudal aristocracy. She learnt the ABC of politics from her father, Zulfaqar Ali Bhutto (1928–79), who was overthrown in a military coup by General Zia ul-Haq in 1977 and hanged in 1979, despite strong international pressure for his pardon. Nawaz Sharif may be said to primarily represent the interests of big business and industry.[25] A protégé of Zia ul-Haq and politically his 'adopted son,' he rose rather quickly through the political hierarchy to become the Punjab's Chief Minister (1984–1990). Benazir Bhutto hails from Sindh and Nawaz Sharif from the more populous and prosperous province of Punjab. Tradi-tionally, with few exceptions, Pakistan's federal power elite have come from Punjab – hence the traditional political rivalry be-tween the Sindhis and Punjabis.[26]

The high political drama created after the unraveling of Zia's military dictatorship brought Benazir Bhutto into the national limelight and to the center of the political stage. She won the

168   FAITH AND FREEDOM

election of 1989, only to be booted out barely a year and half into her five-year term. In her first term in office the young and some-what inexperienced Benazir Bhutto not only had to contend with the contemptuous religious fundamentalist parties, who saw her as unfit to become the head of a Muslim state, issued various *fatwas* against her, and even sued her in court for having referred to her late father as a martyr, *shahid*.[27] She had to face stiff challenges from the opposition, headed by Nawaz Sharif and supported by the president, both of whom were backed by the military. Unable to deliver on her campaign promises, Bhutto was eventually dismissed in August 1990 by the president, who invoked the Eighth Amendment (the handiwork of Zia, this gave the presid-ent executive power to dismiss the prime minister and to dissolve parliament). He brought charges of financial impropriety against her.

The caretaker government of Mustafa Jaoti was asked by Presid-ent Ghulam Ishaq Khan, to man the ship of the state, while both Nawaz Sharif and Benazir Bhutto prepared for an electoral show-down to be held in the October of the same year. Supported by the president, the military, and the fundamentalist Jama'at-i Islami, Nawaz Sharif seized the moment and defeated Benazir Bhutto to win the election of October 1990. Nawaz Sharif was also toppled in April 1993 when the president evidently felt that the prime minister was becoming cocky, and looking for ways to repeal the Eighth Amendment – the sword of Damocles that every Pakistani prime minister feels is hanging over his or her head. Nawaz Sharif faced daunting challenges not only from an offended president and dissatisfied fundamentalist allies, but also from Benazir Bhutto and a strong popular opposition.

It is against this highly complex background of superimposed political, ethnic, and ideological rivalries that I will try to look at the politics of honor rape.

Political Rape, Honor Rape

Although the idea that 'rape is fueled by cultural values that are perpetuated at every level of our society,'[28] was first ventured in relation to Western societies, it can be generalized to other cul-tures. In the context of Pakistani society, Khalid Ahmed, the noted Pakistani journalist, observes, 'Feuds are settled through rapes. Men avenge themselves on each other by raping each other's mothers, wives, daughters and sisters. A brave adversary is supposed to break down under the grief and dishonor of the violation of his womenfolk. At times, women are gang raped, then paraded naked in the streets to show to the society that terminal revenge has been taken.'[29] No one intervenes. Many may feel sad and sorry, but all know the rules of the game.

'Honor,' argues Stewart, 'is a notoriously paradoxical topic, and one of its most famous puzzles is the effect that women's behavior can have on men's honor.'[30] In Pakistani society the concepts of political rape and honor rape are inextricably linked. In this context, honor, *izzat,* is intimately tied in with the sense of a male 'natural' right to possess and control womenfolk. Objectifying honor in the person of a woman, men possess honor, just as they possess gold and land – the three elements that are said to be the most sought-after commodities in Pakistan, and therefore to lie at the root of all conflicts. Logically, it follows, women cannot possess honor in the same way as men. They represent honor; they symbolize honor; they are honor.[31] Objectified into manipulable possessions, symbolic or otherwise, women lose a sense of individuality in the eyes of the community. Raping a woman robs a man of his most prized possession, his honor, but it obliterates a woman's whole being. Once a man's honor is violated, all he can do, all he is expected to do, all he should do is to seek revenge. As for the raped woman, no one cares – or dares to care; she doesn't exist as an individual.

Perhaps the modern political rape resonates historically with the development of separationist political opposition in Pakistan, in which some women also participated. Politics, revenge, and humiliation of the 'enemy' were the motives of a losing Pakistani army during its civil war with East Pakistan, now Bangladesh, in 1971 when Pakistani soldiers sexually assaulted and raped a large number of Bengali women just as their troops were retreating.[32] Symbolically, too, this action was rape of a nation which had dared to defy its big 'brother,' by wishing to assert its autonomy and demanding recognition of its distinct identity.[33]

With the passage of the Hudood Ordinance in 1979 legalizing punishment for adultery, theft, drinking and false accusations, the number of women in police custody has increased dramatically.[34] Under the Hudood Ordinance the boundaries between rape and adultery/fornication, *zina,* have become rather blurred. The women of Pakistan are thus caught in a double-bind: if they report a rape case – assuming that they can overcome all the familial and cultural barriers that militate against disclosure – not only may they not get justice, but there is every chance that they will be accused of adultery.[35] Despite the rape, torture, and abuses that women face in police custody, many are reluctant to speak up or to file charges against the responsible officers for fear of police reprisals. Women's predicament in such situations and their fear-inspired reluctance to pursue justice is complex and multifaceted. This is due partly to the shame many raped women feel, partly to intimidation by the agents of 'law and order,' and partly to the equation of rape with adultery under the Hudood Ordinance. This strongly discourages many women from seeking help, rendering 'sexual justice' practically ineffective in Pakistan.

Theoretically, variations of violence against women have been conceptualized in terms of controlling female sexuality, restricting women's autonomy, keeping them in their place, and maintaining male guardianship and dominance.[36] Concurring with these perspectives, and drawing on my ethnographic field work in Pakistan, I submit that in the case of the women mentioned above, the act of rape is more than a show of dominance through brute force to keep women in their place. It is also more than an instrument of oppression to restrict women's movement and control their bodies. Nor is it merely to make public examples of raped women in order to strike fear in the hearts of other women, thus forcing them to obey the rules of the male power structure, and to remain within certain culturally and religiously specified boundaries. While sharing aspects of these elements, the specificity of the cases of these three women involves an act of *revenge* aimed at humiliating and dishonoring a powerful and potentially threatening rival. Here the 'enemy' was none other than Benazir Bhutto! How is that possible, one might ask: she herself is a woman. Precisely the point. When female members of her party are raped, not only are individual women dishonored, but symbolically Benazir Bhutto herself, the leader of the opposition and the model of womanhood, is 'raped' by association. How could a nation, any nation, choose to have a raped leader? Conversely, how could a leader who is unable to protect herself or her followers protect her country from being invaded by its 'enemies,' real or imagined?

Although out of power in 1991, Benazir Bhutto was considered a great threat by the authorities, particularly in the Sindh province. She was a force to be reckoned with. She had to be brought to her knees. It was not enough that the president had brought law suits against her, all of which were eventually thrown out. Still very popular with the masses, she had to be taught a proper lesson, a lesson all too meaningful for a woman. She had to be dishonored, symbolically and actually.

The unfortunate women who are caught up in this archaic cultural and political feud become the conduit for political action and a culturally meaningful medium for sending a message to a political enemy or rival. It is at the level of individual experience that Pakistani women share the horror of 'bodily violation' with women from other cultures. The premises of human rights are based on the sanctity of the individual, and the inviolability of this sanctuary. So long as the prevailing tribal and feudal ethical system remains strong in Pakistan, chances of meaningful human rights changes for women on a large scale are dim. On a positive note, and painful as the experiences of these women have been, they have confronted Pakistani society with a moral tension, leading to greater public awareness of the issue of violence against women. They have also strengthened the resolve of many Pakistani women activists who are poised to reclaim their bodies and their voices. They are determined to speak out, realizing that remaining silent for any longer is a 'crime.'

Notes

Acknowledgement. I am grateful to Mahnaz Afkhami, Thomas J. Barfield, Anna Enayat, Robert Hefner, Allan Hoben, Charles Lindholm, Farzaneh Milani, Richard Murphy, Kaveh Safa, and Mohamad Tavakoli-Targhi for reading and commenting on this chapter. Thanks are also due to the American Institute of Pakistan Studies that made my field work (1991–3) in Pakistan possible.

1. Kishwar Nahid, *The Scream of an Illegitimate Voice,* trans. from Urdu by Baidar Bakht, Leslie Lavigne, and Derek M. Cohen, (Lahore: Sang-e Meel Publications, 1991), p. 30.
2. Personal communication, 22 May 1993, Karachi.
3. *Herald,* January 1992, p. 42; *Shirkat Gah's Newsheet,* 4, 1 (1992), p. 4.
4. *Ibid.*
5. Although news of rape, violence, and abuses against women had become more or less a part of daily news digest by then, women themselves were seldom involved in such publicity.

6. By 'feudal' in the Pakistani context I mean a relatively small group of big, politically active, and powerful landowners. 'It is also a moral category,' in the sense that Pakistanis often talk of 'feudal attitude,' meaning 'a combination of arrogance and entitlement' (Richard Murphy, personal communication). Honor rape is not limited to feudal vendetta, and is occurring in the society at large. See also Nafisa Shah, 'Of Female Bondage,' *Newsline*, January 1993, p. 36; and her interview with Mariam Palojo, a female leader of Sindhi Movement, on the plight of Sindhi peasant women, *ibid.*, p. 46.

7. Rape of Pakistani women as a form of 'feudal vendetta,' argues Yusuf, is widespread. The most famous − or rather infamous − case is that of Nawabpur 'when three women of a family were forced by the sons of a local landlord to parade naked in the street. This was a form of vendetta against their brother, who had wanted to marry a woman from the land-lord's family.' Zohra Yusuf, 'A Rising Graph?' *Herald*, January 1992, pp. 47−8.

8. Irfanullah Marvat also held the portfolio of home affairs advisor to the Sindh Chief Minister, Jam Sadique Ali.

9. *Herald, op.cit.*, pp. 38−9.

10. According to *Hobson-Jobson Dictionary*, edited by H. Yule and A.C. Burnell (1886, 1989), a *dacoit* is a robber belonging to an armed gang. The term, being current in Bengal, got into the Penal code. By law, to con-stitute dacoity there must be five or more in the gang committing the crime. In 1817, Sir Henry Strachey observes, 'The crime of dacoity has, I believe, increased greatly since the British administration of justice,' p. 290.

11. *Herald, op.cit.*, p. 41.

12. *Ibid.*

13. Pakistani kinship and political social organizations vary according to ethnic groups and from region to region. As such, 'tribal' social organ-ization finds different manifestations and structure in Pakistan. For an analysis of Pakistan's political structure as it relates to a 'tribal' system, see Charles Lindholm, 'The Segmentary Lineage System: Its Applicability to Pakistan's Political Structure,' in Ainslie T. Embree (ed.), *Pakistan's Western Borderlands: The Transformation of a Political Order* (Durham, NC: Carolina Academic Press 1977), pp. 41−66.

14. *Herald, op. cit.*, p. 45.

15. Whether the Islamic revivalist parties or movements should be iden-tified as fundamentalist is a dispute beyond the scope of this paper. It is worthy of note, however, that the Jama'at-i Islami in Pakistan printed the term 'fundamentalism' in its own English political posters during the October 1993 election.

16. *Herald, op. cit.*, p. 43; *Newsline*, December 1991.

17. *Herald, op. cit.*, p. 43.

18. *Ibid.*

19. *Ibid.*

20. *Ibid.*

21. I am thankful to Dr Haroon Ahmed and his wife, Anis Haroon, for their generosity in sharing with me their knowledge and insight about this case.

22. For a description of violence and abuse of women prisoners see Asia Watch and the Women's Rights Project, *Double Jeopardy: Police Abuse of Women in Pakistan* (New York: Human Rights Watch, 1992).

23. Whether or not Pakistan's form of government is democratic has been the subject of some debate. Given the fact that Pakistan has been under military rule for the most part of its young history, some skepticism regarding its fledgling democracy is understandable. Nonetheless, one may categorize it presently as a democracy, however imperfect, because of its functioning parliament, free press, and partial recognition of individual and civil rights.

24. It is interesting to note here that Urdu, Pakistan's national language, is not native to a vast portion of the population. Linguistically, Pakistan is very diverse, with the majority of the population speaking their own mother tongues (Sindhi, Punjabi, Pushto, Sarieki, Baluch, etc.) at home. Urdu, however, is taught in schools. English is spoken even less, and is primarily the language of the elite.

25. As national leaders, both Benazir Bhutto and Nawaz Sharif claim to represent the entire nation, and to some extent this is true. Their moorings, nonetheless, are within the major 'interest' groups identified here.

26. Hamza Alavi, 'Ethnicity, Muslim Society, and the Pakistan Ideology,' in A.M. Weiss (ed.), *Islamic Reassertion in Pakistan* (Syracuse: Syracuse University Press, 1987), p. 25.

27. The court dismissed the case.

28. Susan Brownmiller, *Against Our Will: Men, Women and Rape* (New York: Simon and Schuster, 1975), p. 389.

29. Khalid Ahmed, 'The Sociology of Rape,' *Slogan*, February 1992, pp. 36–7.

30. Frank H. Stewart, *Honor*, (Chicago: University of Chicago Press, 1994), p. 107.

31. Like many complex concepts, *izzat* has multiple connotations and involves overlapping meanings, including respect, honor, esteem, dignity, and reputation. As such, the term may be gender neutral: both men and women can have dignity and honor, but the main component of their honor is affected differently, domestically and publicly. Women's honor is often a component of their chastity, Stewart, *op. cit.*, p. 107. Women's loss of honor bears directly on the honor of their primary male kin, as custodians of women's chastity. In the case of political/honor rape, a woman's own *izzat* (honor, respect) is perceived, by the perpetrators, as immaterial if not irrelevant, giving the trauma of rape greater poignancy.

What is relevant is how it reflects on her men's honor. It is in this sense that the victimized women represent honor, or 'are' honor.

32. See Brownmiller, *op. cit.*, pp. 78–86.

33. For a comprehensive study of the creation of Bangladesh see Richard Sisson and Leo Rose, *War & Secession: Pakistan, India, and the Creation of Bangladesh* (Berkeley: University of California Press, 1990).

34. Asma Jahangir and Hina Jilani, *The Hudood Ordinances: A Divine Sanction?* (Lahore: Rhotas Books, 1990). See also Charles H. Kennedy, 'The Implementation of the Hudood Ordinances in Pakistan,' *Islamic Studies*, 26, 4 (Winter 1987), pp. 307–19.

35. '*Zina*,' writes human rights lawyer, Asma Jahangir, 'includes all forms of extramarital sex which, after the promulgation of the [Hudood Ordinance] is punishable with imprisonment and whipping ... . A victim of rape is caught in a snare: if she complains of rape, she has to make out a watertight case, or else she in turn can be accused of *zina* ... . If a woman who has been raped fails to report the crime she may well be arrested for *zina* in any case, if the crime is discovered,' *Herald, op. cit.*, p. 52b.

36. Susan Brownmiller, *op. cit.*; Pauline B. Bart and Eileen G. Moran (eds), *Violence Against Women: The Bloody Footprints* (California: Sage Publications, 1993); Jalna Hanmer and Mary Maynard (eds), *Women, Violence and Social Control* (New Jersey: Humanities Press International, Inc., 1987); and Gail Omvedt, *Violence Against Women: New Movements and New Theories in India* (New Delhi: Kali for Women, 1990).

10

Muslim Refugee, Returnee, and Displaced Women: Challenges and Dilemmas

Sima Wali

Muslim women bear the brunt of patriarchal male ideology and the contemporary theopolitics that pits them as political pawns in the ideological warfare now raging between extremist Islam and the West. Physical protection of Muslim women, always elusive when defined and administered by men, is further jeopardized in war and civil conflict when law and order break down and social norms are suspended. In the Afghan tribal clan system, for example, rape in the absence of war is rare because the perpetrator faces certain death and his clan and his tribe must endure years of feud during which many male members will lose their lives. The severity of response stems from the nature of the prevailing norms which characterize rape not so much as violence against the woman, but as a direct challenge to the honor of the men of her clan. The suspension of norms in times of conflict, particularly under refugee conditions, leaves women completely unprotected and subject to the most egregious forms of violence and abuses of human rights.

This chapter highlights deficiencies of international policy and charitable organizations' activities in relation to refugee women in general and Muslim refugee women in particular. The Afghan refugee situation is examined as a case in point. The chapter concludes with recommendations for strategies which would address the present gender imbalance in refugee-aid policies.

Overview

Contrary to widespread expectations, the end of the Cold War has not brought an end to conflict, but has actually fostered a new kind of violence.[1] The general weakening of the nation state system and, particularly, the power vacuum created by the break-up of the Soviet Union have led to a re-emergence of ethnic violence and religious conflict. As low-intensity warfare spreads across the globe, people are forcibly uprooted, adding to already existing massive refugee movements across international borders.[2] The sheer volume of uprooted populations, along with a post-Cold War shift in political alliances, has crippled international humanitarian and political response mechanisms. The world community is no longer willing or able to respond systematically to this accelerated humanitarian crisis. The West, especially the United States which is still evaluating its position as the sole remaining superpower in the changing world order, fails to provide the world community with strong and decisive leadership.

Approximately 80 per cent of the world's more than 20 million refugees are women and their dependent children.[3] It is also estimated that 80 per cent of the world's total refugee population is Muslim, mostly Afghans, Azerbaijanis, Palestinians, Iranians, Bosnians, Iraqis, Kurds, Burmese (Myanmar), Somalis, Sudanese and Tajiks.[4] Approximately 75 per cent of Muslim refugees are women and children fleeing from or seeking asylum in Muslim countries.[5] However, discourse on women and human rights in Islam does not include Muslim refugees, and little information is available on population displacement in the Muslim world or on the impact of religion and culture on Muslim women in forced migration.

Afghan Refugee Women – A Case Study

The situation of Afghan refugees illustrates how political considerations override encoded social mores, undermining humanitarian considerations. It also illustrates the transfer of male-led political agendas to sexual politics.

The Afghans are admired in the Muslim world for building a small nation that after a long struggle defeated a large 'godless' (i.e., non-Islamic) superpower. Many Arab countries, especially Saudi Arabia, covertly financed the Mujahadeen in their war against communism. Pakistan, the host country for the world's largest Muslim refugee population, continues to overflow with Arab and non-Arab mercenaries supporting the Mujahadin cause. The most extreme Afghan political factions have been given the majority of resources, diminishing the power and status of the more politically moderate Afghans. These extremist factions have set out to change the prevailing social norms and mores, including attitudes and perceptions about the proper role of Afghan women and girls in society.

In short, Afghan religious leaders capitulated to Pakistani attitudes about women to appease Pakistan, a nation ruled by strict Islamic laws and a major distributor of arms and other resources to the Afghan factions. In 1990, as a member of a delegation representing the Women's Commission for Refugee Women and Children sent to Pakistan to assess the status of Afghan women in refugee camps, I interviewed several Afghan women. They reported stress and trauma typical of life in exile. Afghan city and tribal women are being coerced into the practice of *purdah*, or veiling, which was not previously the custom of their communities. The survival rate, physical protection, nutrition, education, skill development, and psycho-social well-being of female refugees and displaced women fell far below those of their male counterparts, mainly because of inequitable access to resources.

Afghan women refugees cannot collect their food rations in public and therefore suffer from hunger if they have no male relatives or male children to rely on for collecting their rations. Women observing *purdah* cannot leave refugee compounds to receive medical attention. Women, including pregnant women, must rely on medical volunteers coming into refugee camps to offer care.[6] Afghan women bear children under almost intolerable circumstances and pressures. Although themselves malnourished, they bear numerous children in utter disregard of healthy birth-spacing practices.[7] Women of child-bearing age must submit to the male political agenda of replenishing a lost population decimated by war. Male children are preferred. Afghan religious and political leaders argue that family planning is undesirable because large numbers of children are needed by the society. Afghan clan elders in the refugee camps tell women that their greatest contribution to the *jihad* – the holy war – is bearing children, especially male children.

In most Afghan refugee camps women and girls are expected to uphold 'Islamic' virtues. Veiling, seclusion, lack of access to education, and short birth-spacing are regarded as religiously normal practices. Refugee camps, progressively institutionalized along patriarchal lines, are inadvertently supported by the West and by donor policies that often fail to take into account the special needs of women in exile. The argument of cultural relativism, widely used by the international donor community as a reason not to act, in effect buys into the male political agenda of keeping women subservient and victimized.

These policies do not abate when refugees return to their countries of origin if Islamic governments have seized power. In Afghanistan, following the Soviet withdrawal and the take-over by an Islamic government, religious *fatwas* were issued proclaiming Islam the state religion and demanding the immediate expulsion of Afghan women from governmental and non-governmental posts. Throughout the 15 years of warfare, Afghan women, especially war widows, had to take employment outside the home to support themselves. With the new *fatwa*, female wage-earners were ordered to stay at home and, when in public, return to the practice of veiling. This denied them the right to earn their livelihood and showed disregard for a centuries-old Afghan tradition, supported by Islamic principles, that calls for the protection and care of widows and orphaned children.

Although the government ordered women to stay at home on Islamic grounds, its real motive was to provide job opportunities for more than 1.5 million war returnees, the majority of whom were male. This policy served as a powerful political tool, re-warding resistance fighters with employment and access to limited resources in exchange for waging *jihad*. As a result, large numbers of Afghan women fell into poverty. In the name of the liberation movement, men once again reinstated their control and dominion over 'their' women. In effect, *jihad* is being waged against women's mobility, freedom, and human rights. Far from being integrated as active participants in the rebuilding of repatriated societies, women are once again objectified and oppressed.

A similar practice was instituted in Iran when the Islamic regime imposed restrictions on women. Giving control to men over 'their' women was deemed necessary to alleviate heightened male vulnerability over loss of power in the internal economic and political spheres during the war with Iraq.[8] The practice was introduced in the context of Islam in order to discourage dissid-ence. Dissent against God-given laws bears far greater risks than waging war against man-made laws.

Along with social and economic subjugation, women are subject to sexual violence. Reports of rape of Afghan women perceived to be either supporters or family members of rival resistance groups are legion. Afghan men who witnessed the atrocities committed against women during the war, but apparently could not prevent them, have shown grave concern about the phenomenon of sexual violence against women and girls, particularly since its instigators are thought to be their own Muslim brethren. Moreover, the social stigma of rape, especially of virgin girls, is great because it is thought to bring shame not only on the girl's immediate family, but on the larger clan as well. Reports of 'honor killings' of rape victims in Afghanistan are common. They are also found among Bosnian Muslims.

The fate of Afghan women and girls living in asylum in neighboring Pakistan is no better. Atrocities such as selling young virgin girls to Arab countries or forcing them into prostitution in Pakistani brothels continue. These activities are well-financed, organized, and usually secret. Nurses and doctors staffing the Pakistan refugee camps, whom I interviewed informally in 1990, expressed alarm at the high numbers of young female rape victims and women forced into prostitution.

Afghan male leaders in general and refugee leaders in particular are unable or unwilling to confront these atrocities. Those who are not supported by outside powers are not in a position to reveal or combat such gross violations for fear of retaliation or out of shame. Incidents such as the reported burning of Afghan widows' camps in Pakistan[9] demonstrate men's frustration over not being able to protect 'their women' who are often young widows sold into forced servitude. In the absence of an organized, constructive response, these incidents will probably recur.

Some Lessons from the Afghan Refugee Experience

Disregard for Muslim women's and girls' education, training, health, and mental health stems from inequitable social practices exacerbated by economic, political, and social instability. The conditions and status of refugee and displaced women cannot be segregated from the larger socio-economic, political, and cultural contexts. Historically, Muslim women have been relegated to second-class status in their societies. Their status regresses further upon forced migration. In exile, and lacking a government of their own, they are pitted against indigenous as well as foreign male-dominated movements.

Repatriation can occur successfully when war ends only if a democratic and humanitarian government emerges in the country of origin, consistent with the aspirations of the refugees. Repatriation in the absence of peace, security, physical protection, freedom from hunger, and respect for equity is an empty concept, encoding, largely, a political agenda created by the end of East–West conflict, in which refugees have little use for superpower politics. It also denotes a lack of political will to finance refugee care and relief in an ailing global economy. Thus, successful repatriation depends not only on the existence and reliability of internal security, but also on significant financial commitment by the international community. Unless these conditions are met, successful repatriation, rehabilitation, and rebuilding are unlikely. Women bear the brunt of wars and human rights violations, but must depend on men for major decisions affecting their lives. Western as well as UN refugee relief and aid agencies have failed to support activist refugee or displaced women's activities, preferring to finance male-led political service agencies. Thus, even women's access to equitable relief and aid resources is determined on behalf of women by men. In the Muslim world, 'Islamists' perceive the idea that uprooted women should be liberated as a Western hegemonic concept alien to Muslim culture. The belief that Islam is intrinsically 'fundamentalist,' anti-feminist, and undemocratic is developed by the male leadership with the objective of consolidating male power.[10]

In war-devastated societies, the burden of re-instilling values falls upon women. It is the inherited responsibility of Muslim women to put the pieces of their societies back together. Uprooted women in the Muslim world are finally working to challenge patriarchal power structures and to define Islamic history as well as Islamic principles from the perspective of women. They assert that inequitable systems of patriarchy and polity are based on a male world view but not on Islamic principles.

If the contention over Muslim women's liberation was over the 'Islamization' of women and their conduct, problems such as trafficking in young girls, forced prostitution of women and their children, and support for orphans, war widows and the handicapped would be solved in terms of a proper Islamic humanitarian code of conduct. Instead, the focus has been on withholding access to education and training from women and girls by instituting further restrictions on refugee women and by denying them control of resources. Such restrictive measures have significantly contributed to a decline in the status of Muslim women in exile.

Years of languishing in refugee camps have deprived refugee children of education and have led to widespread drug use. Lack of access to resources, especially access to equitable educational facilities, is common to all refugee women and their daughters. However, sex-biased education is more pronounced in societies which assert that sex-biased education is a Muslim practice. The Afghan refugee situation is a case in point, where primary education for young girls is highly restricted. According to a 1992 study conducted by May Rihani of Creative Associates Inc., in a sample of 1,000 rural primary and secondary schools in Afghanistan, the number of girls was 2.7 per 100 students.[11] Tribal religious leaders dictate education policy with a strong bias toward religious and war training at the expense of science, mathematics, and other subjects. Young boys are recruited as early as nine years old to join combat forces rather than remain in school.

Refugee children grow up surrounded by the violence of war and drugs, and distant from the social norms and values that prevail in times of peace. The burden of re-instilling values to counter the culture of violence and drug abuse falls on women, but little regard is paid to women and their daunting task when they return to their war-devastated societies. To date, the international community has, in large part, bypassed the problem of rebuilding the social structures and systems that empower women to play their part in rebuilding the civil and political infrastructure.

Yet despite inadequate access to formal education during more than 14 years of war, Afghans are becoming increasingly aware of political and international affairs. Women, in particular, have sharpened their survival and economic skills as well as their interest in maintaining direct linkages with the outside world. However, they are burdened by the wrong policies and practices of the male leadership and by the persistent misrepresentation of their agenda.

Conclusion

Muslim refugee women must not be viewed as a separate group in discourses on feminism or the women's movement. Neither the Muslim women's movement, nor women's movements in the West, have yet integrated the problems of uprooted Muslim women into their programs. The Muslim world has failed to address major economic or humanitarian problems that are pervasive among uprooted Muslim populations, including adequate support for war widows and orphaned children, adoption facilities and practices, birth-spacing, female-headed households, and the handicapped. Rather, the focus has been on politico-religious strategies which have engendered sectarian divisiveness. Regional Muslim powers have underscored the differences among the Afghan Sunni and Shi'a sects as a means of waging war on rival Muslim supporters. Such rival approaches have exacerbated the tragedy of the Afghan people and have created a male-led populist movement waging war on women.

In contrast to the unity witnessed during the pan-Islamic movement in the early twentieth century, the Muslim world today is becoming ever more fragmented. Often, uprooted Muslims, especially women, are used as pawns in a political game. Widespread economic and political discontent and frustration have resulted in more regressive policies and practices toward refugee, internally displaced, and returnee women. Restrictive laws and practices against uprooted Muslims are inextricably linked to this heightened male frustration. Often, governments and male resistance movements resort to the use of female subjugation as a potent, visible symbol to disguise male economic and political vulnerabilities; and all this is done in the name of 'Islam.'

The tragedy visited upon uprooted populations in general, and upon women and girls specifically, produces unfathomable, lifelong psychological effects. If the international community is to make a difference in ending the prolonged suffering, it must commit itself to supporting a popularly elected platform of leadership committed to democratic values and principles, as well as respect for human rights and equity. Industrial nations, especially the United States which funded the war in Afghanistan, must in turn also finance the process toward peace, democracy and pluralism. Neither politics nor shifting global economies should be used to capitulate to oppression, nor should they dictate and drive humanitarian intervention.

Activists dealing with women, human rights, feminism, and peace must integrate refugee women into their discussions, especially as they bear the brunt of the most egregious forms of human rights abuses. Solutions for women in forced migration must include equitable treatment and equal access to resources. In large part, the women's movement has failed to address and raise consciousness among women at the grassroots level. Western donor policies must reflect the needs and resources of women in forced migration and deal with the acuteness of their situation if they are to build pluralism and civil societies. The Muslim world must institute humanitarian and democratic principles consistent with equitable Islamic policies and practices toward its women. The Western world must recognize gender-based persecution of Muslim as well as non-Muslim women, particularly in asylum policies. Finally, discourses on Muslims in forced migration must be linked to larger issues such as economic restructuring, hunger and poverty, development, pluralism and the building of civil societies.

Notes

1. 'Challenges and Opportunities in the Age of Repatriation: The Role of NGOs'. Report of a conference held at Georgetown University, Washington, DC, 16–17 June 1993.

2. Conference on Mental Health and Well-Being of Refugees and Displaced Persons. Stockholm, 6–11 October 1991. Unpublished proceedings.

3. Rosemarie Rogers and Emily Copeland, *Forced Migration: Policy Issues in the Post-Cold War World* (Medford, Mass.: Fletcher School of Law and Diplomacy, Tufts University, 1993), p. 88.

4. United States Committee for Refugees, *World Refugee Survey 1994* (Washington, DC: United States Committee for Refugees, 1994).

5. Statement submitted by the International NGO Working Group on Refugee Women to the UN Commission on the Status of Women, Thirty-Ninth Session, New York, NY, 15 March–4 April 1995.

6. Deirdre Wulf, *Refugee Women and Reproductive Health Care: Reassessing Priorities* (New York: Women's Commission for Refugee Women and Children, 1994), p. 41.

7. Ninette Kelley, *Working with Refugee Women: A Practical Guide* (Geneva: International NGO Working Group on Refugee Women, 1989).

8. Leila Ahmed, *Women and Gender in Islam* (New Haven: Yale University Press, 1992), p. 232.

9. The Nasir Bagh Camp housing Afghan widows in Peshawar served as a showcase for visiting foreign dignitaries at the height of the Soviet invasion of Afghanistan. The widows' access to resources and living conditions was considerably more humane than in other refugee situations, which led to heightened Afghan male vulnerability over not having decision-making power over 'their women.' Traditionally, a widow is taken as the second or third wife of her husband's brother. In other cases, extended family members, usually from the husband's clan, undertake the caretaking of the widow.

10. Rema Hammami, 'Women, Hijab and the Intifada,' *Women Living Under Muslim Laws Dossier*, 9/10 (November/December 1991), p. 48.

11. Author interviews with Ms Rihani, Washington, DC, 1994.

S.O.S. Algeria: Women's Human Rights Under Siege

Karima Bennoune

The current violence in Algeria is both tragic and deeply alarming in its scope and intensity to all observers, but is especially heart-breaking for those who have followed the country's history for the last 40 years. Algeria was once a symbol of progressive anti-colonial struggle which brought women and men together to fight for their basic human rights. Djamila Bouhired and other women fighters in the war of national liberation became the international symbols of Algeria's freedom struggle and were revered throughout the Arab World. After independence, the country was famous as a supporter of global progressive movements, harboring Black Panthers and exiles from Pinochet's Chile, and spearheading the non-aligned movement. Today, Algeria is on the road to national suicide, complete with terrible atrocities committed by citizens against other citizens, internal corruption, and external manipulation. Algerian women are again shouldering heavy burdens in the conflict, and are once more becoming symbols of the fight for human rights and justice in their country. A nation which paid with the lives of one in seven of its population during its war of independence is again losing its children. The number of people killed since 1992 has been estimated as anything from 4,000 to 30,000. The official Algerian government tally, released in August 1994, counted 10,000 Algerians dead.[1] The Western press now often cites the figure of 30,000 casualties since 1992.[2] Many of these victims have been women who have been increasingly targeted.

While recounting atrocities by itself does not explain the crisis in Algeria, documenting the unfolding horror is a prerequisite to any meaningful discussion of the current problems facing many Algerian women. Consequently, this chapter will begin with an overview of the suffering currently inflicted on Algerian women, primarily by fundamentalist[3] violence. The next step is to look beyond those crimes to the ideology and movement which motivates them, and thereby attempt to understand what is at stake in Algeria today and what the meanings of the country's internal conflict are, both for the nation's future and for women throughout the region.

This article cannot possibly contain a full account of recent events in Algeria, nor does it mean to condone human rights violations by the Algerian government because its focus is on the abuses committed by fundamentalists. According to Algerian human rights organizations, international human rights organizations, and press reports, the violations of the government have included extrajudicial executions, administrative detention and the use of torture. Using respect for human rights as the criterion for evaluating legitimacy would disqualify both the Algerian government and fundamentalist groups from the right to govern Algeria. However, fundamentalist ideology and activity unquestionably pose a unique and overwhelming threat to the lives of Algerian women.

Living in a Waking Nightmare: Fundamentalist Atrocities Against Women in Algeria, from 1992 to the present

'The fundamentalists are hunting women.'[4]

'I thought of buying poison so I can kill myself if taken by them alive, so all they get is a corpse. I am losing my hair from nerves.'[5]

Killings

At the offices of an Algerian newspaper in early December 1994, a woman journalist said with a quiet firmness, 'Go and tell them what is happening here. How shocking it is that so many outside do not know, that so many are ignorant and are silent. In Algeria every day women are being kidnapped, raped, mutilated, tortured to death and killed by members of fundamentalist armed groups which the United States government helped to train and with whom it continues to urge the Algerian government to dialogue.'[6] The principal armed groups are known as the GIA or Armed Islamic Group, the MIA or Armed Islamic Movement and the AIS or Army of Islamic Salvation. Among the armed groups, the GIA is believed to be the leading perpetrator of attacks on civilians.

One of the first women to be assassinated in the current wave

of violence was 21-year-old Karima Belhadj, who worked as a
typist in the youth and sports department of the General Office
of National Security. Karima supported her entire family of eight
with her paycheck and was engaged to be married. She was shot
repeatedly in the head and abdomen while walking home from
work, and died in the hospital on 7 April 1993.[7] Many women
were utterly shocked by the murder of Karima Belhadj and for
many this event represented a new phase in the conflict, a phase
in which the deliberate targeting of women on an ever-widening
scale became the norm.[8] A young woman journalist expressed the
impact of the event: 'We thought at the beginning that women
would be okay. But when they killed a 21-year-old woman who
worked as a secretary in a police station, we realized we were
wrong. Women are afraid. No one is safe.'[9]

What follows is the smallest sampling of the escalation in atrocities against women since Karima Belhadj's murder:[10]

23 January 1994: In the city of Tiaret, Mrs Derouche Mimouna,
28 years old and mother of five children, is decapitated in front
of her family;[11]

25 February 1994: In Sidi Bel Abbes, two sisters, aged 12 and 15,
are kidnapped and raped in the forest;

3 March 1994: In Tlemcen, a 69-year-old woman named Samia
Hadjou is killed by having her throat cut.

23 July 1994: In Chlef, a 37-year-old working woman is killed
in front of her children and her decapitated head is left in the
street as a warning to others. Reportedly, her young children
attempted to run into the street and retrieve their mother's head.

7 November 1994: Birtouta, Blida region: The bodies of two young
sisters, Saida (15) and Zoulikha (21) are found on the side of the
road. They have been gang raped, their fingernails and toenails
have been removed, and, as the final horror, their throats have
been cut. They have been thus 'punished' because they refused to
consent to a temporary marriage or 'Zaouadj el-mouta' with fundamentalist armed men. Their mother Khadidja, who attempted
to protect her daughters, was found 20 days later in a mass grave,
having been raped and killed like her children.

Given the growing frequency of such occurrences, it is understandable why two young women I met expressed the desire to
carry poison with them, so that they might take their own lives if
captured. As journalist Ouessila Si Saber concluded, 'It is not an
easy death, the women victims must suffer first, before dying.'[12]

Despite the danger, Si Saber and many other Algerian journalists continue to sign articles about the attacks on women and to live and work in Algeria. It is largely due to their work, and that of increasingly besieged human rights workers, that documentation of the onslaught against women's human rights is available.

'Dying Beautiful': Violence and the Veil

Having visited Algeria in February and then in December of 1994, I was startled by how greatly the violence against women had escalated.[13] The heightened pressure on women to veil is but one example. In March of 1994, the Armed Islamic Group (GIA) issued a statement classifying all unveiled women who appeared in public as potential military targets. To punctuate this threat, gunmen on a motorbike shot and killed two young high school students, Naima Kar Ali, 17, and Raziqa Melou-Ladjmi, 18, while they were standing at the bus station in Boumerdes, about 40 kilometers east of the capital.[14] Katia Bengana, a 17-year-old high school student in Blida, had already been gunned down in the street while walking with a veiled friend on 28 March 1994.[15] Katia had been warned by local fundamentalists, but refused to veil. Her friend was reported to have been left alive because she was veiled.[16]

The campaign to force women to veil has been relentless. A woman professor who taught at the University of Blida until she stopped recently for security reasons, said that most of her women students had begun to carry a scarf in their briefcases to put on before entering the University campus.[17] She and another woman professor both described the impact of flyers and graffiti. They pointed to one particular slogan which appeared throughout Algiers during Ramadan in 1994. It warned, 'O you woman who wears the *jilbab* (full robes), May you be blessed by God. O you who wears the *hijab* (headscarf), May God put you on the straight road. O you who expose yourself, the gun is for you.'[18] While in Algiers the majority of women remain unveiled, in rural areas and smaller towns, the pressure has forced many young girls and women to begin veiling. As one 22-year-old woman from Tlemcen expressed the mood of many young women students: 'None of us want to wear the veil. But fear is stronger than our convictions or our will to be free. Fear is all around us. Our parents, our brothers, are unanimous: Wear the veil and stay alive.'[19]

The pressure on women to wear the *hijab* highlights the use and misuse of concepts such as 'traditional' in relation to events in Algeria. While Algerian women have worn the *haik*, a white silk cloak covering the head with a lace kerchief over the lower part of the face, for centuries, the *hijab* and *jilbab* which the fundamentalists seek to impose are relatively new, having been brought to Algeria only in the late 1970s. The *chador*, which is worn by only a few women, began to be seen around Algiers in the late 1980s and is also clearly a foreign import. Algerian peasant women have never veiled, but have instead worn scarves tied only over part of their hair.

'Layadjouz': Forbidden Lives

Behavior such as working in non-traditional professions, for example as a school principal or woman activist, is deemed *layadjouz* or forbidden, and has lead fundamentalist armed men to 'execute' women.[20] Women activists have been particularly targeted both with threats and violence. The killing of Nabila Djahnine, a 35-year-old architect who headed a Berber women's group called The Cry of Women, in Tizi Ouzou on 15 February 1995, is but the latest tragic example.[21] Many women activists live in hiding, some moving every few days to avoid attack, and even having to be separated from their spouses, children and families for security reasons.

Paradoxically, while women have been killed for playing 'untraditional' roles, they have also paid with their lives for participating in 'traditional' activities. Working as a fortune teller, running a Turkish bath or *hammam*, or even being a hairdresser have brought death on women because such activities have been deemed immoral by fundamentalists.[22] Other women have been threatened because they are accused of being witches, particularly local traditional fortune tellers.[23]

Another 'punishable offense' is marriage to a non-Muslim man. An Algerian woman married to a Belgian man was 'executed' along with her husband in January 1994.[24] The woman and her husband had lived together in Algeria for 30 years at the time of their deaths.

Rape: 'Nothing is More Traumatizing Than This'[25]

In addition to killings, rape and gang rape are reportedly on the increase. Kheira X, a young Algerian girl from the interior of the country, gave an interview to the Algerian newspaper *El Watan* describing her ordeal when kidnapped by the members of an armed group:

> They threw me in a van without windows and drove for hours on end … They then took me into a kind of cave, where there was already an old woman. A few hours later, three men came to find me. They laid me down on the ground and one by one they raped me. The woman who was close by me was crying quietly. One of them struck her, then they left.[26]

One of the first women to report being gang raped by members of the fundamentalist armed groups was, ironically, the wife of an Imam, Akila Belarbi.[27] This occurred in the town of Maalma, 150 kilometers from Algiers. Later rapes were reported in Jijel, Oran, Ain Defla and M'sla, as well as in Bouira which is only 200 kilometers from Algiers.[28] In Bouira, a 9-year-old girl was the only survivor of the fundamentalist massacre of her entire family, but she was raped and clubbed in the head.[29] In Boumerdes, east of Algiers, a middle-aged woman seamstress was kidnapped by the local 'Emir' and then beaten, tortured and collectively raped, by many armed men. She reported this to the National Human Rights Observatory.[30]

The kidnapping of young girls and women for use as sex slaves by the armed groups became so widespread that, in a totally unprecedented move for a society where sexuality remains a taboo subject of public discussion, three young women between the ages of 15 and 28 who had survived similar ordeals appeared with their fathers on Algerian national television on 22 December 1994, to speak about their experiences. Fifteen-year-old Khadidja told a shocked Algerian public of being kidnapped at gunpoint from her parents' home in front of her family, kept in a 'safe house' for several weeks where she was forced to cook and clean for 'God's warriors' and repeatedly raped.[31]

A 17-year-old girl pseudonymed Ouarda testified in the press of her months in captivity in an armed group stronghold where she also was repeatedly raped until pregnant. After being kidnapped off the street while returning home in downtown Algiers, she was kept with a group of other young girls, one of whom was shot in the head and killed when she tried to escape. 'Ouarda' described the first rape:

They made all the other girls leave and two terrorists came in with me carrying their arms. One ordered me to take off my pants. I refused, saying that what he wanted to do was not good and that God condemned it and we were not married. He threatened me with his knife saying that he would slash me and that he would do whatever he wanted to as God would permit him because he is a *moujahid* and he would marry me later ... . I was really afraid when he placed the blade of his knife against my cheek. I took my pants off, crying. He told me to take off my underpants. I screamed and refused. I begged him, saying that this was shameful in God's eyes but he took a cigarette and lit it and began burning me on the thighs. I screamed and closed my eyes with my back to the wall. He burned me again and I fainted. I did not feel anything else. When I regained consciousness, I was on the ground covered in blood.'[32]

Women survivors are threatened with further punishment, and in the case of rape with shame, in fear and often in silence, even after the assault has ceased. Many of these women have either gone into hiding or fled to other parts of Algeria, becoming part of an increasingly large community of internal refugees seeking safe haven in other cities. Furthermore, the general climate of terrorist violence against women has produced its desired effect: a widespread psychosis and insecurity among the female population at large.[33]

Threats: Words That Change Lives

An even wider group of women than those who have actually experienced violent attacks have been subjected to harassment and threats; and, given the level of ongoing violence, these threats are terrifying and profoundly life-altering. Some women are threatened doubly, as women and also as members of other targeted groups like teachers. Few have paid as high a price as journalists of the print and visual media.[34] A 25-year-old woman journalist recounted the events which sent her into hiding, living in a cramped hotel now used to protect the increasingly vulnerable journalist community.

I found my name on a list in the local mosque. It said that I am an apostate and should be killed. It said that I would be killed in the next few days. Fear is human. I was afraid. I thought of Tahar Djaout (journalist murdered in 1992). He said, 'If you speak out, they will kill you. If you keep silent, they will kill you. So speak out and die.' I won't hide it from you, I was really afraid. I tried to hide and I tried to keep writing.[35]

Teachers and other members of the educational profession have been particular targets as part of the ongoing fundamentalist campaign against modern education. This has included attacks on students and teachers and the burning of hundreds of schools, as well as threats against all who continue to participate in the educational system.[36] A woman school inspector received the following threat in February 1994:

'For [Miss X], School inspector, If you do not solve the problems of Muslims which you have created before the end of Ramadan, you will have your throat cut like all tyrants and sinners, The conditions on you are: 1) Wearing the *hijab* permanently after the first day of Ramadan, 2) asking forgiveness from the Muslims that you have made suffer in your behavior as a tyrant, 3) we are watching you and we know where you live. We are not afraid of the police or the gendarmes but we will cut your throat before the end of Ramadan. If you do not [meet these conditions] before the end of Ramadan, you are responsible. We warned you before cutting your throat.

[Signed] The Islamic Group of El Harrache, Head of the Group Azedine, Long Live Islam, Long Live the GIA, the armed struggle for an Islamic state in Algeria.[37]

The school inspector has been in hiding ever since. She has been forced to alter her work schedule significantly, and to have only extremely limited contact with her family. In the wake of the threat, she experienced terrible emotional stress, remarking in February 1994 that she felt as if she were 'living in a waking nightmare.'[38]

In October 1994, Nadia X, a woman doctor in a suburb of Algiers received death threats from within her hospital. Her husband began accompanying her to and from work and the entire family suffered greatly from stress. The doctor said sadly, 'It is so disturbing after all I've tried to do, remaining a doctor in the public health system, that someone out there hates me that much. You ask yourself: why?' Her daughter, a college student, interrupted angrily: 'There is no reason why.' She softened, and in a quieter tone said, 'A letter like that changes your life.'

Similar threats, and the knowledge that such threats are acted on, have provoked a mass exodus of Algerian professionals to Europe, Canada and elsewhere. Increasing numbers of Algerian women are currently seeking political asylum in the United States, with mixed results. Many are in great conflict over the decision to leave and face the difficult choice of whether it is a stronger stand against intolerance to stay and die or to leave and live.

'Touched for Life': Women as Witness to War

Women have also suffered from violence against family members. In a new twist, men are now being killed for the political views and activities of their wives. For example, Mohamed Redha Aslaoui, a dentist and the husband of Leila Aslaoui, a former judge and government minister who resigned from the current government in protest at its policies and spoke out against the fundamentalists, was assassinated by men who came into his office.

Often, a woman whose family member is killed will receive threats if she identifies the killer to the authorities. Mrs. X Kaddour whose husband was murdered, reported to the National Human Rights Observatory that in July 1993 she was 'condemned to death' for reporting the killing of her husband to the police.[39] She was forced to flee to another area of Algeria. A mother, identified only as B. Rabah, whose son and nephew had been kidnapped, murdered, and dismembered by one of the fundamentalist armed groups received a threatening letter on 14 May 1994, condemning her to death and stating that her other son would be murdered just like his brother if he did not stop singing, because it is sinful.[40]

When not directly attacked themselves, women have had to bear witness to the terrible whirlwind of killing around them. Almost every woman has lost a neighbor, a friend or a family member and they have often had to watch these deaths, unable to stop them. A male journalist described to me the impact of one incident on his wife:

My wife was there [when Abderrahman Cherbou, a journalist was killed]. They put a bag over his head and attacked him with a knife. He still had the bread he had bought in his hand. He tried to run away with the blood spurting from his throat. This is how my wife saw him and she is touched for life by this. He died twenty minutes later from loss of blood.[41]

An overwhelming sense of powerlessness and uncertainty about the future is becoming pervasive. Some women professors have spoken of the growing 'collective psychosis' produced, particularly among women, by the escalation in violence during 1994. Commenting on the horrors about which women survivors had told her, journalist Zazi Sadou remarked:

> Kidnappings, rape, torture, assassinations, 'dishonor', flight, exile, permanent fear of reprisals, nightmares, hopes and futures broken ... .
> Here is a sample of what the soldiers of the Islamic State offer to women and their families, only five years before the dawn of the 21st century.[42]

Roots of the Nightmare: Fundamentalism and Violence against Algerian Women Before 1992

For some, the violence of the Algerian armed groups against women has come as a terrible shock. It is certainly unprecedented in the history of independent Algeria. However, for many Algerian feminist observers and critics of both the fundamentalists and the government, the violations of women's human rights are but the logical conclusion of the ideologies of the political wing of the Algerian fundamentalist movement and the irresponsible policies and corruption of successive Algerian governments which helped to spawn that movement.[43]

Throughout the 1980s, the government of Chadli Benjedid (president 1979–92) collaborated closely with the burgeoning fundamentalist movement. The fundamentalists provided the government with allies against progressive forces and discouraged populist challenges while the public sector was dismantled. Fundamentalist ideology served to harness and deflect popular anger and frustration with the economic devastation wrought by 'reform,' corruption and mismanagement. If the real problems in Algeria were not the housing crisis or the medicine shortage, but rather a lack of religiosity and cultural impurity, the government's major failings could be overlooked. All the regime had to do was allow the fundamentalists to organize, to create its own face of cultural 'authenticity' by enacting the conservative and repressive family code of 1984, having the president's wife appear in public in a *hijab*,[44] and encouraging national assembly deputies to speak of sending working women back to their kitchens as a way of ending unemployment. According to Saida Ben Habylas, the official representative of Algeria to the Arab Regional Preparatory meeting for the Beijing World Conference on Women:

The history of the FIS and other 'terrorist' groups is a series of alliances with a corrupt 'politico-financial mafia' that helped bring about the economic and social inequalities in Algeria during the 1970s and 1980s ... . Political pluralism and democracy could have meant exposure of corruption of the old order. This old order allied themselves with the FIS in the 1980s and agreed to 'share power'.There was a deal.[45]

Popular frustration with the policies of Chadli Benjedid's government and widespread corruption came to a boiling point in the October 1988 riots which the government suppressed by killing and torturing hundreds of civilians.[46] In the aftermath, rather than responding to the predominantly socio-economic demands of the rioters, the regime decided to deflect attention away from its own policies and culpability with political reforms. It legalized opposition political parties, liberalized restrictions on the press and established a timetable for multi-party elections. While in the abstract these are inherently positive developments, given the vast socio-economic problems caused by the government's policies, in this context they served as no more than a formalist figleaf. Furthermore, the Islamic Salvation Front (FIS), the major fundamentalist grouping, was legalized despite the constitutional prohibition on parties founded on the basis of religion. Given the lack of response to the demands of the October uprising and the failure to bring to trial those responsible for the killing and torture, the post-1988 period was the perfect environment for the spread of fundamentalism.

With the benefits of legality, FIS activity and support mushroomed. The negative consequences for women were plain to see. Women of all socio-economic backgrounds began to experience tremendous difficulty walking in their neighborhoods, going out to work and dressing as they chose. The FIS analysis of Algeria's economic problems was summed up by the slogan, 'Our crisis is a crisis of faith and morals.'[47] As such, women's behavior, habits and dress took center stage in the movement's agenda. Any progress made in women's status during the previous twenty years seemed to erode overnight. Thus, a young working woman from a working-class background remarked to me while going through a military checkpoint on the outskirts of Algiers during the summer of 1992 after the military intervention, that she felt less fearful with the soldiers around than she had when the FIS cadres controlled her neighborhood.[48]

While the FIS was a legal party, the number of attacks on

women skyrocketed, on both the individual and mass levels. For example, women's college dormitories were repeatedly besieged by FIS militants who threatened women residents, prohibiting them from entering or leaving. Often the authorities refused to interfere to protect the terrified women students. Though similar attacks occurred at the University of Oran[49] and elsewhere, the worst incidents happened during 1989–90 in Blida, a middle-class town and fundamentalist stronghold about 100 kilometers from Algiers. A group calling itself 'the Redeemers' was established to patrol the conduct of women.[50] According to the Algerian newspaper, *Algérie Actualité*, the slogan of this movement was 'All girls who go out at night will die.'[51] Members of this group constantly harassed women in the Ben Boulaid women's residence at the University of Blida, threatening and sometimes actually physically assaulting them. As a press release written by a group of women residents who experienced these events said, 'These fundamentalists, sure of their strength and egged on by the authorities' silence, have taken the place of those who represent the law and have started to apply their own laws.'[52] In 1990 the situation in Ben Boulaid culminated in a siege by some 300 militants, reportedly including Ali Benhadj, the FIS's second-in-command.

Clearly, the cancellation of elections by the military in 1992 does not, as the Western press frequently claims, mark the beginning of fundamentalist violence in Algeria. Rather, the fundamentalist violence against women was deeply rooted in the group's ideology and practices and its commitment to the 'policing of morality,' even while it was a legal political party participating in an electoral process.

In the 1990 municipal elections, the first multiparty elections in the history of independent Algeria, the FIS won the majority of municipalities, probably due to popular frustration with the FLN and a lack of other viable alternatives. Subsequently, the party used its power to keep women out of various public spaces. They were banned from cultural centers and other public facilities. Buses were forcibly gender-segregated. Women were chased off beaches and mixed marriage ceremonies were prohibited in public hotels. Sports and technical training for women in schools was banned.[53]

On an *ad hoc* basis, fundamentalists implemented their ideological agenda by harassing women who were merely trying to practice their professions. For example, an open letter from a group of women students at the Polytechnical School of

Architecture and Urbanism in Algiers described being barred by
FIS members from houses which the student group was to survey
in Bourouba. The women students were told that their place was
at home and the male students were told to take the women away.
The women students commented: 'We were considered as devils,
we were really insulted and humiliated ... . Now our work has
come to an end ... . '[54]

Other professional women were threatened if they did not put
certain allegedly religious standards above the professional standards required in their work. This included practices necessary for
public health and safety. For example, a woman director of the
department of obstetrics and gynecology at an Algiers hospital
received threats when she attempted to continue implementing
universal standards of sanitary practice in her hospital department.
A women's association commenting on the threats to this doctor
asked:

> Can we accept that student-nurses refuse to wash their arms, on the
> pretext that their religious convictions do not allow them to do so?
> What about the health of patients? Can we accept a husband's refusal
> to let his wife be examined by a male doctor when there is no (female)
> on-duty doctor? In ... medicine, can we accept workers' refusal to
> consult a woman doctor, whose work it is, and who is there to do it?[55]

The fundamentalist commitment to purification led also to
attacks on individual women, particularly widows who did not
remarry and other women who lived alone. These included five
attacks during the same night in Bou Saada and another in
Ouargla in 1989.[56] In the Ouargla attack, the woman victim's
8-year-old disabled son was burned to death when a group of
fundamentalists firebombed his mother where she lived alone with
her children, having been divorced by her husband and made
homeless by the provisions of the Algerian family code.[57] A woman
activist's home was also firebombed in Annaba in November 1989,
leading women's groups to organize demonstrations under the
slogan, 'We Fear For Our Future.'[58]

Women activists argue that too little attention is given to this
terrorism against women which started before the interruption of
elections in 1992 and before the attacks on male intellectuals and
journalists. Had the earlier attacks on women been taken seriously,
they argue, the later violence could have been predicted and
possibly averted. Given the unwillingness of the conservative

regime of Chadli Benjedid to protect women or to see the assault
on them as political, the true nature of the fundamentalist view of
women and its basic relationship to the fundamentalist social
project for Algeria were obscured.

Beyond Atrocities: The Meanings of
Fundamentalist Violence against Women

'How can the murder of a girl or a journalist bring an Islamic
state?'[59]

It is difficult to make sense of movements which, on the one hand,
call for women to be pure and chaste, and yet simultaneously
engage in widespread gang rape. However, there are clear meanings to this seeming madness.

No group of women was as reviled by fundamentalist ideologues
in the 1980s and early 1990s as the women activists who attempted
to organize against the 1984 family code, the 1990 electoral law
and for greater rights for women in Algerian society. When asked
why, in her view, the Algerian armed groups were attacking
women, an Algerian woman professor who used to teach at the
University of Algiers until she was forced by the situation to stop,
responded:

> This is clearly happening because women are refusing to obey in-
> structions they are being given. Women threaten the communitarian
> vision of the armed groups and raise the issue of equality. Some women
> are refusing to be assimilated into this project and continue to insist on
> protecting their individual identities and rights. The armed groups are
> disturbed by women's groups which break their vision. Especially
> women activists. They are in this view, the absolute worst. They are
> 'public women.'[60]

These 'public women' were branded as 'the avant-garde of
colonialism and cultural aggression' and, because they opposed
the family code which legalized polygamy, they were dubbed, 'the
women who want to marry four husbands' by the fundamentalists.
In an interview with Agence France Presse in 1989, Abassi Medani,
the leader of the FIS, stated that the recent anti-fundamentalist
demonstrations of women were 'one of the greatest dangers threatening the destiny of Algeria.' This is because the women participants were 'defying the conscience of the people and repudiating

national values.'[61] Arguably, this level of venom and misunder-
standing represents the ideas of which the throat-slitting and gang
rape of today are but the logical conclusion. When dress and
behavior standards are imposed on women by 'death sentences,'
and all ability to engage in educational, professional or political
activity construed as foreign, women who challenge such a regime
of morals become the 'other', the *kafr*, the apostate, and, in the
literal and backward interpretation of the fundamentalists, an
obvious target. Many of the women whose lives have been claimed
by fundamentalist violence are not accidental victims, but are
carefully chosen prey because their lives, activities and voices are
a threat to the fundamentalist order. As H. Zerrouky argued in
the Algerian newspaper, *Le Matin,* the roots of this violence go
even deeper:

> In fact, what is shocking about these young men who kill women when
> we know that they have been raised on misogyny since primary school?
> A misogyny relayed [to them] again by Abassi Medani who speaks of
> women 'democrats' as 'spies of neocolonialism.'

> These assassinations are finally nothing more than the culmination of
> the way in which women are treated in the country. After trying to
> close them in, to marginalize those who seek to reclaim their rights,
> we have moved to the ultimate stage.[62]

The Other Algeria: Women's Struggle Continues

'You must know that there are Algerian feminists and we are now
fighting for the right to life and the rights of women. We need the
maximum solidarity.' Algerian Woman Activist

'Neither the *hijab* nor the *jilbab*, neither Iran nor the Sudan.'
(Slogan from women's protest against the violence, 8 March 1994.)

Despite the firestorm which surrounds them, Algerian women
continue to defy the Emirs and their cohorts. They are doing this
at both the collective and individual level. Collectively, women's
organizations continue to issue press releases, to meet in secret
whenever possible, to try to provide solidarity to women survivors
of violence and to women who have lost family members, to go
on speaking to the foreign press, and to reproduce and distribute
press articles on the current situation of women. Up until recently,

they continued to hold demonstrations which have become a
seriously life-threatening endeavor.[63] Women's groups were key
organizers of the nationwide demonstrations against violence on
22 March 1994, and many of the participants were women.[64]

On an individual level, women perform what Fatima Mernissi
has called 'daily battle' by continuing to go out to work and to go
to school, by refusing to wear the *hidjab*, by continuing to write
and publish, and by attempting to care for their families in a
situation increasingly fraught with peril and economic deprivation.

Many such women with whom I spoke while in Algeria were
deeply concerned that the outside world thought of Algeria only
in terms of the *chador* and the fundamentalists. They expressed the
hope that the outside world should know that they do exist, that
they represent another Algeria, which retains its commitment to
progressive values and tolerance. As one woman intellectual said,
'It is important for people to know that a democratic Algeria exists
in the women's movement and elsewhere. If these values did not
exist, there would be no struggle in Algeria.'[65]

Algeria's Turmoil in the Larger Context:
Meanings and Messages

> I have to believe that you Americans do not understand us or the full
> importance of our problem. Those whom you supported or still support
> in Afghanistan and Saudi Arabia are full of scorn for you. They believe
> that American women are filthy whores. I do not believe this and
> neither do my friends. We do not want to be like you, but we want to
> live in a country where we can be like you if that is what we please, or
> be like ourselves, or even wear a veil if we want to. But the Islamist
> terrorists, after they have turned Algeria into another Iran, will not
> give us any choices at all.[66]

It is disturbing that the conflict in Algeria is most frequently
discussed in the mainstream Western media in terms of its potential to generate waves of refugees who are not welcome in Europe.
In an era when Huntington is attempting to split the world into
cultural spheres, basically divided into 'the Muslim world' and
'us,' when Islam has replaced communism as the great post-Cold
War whipping boy, the hysteria about the Muslim hordes has
totally obscured the reality of what is happening on the ground in
countries like Algeria.

On the other hand, while an anti-racist analysis is crucial to debunking such a demonology, one cannot fail to face up to the implications and nature of fundamentalism as practiced and experienced on the ground. To confuse fundamentalism with some sort of 'essential' or 'true' or 'authentic' Islam as a culture or religion, whether from an antagonistic or sympathetic perspective, is an incredible mistake. Similarly, to assume that those who oppose fundamentalism are 'Western' or 'elite' or lose their 'authenticity' as a result is equally misguided. In fact, 'anti-fundamentalists', for lack of a better term, have defended such 'indigenous' aspects of Algerian culture as Andalus and Rai music, and dancing at weddings. On the other hand, as documented above, the armed groups have actually violated nearly every principle of *Islamic* humanitarian law as well as international norms.[67] Thus, the major dangers of Muslim fundamentalism are not for the 'West' or 'Western civilization' or even Western interests, but for the Muslim world and the people who live there. What is needed is a very careful political analysis which is not simply based on construing the enemy of one's enemy to be friendly or worthy of support.

When I arrived in Holland after my last trip to Algeria, a Dutch man responded to my description of what is happening there by saying that an Islamic State would not change life for the majority of the country's women. While this might be an attempt to critique the mainstream Western discourse on 'Islam,' it is a deadly analysis with terrifying consequences for those who will actually be ruled by any future Islamic state. It utterly ignores the track record of the Algerian fundamentalist movement as documented in this chapter.

The most incredible omission in much mainstream discussion of Muslim fundamentalism in the US is the role of the United States itself and other Western governments in promoting it, both actively and tacitly, as an option. The well-known US training of Algerian and other Arab Muslim fundamentalist armed men in Pakistan and Afghanistan during the 1980s is the most concrete example. Western support of the destruction of the Algerian economy via the dismantling of the public sector is another example. As one woman activist said, 'The West indirectly supports the FIS with its IMF and World Bank demands on Algeria. It is weakening the middle class and making the poor poorer and the rich richer.'[68] Despite these realities, Mark Parris, acting assistant secretary for Near Eastern Affairs, in a statement before the Subcommittee on

Africa of the House Foreign Affairs Committee in March of 1994,
claimed that 'Algeria's crisis is largely homegrown' and the product
of 'socialist mismanagement.'[69] Ironically, in this very statement
he alludes to the pressures put on Algeria by the US to reform its
economy and to restructure its debt which he admits 'might create
hardship in the short term.'[70] A former Algerian prime minister
was told by a visiting American delegation that the continued
existence of a public sector in Algeria is considered a far greater
problem than fundamentalism or fundamentalist violence.

The Way Forward

> I am no intellectual, but I believe other people were told, elsewhere in
> other times that the evil and fear around them would pass. As far as
> I know, it did not pass. It got worse. I believe it will get worse unless
> someone hears us.
>
> Fatima B.

At this writing, the violence in Algeria is escalating yet again.[71]
The Armed Islamic Group set off a bomb in downtown Algiers,
blowing up a bus, killing 42 people, and wounding 256 others on
30 January 1995. This was the single largest deliberate killing of
civilians in the conflict so far and represented yet another new
stage in the conflict. The GIA statement which claimed responsibility for this attack timed to mark the beginning of the Muslim
holy month of Ramadan, opined in frightening language that:

> There will be no peace, no truce and no compromise, because this
> holy month of Ramadan is a time for killing and fighting, for victories
> and breakthroughs, and it is the duty of all fighters to intensify military
> work and religious struggle.[72]

In one week in February 1995 alone, fundamentalist armed
groups took responsibility for the killings of 11 intellectuals, including the director of the national theater, a composer of Algerian
Rai music and feminist leader Nadia Djahnine.[73] On the other
hand, a prison riot of fundamentalist prisoners was quashed in
late February 1995, killing nearly 100 prisoners. The spiral of
violence seems to move only upward. Meanwhile, the economy, a
root cause of many of these problems, continues to flounder, producing an unemployment rate of nearly 40 per cent.
    One of the biggest fears of many women is that, in any

settlement with the fundamentalists, their status is perhaps the most likely concession. This leads to what one woman described as the 'key paradox' in the Algerian drama: 'how to deal democratically with a movement which believes that democracy is heresy and which proposes a new power structure based on religious legitimacy, determined by a hegemonic vision.'[74]

However, one of the very strong appeals of fundamentalism is its hegemonic and clearly articulated vision. One of the key challenges, therefore, is the clear articulation of an alternative, a third way, which represents neither the military-backed government and its allies in the 'mafia' nor the fundamentalists. As a woman intellectual envisioned this project,

> The democratic movements and activists need to put a democratic front together, a front of those who oppose an Iranian-style regime in Algeria. This movement must pose concrete alternatives. The fundamentalists have been selling heaven and dreams. So the democratic movement must also sell a dream.[75]

However, this is no easy task and many of those who could be key players in such a project, being critics of both the government and the fundamentalists, have either been killed or are in hiding. In addition, given the pressure placed on Algeria by IMF-induced austerity measures, it will become increasingly difficult to offer a real alternative as life becomes materially worse for people.

The final session of the Arab Regional Preparatory Meeting in Amman, Jordan for the upcoming Beijing Conference on Women passed a resolution condemning the violence against women in Algeria over the vociferous objections of the Sudan and despite the nervousness of many governments to raise the issue. After strong pressure from the non-governmental organizations present, including a petition drive among delegates, the resolution was passed. It reads as follows:

> We declare and affirm our solidarity with Algerian women, who are confronted with a fierce battle against their existence, thinking, education and right to life, a battle aimed at keeping them from participating in the development of their country and waged by the forces of extremism and backwardness, which chose the language of violence and terrorism instead of the language of dialogue. Those forces are committing the most heinous crimes in violation of the rights of women and children, just to achieve their goal of doing away with the gains of Algerian women and undermining the achievements of the Algerian

revolution in which women participated effectively, made sacrifices and became a model for Arab women in their struggle for their country's freedom, progress and stability.

Women of the world are called upon to show solidarity with Algerian women in their just struggle to protect their gains and rights to life and peace, for those are imperative conditions to insure world peace.[76]

One can only hope that the violations of Algerian women's human rights are recognized as key to the problems facing the country, and that any solution to the crisis deemed 'peaceful,' guarantees, as the above resolution indicates is necessary, women's rights and equality.

Notes

1. See e.g., *Human Rights Watch World Report 1995: Events of 1994* (Human Rights Watch), p 256.

2. See e.g., Youssef Ibrahim, 'As Islamic Violence Accelerates, Fears of a Showdown in Algeria,' *New York Times*, 22 February 1995, p. A6.

3. This is a somewhat problematic and controversial term. However, the author greatly prefers it to 'Islamist' which seems to imply that there is something unique to the Muslim religion which captures the essence of such movements. The term 'fundamentalist' puts the phenomenon in the context of similar movements in other religions, which, although each shaped by its specific socio-economic context, share a particular historical moment. For a well-thought-out discussion of definitions of fundamentalism, see Ayesha Imam, 'Women and Fundamentalism,' in *Women Living Under Muslim Laws Dossier*, 11/12/13, p. 13.

4. Interview with woman journalist who asked that her name not be used, conducted by the author at La Maison de la Presse, Algiers, 28 November 1994. Many of the names of women quoted or discussed in this article have been omitted, shortened or changed altogether for reasons of security. This was often done by the author at the direct request of the woman informer and is either clear from the text or has been noted.

5. Interview with woman journalist, La Maison de la Presse, Algiers, 28 November 1994.

6. See F.B., 'USA: Pour la poursuite du dialogue?' *El Watan*, 6 November 1994, p. 3.

7 See 'Deliberate and Arbitrary Killings of Civilians by Armed Political Groups in Algeria: Repression and Violence Must End,' Amnesty International, October 1994, AI Index: MDE 28/08/94. See also, National Human Rights Observatory, 'Attentats contre les personnes,' Table containing a partial listing of women killed, raped and attacked between October 1992 and March 1994. The National Human Rights Observatory

was originally founded by the Algerian government but has proved to be independent, objective and dedicated in its human rights work. Twelve of its 42 board members are selected by nongovernmental human rights organizations. See also, Selim Ghazi, 'Terrorisme: ces femmes qu'on assassine,' *El Watan*, 8 March 1994, p. 1.

8. The targeting of women was one prong of the fundamentalist armed groups' strategy, a strategy which included the deliberate targeting of intellectuals, journalists, teachers, athletes, musicians, writers, professors, lawyers and other civilians of both genders. See Flora Lewis, 'The War on Arab Intellectuals,' *New York Times*, 7 September 1993, p. A15.

9. Interview conducted by the author with Naziha X (pseudonym), Algerian woman journalist at La Maison de la Presse, Algiers, 27 November 1994.

10. While only a few of the attacks on Algerian women have received press coverage in the United States, the phenomenon has filled the Algerian press. See, e.g., Algerian Press Service, 'Terrorisme: vingt-cinq femmes assassinées,' *El Watan*, 7 March 1994, p. 1; Mahfoud Bennoune, 'Comment l'intégrisme a produit un terrorisme sans précédent,' *El Watan*, 6 November 1994, p. 7; Ahmed Ancer, 'Journée internationale de la femme: 8 mars de deuil,' *El Watan*, 8 March 1994, p. 1.

11. For all these cases, see National Human Rights Observatory, 'Attentats contre les personnes,' *op. cit.*

12. Ouessila Si Saber, 'Birtouta: la mère des deux filles a été retrouvée: de nouveau l'horreur', *Le Matin*, 27 November 1994, p. 1.

13. For example, compare, Karima Bennoune, 'Algerian Women Confront Fundamentalism,' *Monthly Review*, September 1994, and Karima Bennoune, 'The Struggles of Algerian Women in 1995: To Be or Not To Be,' in *Newsletter of the Association for Research on Algerian Women and Cultural Change (ARAWOC)*, Winter 1995, No. 1.

14. See Salim Ghazi, Boudouaou, 'Deux lycéennes assassinées,' *El Watan*, 31 March 1994, p. 1. See also, Youssef Ibrahim, 'Bareheaded, Women Slain in Algiers: Killings Follow Islamic Threat,' *New York Times*, 31 March 1994, p. A3.

15. See 'Algeria: Amnesty International Concerned by Growing Number of Killings,' Amnesty International, AI Index: MDE 28/WU 02/1994, News Service 57/94.

16. Howard LaFranchi, 'Algerian Women Wary as President Renews Dialogue With Islamists,' *Christian Science Monitor*, 13 April 1994.

17. Interview with Professor Fatiha X (pseudonym), conducted by the author in Amman, Jordan at the Arab Regional Preparatory Meeting for the Beijing International Conference on Women, 6 November 1994. Professor Fatiha stressed that women are still teaching at the University of Blida despite the tremendous risks and constant threats.

18. Interview conducted by the author with Professors Fatiha X and Zohra X in Amman, Jordan, 5 November 1994.

19. Fatima B, 'Perspective on Human Rights: Wearing the Veil, Under Penalty of Death; In their Quest to Root Out 'Western Corruption' Islamic Fundamentalists Declare Open Season On Algerian Women,' *Los Angeles Times*, 1 April 1994, p. 7. Fatima B. is the pseudonym of a 22-year-old Algerian woman. The article was translated into English by the French Committee for Intellectuals.

20. For example, Z'hor Meziane, director of Si El Haoues primary school in Birkhadem, a suburb of Algiers, was shot and killed inside her school on 27 February 1994. Ms Meziane, who was married and had three children, was a veteran of the war of national liberation and a practicing Muslim. She had been a teacher for 20 years and had served as school principal since 1980. Prior to the attack, she had received death threats. See Hassane El-Cheikh, 'Terrorisme, une directrice assassinée: le corps enseignant visé,' *L'Hebdo Libere*, reprinted in Rassemblement Algérien des Femmes Democrates (RAFD), *Pour une Algérie debout*.

21. See 'Militants Suspected of Killing Feminist,' *New York Times*, 16 February 1995, p. A7.

22. A 60-year-old woman fortune teller was raped and had her throat cut in Kherrouba near Boumerdes on 15 December 1993. See Ghazi, 'Terrorisme: ces femmes qu'on assassine,' *op. cit.*, p. 1. A 38-year-old woman from Berrouaghia who ran a small business as a herbalist reported that she had received a letter containing death threats and accusing her of witchcraft. 'Fiche de Synthèse de Zohra X,' October 1994, ONDH.

23. See, e.g., National Human Rights Observatory, 'Fiche de Synthèse, Affidavit of Zohra A., 38 years old and a widow.' Complaint from 10/94.

24. See Bennoune, 'Algerian Women Confront Fundamentalism,' *op. cit.*, p. 28.

25. Comment from Ouessila Si Saber after attending the exhumation of the body of the mother from Birtouta, described above.

26. Amel Boumedienne, 'Quand les femmes sont un butin de guerre: le martyre de Kheira,' *El Watan*, reprinted in *Le Nouvel Observateur*, No. 1576, p. 30.

27. See National Observatory of Human Rights, 'Attentats contre les personnes,' *op. cit.* See also, Ghazi, 'Terrorisme: ces femmes qu'on assassine,' *op. cit.*, p. 1.

28. See 'Attentats Contre les Personnes,' *op. cit.*, which among other atrocities, details the rapes of a 60-year-old fortune teller named Zohra Semmir in December 1993 in Kherouba and two 17-year-old girls, identified only as Fadhila and Fatma B, on 5 December 1993 in Relizane. The rape of Fadhila and Fatma is also discussed in Ghazi, 'Terrorisme: ces femmes qu'on assassine,' *op. cit.*, p. 1.

29. See 'Le Martyre de Kheira', p. 31.

30. National Human Rights Observatory, 'Fiche de Synthèse,' 26 October 1994, on file with author.

31. Zazi Sadou, 'Les ravages de l'intégrisme: le martyre des femmes violées,' *El Watan*, 24 January 1995, p. 3.

32. *Ibid.*, p. 1.

33. This is exactly the condition described by a young woman participating in the large 22 March 1994 anti-fundamentalist demonstrations in Algiers. She was quoted as saying, 'There's a national psychosis.' 'Algeria: Terror at Large,' *The Economist*, 26 March 1994, p. 46.

34. Most recently, on 21 March 1995, television journalist Rachida Hammadi, 32, was seriously injured by gunmen when leaving her parents' home. Her sister Meriam, 36, was killed when she tried to protect Rachida by throwing herself in front to shield her. See Nora Boustany, 'Journalism: Algeria's Fatal Profession,' *Washington Post*, 23 March 1995.

35. Interview conducted at La Maison de la Presse, 28 November 1994, Algiers with Nabila X.

36. See Human Rights Watch, *op. cit.*, p. 257.

37. This threat was shown to author in February 1994. See Bennoune, 'Algerian Women Confront Fundamentalism,' *op. cit.*, p. 28.

38. Interview with Sadia X, Algiers, February 1994.

39. Affidavit, 'Menaces de mort,' document from the National Observatory of Human Rights, on file with the author.

40. Fiche de Synthèse, 'Menace de mort,' on file with the National Human Rights Observatory in Algiers, Algeria. Affidavit taken on 16 May 1994.

41. Interview conducted by the author in La Maison de la Presse, Algiers, 28 November 1994.

42. Sadou, *op. cit.*, p. 3.

43. For more background, see generally Karima Bennoune, 'Between Betrayal and Betrayal: Fundamentalism, Family Law and Feminist Struggle in Algeria,' *Arab Studies Quarterly*, Winter 1995.

44. See Aicha Lemsine, 'Women in Algeria: Stake or Alibi' (Part II), *Friends of Algeria*, 1, 3 (1993), p. 1.

45. See Miriam Shahin, 'Algerian Women fight Terror,' *The Jordan Times*, 13 November 1994, p. 1.

46. See generally 'Comité National Contre la Torture,' *Cahier Noir*, (October 1989) and *Abed Charef*, (October 1989).

47. Cited in Nora Boustany, 'Muslim Right Presses for Battle in Algeria,' *Washington Post*, 5 January 1993, p. A12.

48. The author does not mean by including this statement to condone the military intervention which halted the elections in 1992. However, it is important to listen to divergent perspectives on the impact of this event on many Algerian women.

49. On this incident see, 'Des 'Justicier' aux portes de la cité,' *Alger Républicain*, 1 January 1991, p. 1.

50. See 'Existe-t-il des milices islamiques à Blida?,' *Algérie Actualité*, 12–18 April 1990.

51. *Ibid.*

52. 'Papers from the Algerian Women's Movement,' in *Women Living Under Muslim Laws Dossier*, 11/12/13 (May 1993), p. 22.

53. See, e.g., 'Sports for Women: Banned at Tiaret University,' *Alger Republicain*, January 1990, reprinted in *Women Living Under Muslim Laws Dossier, op. cit.*, p. 27. This article details how a 19-year-old student and member of the national judo team was physically assaulted and thrown out of the university's sports hall when she attempted to continue training despite the ban imposed on women's sports. When the male president of the sporting association attempted to assist her, he too was assaulted.

54. Open Letter from the students of the Polytechnical School of Architecture and Urbanism, printed in *AITDF Bulletin*, reprinted in *Women Living Under Muslim Laws Dossier, op. cit.*, p. 22.

55. 'Intolerable Pressure,' Independent Association for the Triumph of Women's Rights, press release, reprinted in *Women Living Under Muslim Laws Dossier, op. cit.*, p. 27.

56. See Bou-Saada, 'Cinq veuves et leurs enfants violemment agressés a l'heure du f'tour,' *Horizons*, 11 April 1990.

57. Zenati, 'En Algérie, le débat sur la mixité tourne au dialogue de sourds,' *Agence France Presse*, 27 August 1989, reprinted in M. Al-Ahnaf *et al.*, *L'Algérie par ses islamistes* (1991), p. 253.

58. *Horizon*, 22 November 1989, Reprinted in *Women Living Under Muslim Laws Dossier, op. cit.*, p. 29.

59. Interview conducted by the author with Algerian woman journalist, La Maison de la Presse, Algiers, 28 November 1994.

60. Interview with Zohra X, *op. cit.*

61. See 'What the FIS is Saying,' *GET NEWspaper*, 14–20 December 1989, reprinted in *Women Living Under Muslim Laws Dossier, op. cit.*, p. 28.

62. H. Zerrouky, 'Femmes: l'edito,' *Le Matin*, August 1994, reprinted in RAFD, *Pour une Algérie debout*. The particular impact of misogyny in education to which Zerrouky refers was magnified by the large numbers of fundamentalist teachers. Many of these were immigrants from Egypt whom Nasser was trying to get rid of by exporting them to Algeria, which lacked Arabic-speaking teachers after independence given the impact of French cultural imperialism. During the 1980s, the Algerian press reported that some fundamentalist teachers were asking school children about their parents' activities and telling them that their parents were going to hell because their mother appeared in a bathing suit at the beach.

63. A grenade was thrown into the June 1994 demonstration of the MPR (Mouvement Pour la République), killing two people and injuring many others, including feminist organizer Khalida Messaoudi, President of the Independent Association for the Triumph of Women's Rights. Professors Fatiha and Zohra stressed to me that this demonstration had

continued after the grenade attack, largely at the insistence of women participants. However, the attack has somewhat chilled the atmosphere for demonstrations.

64. On women's demonstrations, see also, LaFranchi, *op. cit.*, p. 5. Popular demonstrations against the violence have been frequent despite the associated risks. Some of these have clearly been government-organized, while others appear to be the spontaneous response to various atrocities. See, e.g., 'Marches populaires: le défi au terrorisme,' *El Watan*, 9 November 1994, p. 3.

65. Interview with Fatiha X, *op. cit.*

66. Fatima B., *op. cit.*, p. 7.

67. On Islamic humanitarian law, which includes prohibitions on the killings of women, children and other non-combatants during war, see Karima Bennoune, 'As-Salaamu 'Alaykum: Humanitarian Law in Islamic Jurisprudence,' *Michigan Journal of International Law*, 15, 2, p. 605.

68. Shahin, 'Algerian Women fight Terror,' *op. cit.*, p. 1.

69. 'Update on the Crisis in Algeria,' printed in *Middle East Policy* (sometime between April 1994 and September–November 1994), pp. 188–9.

70. *Ibid.*, p. 189.

71. Ibrahim, 'As Islamic Violence Accelerates, Fears of a Showdown in Algeria,' *op. cit.*, p. A1.

72. Originally published in the London-based Arabic language newspaper, *Al Hayat*, the statement was reprinted by Youssef Ibrahim, 'Islamic Rebels Say They Set Off Bomb in Algiers,' *New York Times*, 6 February 1995, p. A5.

73. Ibrahim, 'As Islamic Violence Accelerates, Fears of a Showdown in Algeria,' *op. cit.*, p. A1.

74. Interview with Zohra X, *op. cit.*

75. Interview with Fatiha X, *op. cit.*

76. Declaration of the Participants in the Arab Regional Preparatory Conference for the Beijing Conference on Women, Amman, Jordan, 3–10 November 1994.

12

Women's Human Rights
on Trial in Jordan:
The Triumph of Toujan al-Faisal

Nancy Gallagher

During Jordan's 1989 parliamentary elections, two Islamists asked an Islamic court to bring a parliamentary candidate to trial for the crime of apostasy from Islam. The case is important because it throws into relief some of the major issues in the women's human rights movement in Jordan and the wider Middle East. Islamists and non-Islamists hold widely differing views on the proper roles and status of women in public life, but all parties claim to speak on behalf of human rights. For most Islamists, also called 'fundamentalists,' human rights derive from Islamic law, based on the Qur'an and other sources. In Jordan they are embodied in the laws of personal status governing marriage, divorce, child custody, alimony, and inheritance. For most non-Islamists human rights in Jordan are based on its Constitution of 1946, the United Nations Charter of 1946, and the United Nations Universal Declaration of Human Rights of 1948 to which Jordan is a signatory. Article 6: 22–23 of Jordan's Constitution gives considerable authority to the king, but grants women 'political, economic, and social equality.'[1] The United Nations Charter in its preamble reaffirms 'faith in fundamental human rights, in the dignity and worth of the human person, in the equal rights of men and women and of nations large and small.'[2] Article 2 of the Universal Declaration of Human Rights states that 'Everyone is entitled to all the rights and freedoms set forth in this Declaration, without distinction of any kind, such as race, color, sex, language, religion.'[3] Fatima Mernissi, the noted Moroccan sociologist has already noted the contradiction:

> When we speak about the conflict between Islam and democracy, we are in fact talking about an eminently legal conflict. If the basic reference for Islam is the Qur'an, for democracy it is effectively the United

Nations Charter, which is above all a superlaw. The majority of Muslim states have signed this covenant, and thus find themselves ruled by two contradictory laws.[4]

The charge of apostasy, a crime punishable by death (or merely by forced divorce according to some interpretations of Islamic law), was almost unheard of until recent years when Islamists have used it in attempts to silence women's rights activists and others. In 1990, for example, it was used against women drivers in Saudi Arabia, where it carries the death penalty.[5] It has also been used against feminists in Morocco.[6] In Egypt, Islamist lawyers, believed to be allied to the Muslim Brotherhood, unsuccessfully sought a court order to force a professor of French literature at Cairo University to be divorced from her husband, a professor of Arabic known to be critical of Islamist views, or be considered guilty of adultery, since it is illegal for a Muslim to be married to a non-Muslim.[7] The international media have sensationalized certain cases of apostasy or of 'crimes against Islam,' notably that of Salman Rushdie and the Bangladeshi author Taslima Nasrin, and have often rushed to condemn 'Islam' because of them. The Jordanian case demonstrates that the causes are better sought in contemporary political and socio-economic realities.

The legal system in Jordan, as in most Muslim societies, is based on two law codes, civil and Islamic. The Islamic courts administer only laws of personal status pertaining to matters of marriage, divorce, child custody, alimony, and inheritance. Although Jordan does not have an apostasy law, its Islamic courts have considerable latitude in interpreting the personal status laws in their jurisdiction.

The Status of Women in Jordan

Women make up 52 per cent of Jordan's approximately 4 million inhabitants.[8] The legal age of marriage is 15 for girls, and 23 per cent of divorces involve women under 19. Women make up only 11.5 per cent of the salaried labor force (men make up 70 per cent) and most of these are teachers, nurses, and secretaries: unemployment is 34 per cent (for men it is 14 per cent). Informal employment of women in agriculture and other areas is very common.[9]

Polygyny is allowed – men are allowed to marry up to four wives, though few do: more than 90 per cent of marriages are monogamous. It is far easier for a husband to divorce his wife than the reverse; child custody laws also favor the father, and alimony is limited.

Unlike Egypt which had an active feminist movement well before the First World War, Jordan had almost no women's groups until after the Second World War.[10] The first women's organizations were charitable: in 1944, the United Women's Social Organization was founded to help needy children; in 1945, the Organization of United Jordanian Women was established to raise the social status of women.[11] In 1949, these two organizations merged into the government-sponsored Jordanian Women's Hashemite Union, but it was dissolved the same year. In 1955 women received the right to organize and campaign for male candidates in municipal and parliamentary elections, and formed the Organization of Arab Women to organize these activities. They themselves could not vote, however.[12]

In the 1960s, overt opposition to the Jordanian government intensified. Activists were influenced by a series of regional and international conflicts including the Suez Crisis (1956), the Algerian War of Independence (1954–62), the liberation movement against the British in Yemen (1963), the Six Day War (1967), the Dhofar revolution (1971), and, above all, the Palestinian–Israeli struggle which had resulted in the migration of hundreds of thousands of Palestinians to Jordan, until more than half of Jordan's population were immigrants from Palestine. Many were associated with political parties and resistance organizations such as FATAH, the PFLP, the Nasserist forces, the Ba'th, and the Communist Party. Women participated in these political activities, but for nationalist rather than feminist goals.

Following the defeat in 1967 the Jordanian government imposed martial law and overt political activism came to an abrupt end, but new ideas continued to circulate just below the surface.[13] During this era, a few Jordanian women, mostly educated professionals based in the capital Amman, began to distinguish their interests from the nationalist struggles and to organize on behalf of feminist issues such as the right to equal employment. Inspired by feminist activists in the Middle East, especially Egypt, in Europe, and in North America, in 1971 they established the Arab Women Organization, to promote the status of Jordanian women by sponsoring literacy classes, vocational training, women's rights, Palestinian rights, environmental projects, and family planning.[14]

The government responded to the new social activism by giving women additional rights. In 1974, it formed the Women's Federation which immediately called for the right of women to stand for elections in municipal councils and for a say in Jordan's new labor laws. The federation also asked that Jordan adopt Arabic and international conventions calling for the abolition of all forms of discrimination against women.[15] In keeping with its 'controlled state feminist' policy, the government in 1974 promptly changed its Electoral and Municipal Laws and granted women the right to vote in national elections.[16] On 3 December 1980, the Jordanian government signed but did not ratify the United Nations Convention on the Elimination of All Forms of Discrimination against Women (CEDAW).

In the 1980s women in Jordan, many of Palestinian origin and influenced by the Palestinian women's movement, demanded that the government take steps to raise the status of women. In 1981, the Women's Federation was dissolved on the grounds that it was working on issues not covered by its by-laws, and a new organization, the Jordanian Women's Union, was created to replace it.[17] The new organization was placed under the Ministry of Social Development, so many members quit on the grounds that it was controlled by the ministry. In 1982 women received the right to stand for office in national and regional elections.[18] In the mid-1980s a group of university-educated women established the Women's Research Center, an independent group that met regularly at the University of Jordan to study feminist issues. Many also participated in the University Women Graduates' Club, which organized regional seminars and workshops on such topics as child abuse and educational and legal reform.[19]

Legal reform quickly became a *cause célèbre*. Activist women argued that while other aspects of Islamic law, such as the bans on usury and on alcohol, had been abandoned, the personal status laws which disadvantage women had been retained. In 1984, the University Women Graduates Club drew up and presented a petition calling on parliament to reconcile the laws of personal status with the constitution, but parliament did not respond.[20]

Jordan's Economic Crisis

Beginning in 1986, Jordan suffered from economic recession following a reduction in subsidies from the oil-producing countries and remittances sent by Jordanian and Palestinian workers abroad. The foreign debt was one of the highest per capita debts in the world. Between October 1988 and June 1989 the Jordanian dinar was devalued by about 35 per cent. The World Bank and the International Monetary Fund insisted on austerity measures.[21] The economic crisis stimulated new levels of political activism from Islamists and secularists alike.

The Muslim Brotherhood (*Ikhwan al-muslimin*), the largest and most prominent of the Islamist organizations, called for a government and legal system based on Islamic rather than secular law. The Jordanian branch of the organization, which had originated in Egypt in the late 1920s, advocated sex-segregated schools, the banning of alcohol, strictly censored television, job market priority for men over women, and pressure on women to cover their heads. Tahrir (Liberation), an Islamist organization founded by a Palestinian religious leader, called for the re-establishment of a pan-Islamic caliphate.[22] In 1956 the government banned all political parties with the exception of the pro-monarchy Muslim Brotherhood, which was allowed to function in an effort to counterbalance the oppositional Arab nationalist and leftist forces. Tahrir was banned along with other political parties, but it remained informally organized. The Islamists claimed to be upholders of tradition and of religious authenticity and morality, and promised religious and moral solutions to Jordan's growing political, social, and economic problems.

Many women were attracted to the Islamist groups, especially to the Muslim Brotherhood, largely because of its social programs. Some 'Muslim Sisters' formed auxiliary groups and worked for social welfare organizations and medical care facilities.[23] Over time the Muslim Brotherhood tempered its pro-government stance and began to seek power and influence for itself.[24]

At the same time, other political forces also gathered steam, as people began demanding a genuine voice in politics and a more democratic society. They called for universal human rights, individual equality, personal freedom, and legal reform. In April 1989, in response to the economic austerity measures, food riots broke out. In response, King Hussein called for parliamentary elections to be held on 8 November 1989. They were to be the first since the 1967 Six-Day War.[25]

The Jordanian parliament has an upper house whose members (senators) are appointed by the king, and a lower house whose members (deputies) are elected for four-year terms. Parliamentary seats are allocated to Muslims, Christians, Bedouin, Circassians, and Chechens (Circassians and Chechens are Sunni Muslims from the Caucasus region who were settled in and around Amman by the Ottoman government in the late nineteenth century)[26] according to their numerical representation in each of Jordan's five governorates.[27] In 1967 parliament had sixty seats divided between the East and West Banks of Jordan. In 1974 parliament was suspended when the Arab League declared the Palestinian Liberation Organization the sole representative of the Palestinian people. In 1984 parliament was reconvened by royal decree and by-elections were held to fill the seats of the eight members of parliament who had died during the ten-year hiatus.[28] The 1984 by-elections were the first in which women were able to vote, a right that was taken seriously.[29] Shortly before the 1989 elections, the government dissolved parliament. Candidates for the 80 seats in the newly enlarged parliament then registered their names (in 1989 Jordan did not have members of parliament from the West Bank, having renounced its ties to the region).

Twelve women were among the 650 candidates who stood for election to parliament. They were of widely different political persuasions, but none ran on an Islamist platform. With the exception of the Islamic Action Front, the political arm of the Muslim Brotherhood, political parties were illegal in 1989, so candidates for parliament had to run independently, loosely associated with the various groups that substituted for political parties.

At the outset of the electoral campaign, the government dissolved the Women's Union along with all women's organizations linked to politics, and formed a new organization, with new by-laws, that would include women from both urban and rural areas. This new union rapidly expanded its membership from 5,000 to 15,000 during the electoral campaign.[30] Like the earlier groups, the union was carefully controlled by the government, but it contained a substantial grassroots representation.

Perhaps because of this unprecedented opportunity to participate in the national elections, women were very active in the campaign. More women than men registered to vote. Secular women in Western dress attended election rallies and campaigned energetically for their candidates. Islamist women wearing head scarves, children wearing green headbands, and bearded men passed out leaflets.[31] The variety of views could be found in all sectors, but represented in part Jordan's economic and social divisions: the secular candidates tended to represent the more affluent, Westernized sectors and the Islamist candidates the poorer, less-Westernized sectors.

Of a total of about 650 candidates for the 80 seats in the parliament, about 8 per cent represented the Islamist groups, ranging from those who wanted Jordan to be a theocracy to those who wanted Islam merely to shape social values. The Muslim Brothers Islamic Action Front registered their candidates in many districts throughout the city and country. They could not, of course, run candidates for the Christian seats, but they ran Christians who were willing to support them, usually as a way of counteracting leftist candidates.

From the outset, the Islamists eagerly seized the opportunity to expand their political influence and their legislative power. They hoped for a majority in parliament and especially coveted the minister of education portfolio to enforce sex segregation in the schools. They also hoped to strengthen Jordan's laws of personal status. While many candidates opposed the Islamists, one of the women candidates came to embody that opposition.

This candidate, Toujan al-Faisal, was a well-known Jordanian television talk-show host. From a middle-class Circassian background, she majored in English literature at the University of Jordan. In 1971, when Jordanian television announced auditions to choose a host of an Arabic-language cultural program, friends had urged her to apply – more for her ash-blond hair, hazel eyes, and attractive appearance than for her educational background or journalistic experience. She applied and was selected.[32] In her years on television, first on the cultural program, called 'Spotlight,' than as a free-lance reporter, and finally as talk-show host of a program called 'Women's Issues,' she gradually became known for her discussions of controversial topics. In 'Women's Issues,' broadcast in 1988–9, she discussed issues such as women's property ownership, inheritance rights, and domestic violence. Her ideas were shared by some of her viewers, but many others, especially those educated in Islamic schools and living in conservative areas, found them sacrilegious. When she planned a program on the abuses of polygyny, the program directors, under fierce pressure from Islamist forces, refused to broadcast it. In response, in early 1989, she resigned from television.

Faisal was not associated with any political group or a member of the Women's Union, but was a member of the University Women Graduate's Club and had organized, moderated, and participated in its workshops and seminars on legal and educational reform, and had spoken on newly recognized issues such as child abuse.[33]

On 21 September 1989, at the outset of Jordan's electoral campaigns, Faisal published an article entitled 'Yushtimunana wa nantakhibuhum,' (They insult us … and we elect them!!) (see Appendix) in al-Ray (Opinion), a government-owned newspaper with a circulation of about 1,000,000, the largest in Jordan.[34] In it, she criticized the Islamists who subscribed to a well-known hadith that 'woman by nature is deficient in intellect and religion' and who believed that 'women were predictable and guided by their emotions, legal minors who need a male guardian to run their affairs.'[35] She sarcastically remarked that since the Islamists believe that women are limited by their reproductive functions the best women must be those who are not mothers! She complained that they sugarcoat their views on women's deficiencies with euphemisms praising women's femininity and decency, but when women demand their freedom and equal rights they accuse them of wanting to abandon tradition.[36]

A few days after the article appeared, she decided to run for parliament. She registered, paid her 500 dinars, and was officially a candidate.[37] Amman Circassians had two seats, in the Third and Fifth districts; her opponent in the Third district would have been a progressive, so she chose to run in the Fifth in order to run against a Circassian candidate of the Muslim Brothers.[38]

A few days after she announced her candidacy, Nuh al-Qidha, the mufti of the armed forces, sent a Circassian army officer to warn her that 'there was no limit to what they could do to her, so she had better withdraw from the elections.'[39] The Circassian, who had been her classmate at the university, told her that he had delivered the message because he was afraid for her. She ignored the warning. She then received anonymous telephone calls warning her to withdraw.

Three weeks after the publication of her article, two bearded men (beards are commonly worn by Islamist men) knocked at her door. She and her sister, who was her campaign manager, were there answering telephone calls from supporters, most of whom were men and women from the educated middle class of her district. The two men entered and said that some people were *haram* (unlawful or evil in a religious sense) and should not be allowed to write. They then demanded that Faisal apologize for her article and withdraw from the election. If she refused, they said they would take her to court and ask for legal authority to shed her blood. She put a call through to her brother, a lawyer, to ask for help. When he arrived he asked the two men who had sent them, and they replied that they were ready to swear on the Qur'an that they did not know. Faisal commented to me:

> I regret to this day I did not give them the Qur'an. I have it here. I said to them, 'If I stopped you and asked you to take something to such and such an address would you do it?' They said 'No.' I said, 'why, because I am wearing this jeans skirt and short-sleeved shirt?' They said 'Yes.' I said, 'Can anybody come to you in Islamic dress and you obey them? How many Israelis deceived the Palestinians in this way?'[40]

The following day she received a subpoena to appear at the south Amman Islamic court on Tuesday, 17 October 1989. The two plaintiffs were an assistant mufti and a private in Jordan's armed forces. The charge was apostasy from Islam. Jordan, however, has no apostasy law and several Islamic courts, including the one in Wadi Sirr, nearest to Faisal's residence, which handled cases in her district, had refused to accept the case. After a search of several days, the Islamic court in Wihdat, in south Amman, had agreed to hear it.[41]

On 17 October, a *faqih* whom the two plaintiffs had made their *wakil* (legal representative) brought the case before the south Amman *shari'a* court. Neither Faisal nor her husband attended, the presence of the defendant not being required in Jordan, because they did not believe she would be treated fairly. The *qadi* asked the two plaintiffs to present further information at a second session he set for 28 October 1989.[42]

As news of the case spread, other parliamentary candidates, lawyers, intellectuals, members of women's organizations, the Arab University Graduates Club, and members of the Jordan Bar Association rushed to offer their support. Jordan's Amnesty International chapter took up the case. Asma Khader, a prominent Amman lawyer and a member of the Legal Committee for the Arab Organization for Human Rights, lent her support. Zulaykha Abu Risha, a well-known journalist and poet who was herself an outspoken opponent of the Islamists and their frequent target, notified journalists of the 28 October session and urged them to attend.[43] Abu Risha also notified the Women's Research Center, which drew up and circulated petitions addressed to the king, the prime minister, and various candidates in the election. Written in similar terms, the petitions summarized the main lines of the case, expressed the outrage of the signatories, and asked that the recipients take steps to prevent the use of religion to terrorize people.[44] Within a very short time, its members had collected over 700 signatures, a task facilitated by the numerous election rallies at which the petitions could be circulated.

At the hearing, women from the various groups filled the courtroom. Many others stood outside, unable to enter.[45] The plaintiff's lawyer accused Faisal of apostasy, heresy, ridiculing the Qur'an, the *hadith*, and the *shari'a*. He added that 'men of religion had tried to warn her of the danger of her words and had asked her to write an article asking for forgiveness and expressing her repentance, but that she had persisted in her infidelity.' He asked the court 'to declare her an apostate, to divorce her from her husband, to refuse her repentance, to ban her articles, to prevent the media from dealing with her, and to grant permission to spill her blood.' He also asked the court to try her brother, Muhammad al-Faisal, as well, since he had defended her when the two men had first called at her home. The two plaintiffs then signed a document, submitted it to the court and their *wakil* had a copy presented to Faisal's lawyer. The *wakil* then began his statement to the court:

> the accused is Muslim, descended from Muslims and married to a Muslim, and is therefore guilty of apostasy from Islam for having attacked the honor of the Prophet ... no one before her had had the audacity to speak against the Prophet and his religion ... [in her article] she mocked the obligation of a woman to be obedient to her husband, to live with him, and not to leave the house without his permission ... she criticized the *hadith* that stated that 'woman by nature is deficient in intellect and religion,' and she opposed the requirement that a woman have a guardian and that her duty is to cook, clean, and serve the members of her family with maintenance as compensation. She asked for four husbands for one woman.[46]

He continued speaking for two and a half hours and concluded by asking the court to find Faisal guilty of apostasy and to sentence her according to Islamic law.[47]

While the *wakil* was speaking, the *qadi* was busy signing other papers and made no comment. When the *wakil* concluded, the *qadi* announced that this case was the first in the history of the Jordanian judicial system in which a defendant was accused of apostasy and that Jordan had no law of apostasy. He then set another session for 9 November 1989, the day after the elections, to rule on the court's competence to deal with the case.[48] This guaranteed that the case would continue to simmer during the two weeks remaining in the electoral campaign. His agreement to study the question of apostasy when Jordan had no apostasy law suggested his interest in expanding his court's prerogatives and his sympathy with the plaintiffs.

As the plaintiffs were leaving the courtroom, a woman spectator called out to them, 'Why pick on Toujan?' One of the two replied, 'The queen is next,' a reference to King Hussein's American-born wife and presumably her Western ways.[49]

The charge that Faisal had advocated a woman have four husbands caused a sensation, though nowhere had she written such a thing, and she categorically denied having said it.[50] Several people, however, remembered her asking the facetious question, 'If men can have four wives why not women four husbands?' by which she meant to oppose both.[51]

The day after the 28 October hearing, Jordanian newspapers broke the story, and the international media picked it up. Journalists from all over the world rushed to interview Faisal, who suddenly became a celebrity. The plaintiffs, perhaps understanding that international sympathy was generally with Faisal, refused all interviews. Wakalat al-anba' (an Arabic news agency) wired stories throughout the Arab world. The BBC and the Voice of America discussed the case. Newspapers throughout Europe and North America carried articles. The *Christian Science Monitor* television station devoted an entire program to it.

Nearly every Jordanian had an opinion. Some took it as a joke.[52] A few compared it to the Salem witch hunts or the Salman Rushdie case.[53] Some thought it was a warning to women close to the palace known for their secular views that they were 'going too far.'[54] One journalist simply stated that it highlighted the differences between conservatives and women who wanted to play a wider role in public life, and argued that it was a means of 'preserving the Jordanian personality and keeping the country intact, conservative, and not so liberal as Western societies.'[55] One woman obstetrician at the Islamic Hospital in Amman, a member of the Islamic Action Front, commented that Faisal should not have criticized parts of the religion while accepting others because, 'Islam is a whole religion, a guide for all aspects of life and should not be undermined.'[56]

Faisal insisted to the *Jordan Times* (an English-language newspaper with a circulation of about 2,000), that the charges were political rather than religious. She pointed out that they had waited three weeks after the publication of her article, until just before the election, to attack her. She stated that 'I am a Muslim and I say that God is one and Muhammad is the Prophet of God. So they have no ground for their case in Islam, because only God can judge if a person is sincere.'[57] She said they attacked her because she drew on Islamic laws to defend women's rights and had threatened them in their own domain: they wanted to make an example of her and to intimidate those who held opinions different from their own.[58] Ibrahim Muhammad Abu al-Adl, Faisal's husband, told the *Jordan Times* that he was proud of his wife's stand and that 'he was shocked and surprised that there are still people in Jordan who harbor such extremist views in today's civilized world.'[59] Faisal herself admitted that she had underestimated her opposition and had not expected such a reaction.[60]

For the king, the case was a public relations disaster. The elections were intended to project an image of a progressive, democratic Jordan, and here was a case that seemed to suggest the opposite. The two plaintiffs were both from the army, his most loyal institution. When Layla Sharaf, formerly Jordan's minister of information, currently a senator, and long a prominent women's rights advocate, sought to arrange a meeting with Faisal's supporters to discuss the petition, the ramifications of the case, and the political activities of the Islamists in general, the king quickly agreed.[61] Sharaf submitted a list of names and points to be discussed, and, on 1 November, a group of twelve met with King Hussein, Prime Minister Zaid bin Shakr, Crown Prince Hasan, and other ministers and officials.

At a press conference following the meeting, the king warned of extremist tendencies, the 'dark side of democracy,' and called upon voters to 'foil what is being hatched against them.'[62] He warned against those who 'exploit religion for political designs' and urged Jordanians to oppose restricting the potential of half the society and to condemn 'the supercilious attitude toward our mothers, daughters, and sisters.'[63] After the meeting, Prince Hasan asked the *qadi al-quda* (chief justice of Islamic courts) to form a

committee to look into reforming the laws of personal status. The
Women's Research Center lobbied to get women sociologists and
psychologists appointed to the committee, and a woman was eventually named to it.[64]

In the meantime, Faisal continued her campaign. When she
was asked if she thought Islam was the solution to Jordan's problems, 'Islam is the solution' being a common slogan of the Islamic
Action Front and other Islamist groups, she replied that she did
not agree because the slogan came from 'a political party claiming
heavenly power.'[65] She continued to insist that she was not campaigning as a feminist – in the Middle East 'feminist' suggests
pro-Western attitudes – but rather as an advocate of human rights
for men and women alike. She insisted that she was not alienated
from her culture and religion and argued that her Islamist opponents considered her a threat because she was well-versed in the
Qur'an and *sunna* and could answer them 'on their own terms.'[66]

As the campaign heated up, young male Circassians began
attending her political meetings to defend her against possible
violence, but this proved unnecessary. The campaign proceeded
peacefully.[67]

The outcome of the 1989 campaign surprised many: the Islamists won the largest bloc of parliamentary seats. The Islamic Action
Front won 20 seats, and independent Islamists between 10 and 14
seats. The rest were won by leftists, Arab nationalists, reformists,
liberals, Bedouin leaders, former officials, and other independ-
ents.[68] Many government-supported candidates were defeated. In
Faisal's district, the Islamic Action Front's Circassian candidate
won handily. All 12 women candidates lost.

The results were a disappointment for the palace, for secularists,
liberals, and leftists, and for those who hoped to see women elected
to parliament for the first time. They were a resounding success
for the Islamists. Still, according to official figures, only 10 per
cent of the 1.6 million Jordanians eligible to register for the election
actually voted for Islamists, and only 25 per cent of those voted for
the Islamic Action Front, reflecting the splintering of the majority
vote among the numerous independent candidates and the ability
of voters to vote for a bloc or slate of candidates. The number of
votes received by the twelve women candidates was less than one
per cent of the total votes garnered by all candidates. About
555,000 of Jordan's 1.4 million eligible voters actually voted.[69]

On 9 November 1989, the day after the election, the judge
ruled that the Islamic court did not have the competence to decide
her case, but the plaintiffs did not give up. In January 1990, Faisal

received another summons. A court of appeal had agreed to hear the part of the case concerning divorce from her husband because of her apostasy, which was within its competence. This time Faisal simply repeated the *shahada* before the *qadi* signifying that she was a Muslim. She neither rescinded nor apologized for her views. After hearing Faisal's statement, the court found no proof of apostasy and declared her innocent of all charges.[70]

Many Jordanians believed that the king had intervened and that the chief justice of the Islamic courts, under instructions from the palace, simply told the court to put an end to the case. A few weeks later, the plaintiffs, who apparently shared this opinion, complained to parliament, now with an Islamist majority, that the courts were being infiltrated by the palace and asked for a new trial. The parliament discussed the matter but took no further action.[71] In 1993, the plaintiffs' *wakil* sued the first 27 signatories on the first page of the petition for libel. This case is still pending.[72]

Reasons for the Apostasy Case

It was not clear who was behind the original case. Faisal herself believes that Nuh al-Qidha, the *mufti* of the armed forces, was acting on behalf of certain wealthy people in and out of the armed forces who were 'trying to protect and to further their economic interests and political and personal privileges against populist reforms.'[73] She has copies of letters sent by the Muslim Brotherhood to supporters in the army that suggest complicity in the case.[74] However, the spokesman of the Muslim Brotherhood, Ziyad Abu Ghanima, an administrator at the Islamic hospital in Amman, categorically denied any links to the two plaintiffs. He said that the two plaintiffs were good Muslims, that the Muslim Brothers neither agreed nor disagreed with the case, and that it was 'a piece of theatrics which gave a bad image to the Islamist movement,' a 'tempest in a teapot.'[75] He denied that the Muslim Brothers had had any part in the trial, and added that 'the Brothers were not interested in such small cases and that people like Toujan, who caused such hurricanes, served its interests.'[76]

Faisal's accusers were certainly not representative of a unified Islamist viewpoint; many Islamists expressed their reservations about the case. One, a student at the University of Jordan, commented that 'Toujan reacted against the situation here. Our leaders don't understand women's problems.'[77] More than one

Islamist contacted her after the final hearing to apologize: 'God
will not forgive us unless you forgive us.'[78]

Was Faisal an easy target because, as a member of a minority,
she was not in a strong position to fight back? The Circassians are
resented by some Jordanians for their prosperity, their preponder-
ance in elite professions, and their Westernized outlook. Kamal
Abadha, the former editor-in-chief of *Sawt al-Sha'b*, a partially
government-owned newspaper with a circulation of about 20,000,
and a prominent member of Jordan's Circassian community, commented to me in 1992: 'The Muslim Brothers made this case in
order to succeed in the elections and to divide our nation and
chose her because she belonged to a minority group. If she were
of Arab descent they could not do any harm to her.'[79]

On the other hand, few Jordanians mentioned Faisal's Circassian origins. Married to an Arab Jordanian and identifying herself
as a Jordanian, she did not campaign on Circassian issues. Many
Circassians, however, worried that her controversial views made
the entire community suspect and wished she would be more
circumspect.[80] Her Circassian identity may have given her an
insider/outsider status that allowed her to criticize her society from
within and without, but it also may have increased the resentment
which was, in any case, already intense. In short, the 'Circassian
factor' was unspoken but present throughout the electoral
campaign.

Social class also contributed to the dynamics of the case. Faisal
was in both appearance and background different from the majority of Jordanian women and men. Urbane and well-educated, her
world view was very different from those who were not. When she
made statements seemingly critical of their religion, resentment
became part of the popular reaction to the case.

Finally, Faisal did not have the support of a political machine
comparable in any way to that of the Muslim Brothers. She was
by far the most vulnerable of their opponents, and therefore likely
to be their target.

The case damaged Faisal's electoral campaign and perhaps the
wider struggle for women's rights, though Senator Layla Sharaf,
Jordan's most prominent feminist, believes that 'the women's
movement in Jordan was more generally weakened by the lack of
common ground between educated and uneducated women, by
differences in their aspirations, their goals, and their perspectives
on how to deal with the problems of women and how to particip-

ate in women's movements, and by the inclination of women to personalize the struggle.'[81]

While the case may have contributed to the defeat of the women candidates and at least temporarily set back the women's rights movement, it also led to the formation of the Committee on Personal Status Laws following the 1 November 1989 meeting with the king. The committee subsequently prepared a document recommending legal reforms and submitted it to parliament.[82] The document, which advocated reforms relating to rights in the work place, marriage, divorce, inheritance, child custody, nationality, and travel, is still being studied.[83] The government appointed several of the participants in the 1 November meeting to influential government positions.[84]

In early 1992, parliament, by then dominated by the Islamists, abruptly changed a long-standing law held over from Ottoman times which allowed women to inherit equally with men, to *shari'a* law which gives the woman only half the man's share. The new parliament also increased sex segregation in the schools and for a time eliminated 'fathers and daughters' festivities.

On 1 July 1992, the Jordanian government strengthened its commitment to women's human rights with its ratification of the United Nations Convention for the Elimination of All Forms of Discrimination against Women (CEDAW) with reservations on three articles. Women's groups hailed the ratification as a victory and set out to remove the restrictions, which centered on the primacy of the family and women's roles within it. Despite the three reservations, women's groups celebrated the ratification.[85] A few days later, in an apparent effort to strengthen his ties to the Islamists, the king gave Nuh al-Qidhah, *mufti* of the armed forces and presumed instigator of the case against Faisal, an award for meritorious service. The award ceremony was broadcast on Jordanian television, with the *mufti* receiving the award from the king's hand.

In mid-July 1992, Islamist women went to court to challenge the election of the secular Women's Union governing board on the basis of unclear membership and voting requirements. Islamist members of the Women's Union won a decision by Jordan's Supreme Court that abrogated the election of the governing board. That enabled them to elect a new board on which Islamist women predominated.[86] Subsequently, however, the case was appealed and won, and in early 1993 the Women's Union returned to the original leadership.[87] The king then made Nuh al-Qidah, *mufti* of the armed forces, chief justice of Islamic courts. A tug-of-war between Islamists and non-Islamists ensued.

Meanwhile, it seemed Faisal's political career had come to an end. She no longer appeared on television and was unable to find work: she was often informed that she had been hired to teach English literature only to learn later that she had been eliminated for unspecified reasons. Her husband's medical practice failed, and he left Jordan to practice in Libya. Faisal believes that Islamists harassed both his patients and his landlord, forcing his newly launched practice into bankruptcy.[88] Remaining in Amman with their three children, she published weekly articles in non-government newspapers and began writing a book about the case. Her first venture into electoral politics had been eventful but brief.

The 1993 Parliamentary Elections

In summer of 1993, the government announced new parliamentary elections for 8 November. In an attempt to limit the Islamist presence in parliament, it introduced a temporary 'one person, one vote' law in place of the old system of bloc voting. The new electoral system reduced the likelihood of persons voting for a slate of candidates, which would make it less likely for a bloc of Islamists to win.[89] The government also prohibited the use of mosques for political campaigning.

In the spring of 1993, Toujan al-Faisal emerged from her retreat to challenge a minister appointed to oversee women's rights, asking on what basis he claimed the right to represent women.[90] She subsequently surprised many political observers by again declaring her candidacy for parliament. Though political parties were now legal, she ran as an independent, this time in the more progressive Third District. Several of Jordan's newly formed parties had asked her to run as their candidate, but she decided to remain an independent rather than 'win the votes of one party and lose the rest.'[91]

Once again, the seats were enthusiastically contested, but a second Islamist sweep was widely predicted. While her defeat was also predicted, Faisal had learned from her earlier campaign to marshal her supporters, especially female precinct workers. Her family, including her husband, now back from Libya and rebuilding his medical practice, gave indispensable support. She spoke in crowded hotel ballrooms, trade union halls, and neighborhood

living rooms, explaining her platform and stating that she was not
an atheist and did not advocate four husbands for women. She
again campaigned on behalf of universal human rights.[92] Rami
Khuri, a well-known journalist and general manager of al-Kutba
Publishers, commented that 'her public meetings were an extra-
ordinarily refreshing sight [attended by] men and women, old and
young, all income and education brackets, all religions and ethnic
groups, and perhaps most important as an indicator of future
trends, many young, single men and women who came to hear
this intriguing new brand of Arab voice.'[93] When the Islamists
again attacked her for apostasy, she had more time to answer
them and, being more experienced, did so effectively. She was
supported by a wide range of people who voted for her not only
to express their disapproval of the earlier case against her, and
their appreciation of her courage in running again, but even more
to show their support for her political platform and her advocacy
of universal human rights.

In the four years that had elapsed since the Islamists had won
their voting majority in parliament, they had not met the high
expectations of their supporters: while Jordanians were concerned
with unemployment, the Islamic Action Front focused on opposing
the Israeli–Palestinian peace process. Tahrir, despite its high
profile, may have lost support with its refusal to be licensed as a
political party on the grounds that the government was 'un-
Islamic' and henceforth illegitimate.[94] To many people, the Islamists had lost touch with issues of popular concern. Meanwhile
Faisal had remained a symbol of opposition to the Islamist
politicians, and supporters of other social visions, including
moderate, pro-monarchy traditional leaders and businessmen, had
had time to organize.

The Third District candidate of the Islamic Action Front ran
a weak campaign, a second woman candidate was eclipsed by
Faisal in face-to-face debate, and another candidate, the progressive elected in the 1989 elections, lost ground to Faisal in the final
days of the campaign, despite last-minute support from the Islamic
Action Front which hoped to forestall a Faisal victory.[95]

In a major upset, Toujan al-Faisal garnered 1885 votes, substantially more than her opponents (each Amman district contains
only a few thousand voters).[96] She had triumphed over her
adversaries to become the first, and to date the only woman
elected to Jordan's parliament.

Once again Faisal was a celebrity.[97] It was a victory that surprised many political observers who had come to view the Islamist
advance as inexorable. Faisal herself commented that 'all Arab
women feel this is their victory. The hope that women can make
it has spread in the Arab world.'[98]

Shortly after the elections, King Hussein appointed one more
woman to the Senate in addition to Layla Sharaf. A woman was
appointed minister of economics, and another as advisor to the
prime minister for women's development.

In February 1994, Jamal al-Quraysha, a Bedouin notable and
a member of parliament, exploded in anger at Faisal during a
parliamentary committee meeting, cast aspersions on her Circassian origins and threw an ashtray that narrowly missed her. She
asked parliament to remove his immunity so she could sue him,
but parliament refused. Faisal considers physical intimidation to
be a key weapon used by opponents of women's participation in
public life.[99]

Jordanian women have continued to press for women's rights,
even in Islamist groups. In March 1994 Nawal al-Fa'uri became
the first woman elected to the *Shura* (governing council) of the
Islamic Action Front. Toujan al-Faisal called it a 'great break-
through in Islamic society.'[100] Faisal continued to be active in
parliament, forming voting alliances in order to support new
legislation to reform Jordan's laws of personal status.[101]

The Jordanian apostasy case illustrates the key question in the
debate between cultural relativists and advocates of international
human rights: where to look for authority? To the United Nations,
to the Constitution, to the Qur'an, culture, and customs, and if
so, to whose interpretation of the Qur'an, culture, and customs?
Who decides what are a given society's culture and customs? The
government? Local political representatives? Religious leaders?
The wealthy? The poor? Men? Women? Children? Minorities or
majorities? The aged or the young? Intellectuals?

In the apostasy case, the role of the state and 'state feminism'
was clear. In an effort to modernize society and to build support
for the government, the state had opened a carefully controlled
space for women activists; sponsored education for women, encouraged women professionals, politicians, entrepreneurs, and
factory workers; and begun a democratization process in which
women could participate. As a result, a genuine grassroots activism
had emerged. The monarchy functioned as a cultural arbitrator,

weighing in sometimes on one side, sometimes on the other, above all seeking to strengthen its own international and domestic legitimacy. But organizations and grassroots advocates proved to have powers of their own.

The outcome of the case illustrates the intensity of the confrontation between advocates of widely differing views on the status of women in Jordan but also the effectiveness of a public debate and a political process that utilize local and universal legal concepts in resolving that confrontation.

Notes

Acknowledgement. I would like to thank all those who generously gave their time in formal and informal interviews and the scholars who discussed this chapter at various stages: Mahnaz Afkhami, Abla al-Amawi, Kum-Kum Bhavnani, May Seikaly, and the members of the Feminist Focus on the Middle East and Africa. It was funded by the MacArthur Foundation's Program for International Peace and Security and by the Academic Senate of the University of California, Santa Barbara. The views expressed are entirely my own.

1. Linda L. Layne, *Home and Homeland: The Dialogics of Tribal and National Identities in Jordan* (Princeton: Princeton University Press, 1994), p. 124, note 8.

2. *Yearbook of the United Nations,* vol. 46 (Dordrecht: Martinus Nighoff, 1992), p. 1187.

3. *Yearbook of the United Nations* (New York: Columbia University Press, 1948–9), p. 535.

4. Fatima Mernissi, *Islam and Democracy: Fear of the Modern World* (Reading, Mass.: Addison-Wesley Publishing Company, 1992), p. 60.

5. Judith Caesar, *Christian Science Monitor,* 4 January 1991, p. 18.

6. Abraham Serfaty, 'For Another Kind of Morocco,' *Middle East Report* (November–December 1992), p. 27.

7. Deborah Pugh, *Christian Science Monitor,* 24 June 1993.

8. 'Jordanian Women: Achievements and Challenges,' Brochure of The Arab Women Organization of Jordan, P.O. Box 6864, Amman, Jordan; Kamal Salibi, *The Modern History of Jordan* (London: I.B. Tauris & Co., 1993), p. 3.

9. *Ibid.*

10. *Ibid.*

11. *al-Ufuq* (The Horizon) (15 July 1992), pp. 37–9.

12. For an extended discussion see Suhayr Salti al-Tall, *Muqadamat hawl qadhiyyat al-mara't wa al-harakat an-nisa'iyyat fi al-urdunn* (Introduction to the woman's question and the women's movement in Jordan) (Amman: Foundation for Arab Studies and Publication, 1985).

13. Salibi, *op. cit.*, pp. 197–242.

14. Brochure of the Arab Women Organization, *op. cit.*

15. *al-Ufuq*, *op. cit.*, pp. 37–9

16. Linda L. Layne, *Home and Homeland: The Dialogics of Tribal and National Identities in Jordan* (Princeton: Princeton University Press, 1994), p. 124, note 8.

17. *al-Ufuq*, *op. cit.*, p. 37.

18. Layne, *op. cit.*, p. 124.

19. Arwa al-Amiri interview, 15 July 1992, Amman.

20. Toujan al-Faisal interview, 15 July, 1992, Amman.

21. Abla Amawi, 'Democracy Dilemmas in Jordan,' *Middle East Report* January–February 1992, pp. 26–7; p. 29, note 4.

22. Salibi, *op. cit.*, p. 175.

23. Interview with Hani Hourani, 24 July 1992, Amman.

24. Salibi, *op. cit.*, p. 175.

25. For detailed accounts of the 1989 elections, see Milton Viorst, 'A Reporter at Large: The House of Hashem,' in *The New Yorker*, 7 January 1991, pp. 32–54; and Abla Amawi, 'Democracy Dilemmas in Jordan,' *Middle East Report*, January–February 1992, pp. 26–9.

26. For further information see Seteney Shami, '19th Century Circassian Settlements in Jordan,' *Studies in the History and Archaeology of Jordan*, vol. 4 (Amman: Department of Antiquities in cooperation with Maison de l'Orient Méditerranéen, 1992), pp. 417–18.

27. The entire plebiscite within each governorate could vote for candidates running for each of the reserved parliamentary seats (Layne, *op. cit.*, pp. 110–11).

28. The six vacant seats from the West Bank were filled by internal election (Layne, *op. cit.*, p. 111.)

29. Linda L. Layne, 'Tribesmen as Citizens: "Primordial Ties" and Democracy in Rural Jordan,' in Linda L. Layne (ed.), *Elections in the Middle East: Implications of Recent Trends* (Boulder: Westview Press, 1987), pp. 132–3.

30. *al-Ufuq*, *op. cit.*, pp. 37–9.

31. *Middle East International* (17 November 1989), p. 3.

32. Toujan al-Faisal interview, 15 July 1992.

33. *Zawaya*, 1, 4 (Paris: Société arabe de presse et d'éditions, March–April 1990), p. 21.

34. *al-Ray*, 21 September 1989.

35. *Ibid.*

36. *Ibid.*

37. Toujan al-Faisal interview, 15 July 1992.

38. *Ibid.*
39. *Ibid.*
40. *Ibid.*
41. *Ibid.*
42. Petition of 24 October 1989 to King Hussein, personal papers, Zulaykha Abu Risha.
43. Interview with Zulaykha Abu Risha, 14 July 1992.
44. Personal papers, Zulaykha Abu Risha.
45. *Jordan Times,* 30 October 1989.
46. Court record published in *al-Ray,* 29 October 1989.
47. *Ibid.; al-Watan,* 29 (1989); *Jordan Times,* 30 October 1989.
48. Court record, published in *al-Ray,* 29 October 1989, and reporter's handwritten transcript of case and notes in the personal archives of Zulaykha Abu Risha.
49. Toujan al-Faisal interview, 15 July 1992.
50. *Ibid.*
51. Informal recollections from Kamal Abadha, Abla Amawi, and Layla Sharaf, 1992–1993.
52. *al-Ray,* 29 October 1989.
53. *Jordan Times,* 30 October 1989.
54. *al-Ray,* 29 October 1989; *Jordan Times,* 30 October 1989; *Christian Science Monitor,* 2 November 1989.
55. *al-Watan* (The Nation), 29 October 1989.
56. Interview with Najat Bseiso, 18 July 1992, Amman.
57. *Jordan Times,* 30 October 1989.
58. *Ibid.; Zawaya* (March–April 1990), pp. 18–20.
59. *Jordan Times,* 30 October 1989.
60. Toujan al-Faisal interview, 15 July 1992.
61. Interview with Arwa al-Amiri, Amman, 15 July 1992; interview with Layla Sharaf, Vienna, 19 July 1993.
62. *al-Ray,* 2 November 1989.
63. *Christian Science Monitor,* 2 November 1989.
64. Arwa al-Amiri interview, 15 July 1989.
65. Toujan al-Faisal interview, 15 July 1992.
66. *Ibid.*
67. Interview with Seteney Shami, 23 July 1992, Amman.
68. *Middle East International,* 17 November 1989, p. 3.
69. *Ibid.; Facts on File,* 24 November 1989, p. 882; Hani Hourani interview, 24 July 1992.
70. *Zawaya* (March–April 1990), pp. 18–19.
71. Toujan al-Faisal interview, 15 July 1992.
72. Layla Sharaf interview, 19 July 1993.
73. *Zawaya* (March–April 1990), pp. 20–1; *al-Watan,* 29 October 1989.
74. Toujan al-Faisal, personal communication, 11 September 1994.

75. *Jordan Times,* 30 October 1989; Interview with Ziyad Abu Ghanima, 19 July 1992, Amman.

76. *Ibid.*

77. Informal conversation with students at the University of Jordan, 17 July 1992.

78. Toujan al-Faisal interview, 15 July 1992.

79. Kamal Abadha interview 13 July 1992, Amman.

80. Seteney Shami interview, 23 July 1992.

81. *al-Ufuq,* 15 July 1992, p. 39.

82. Arwa al-Amiri interview, 15 July 1992.

83. Layla Sharaf interview, 19 July 1993.

84. Arwa al-Amiri interview, 15 July 1992.

85. Brochure of the Arab Women Organization.

86. *al-Dustur,* 13 July 1992.

87. Layla Sharaf interview, 19 July 1993.

88. Toujan al-Faisal interview, 15 July 1992.

89. *Middle East International,* 28 August 1993, pp. 11–12.

90. Layla Sharaf interview, 19 July 1992.

91. Toujan al-Faisal interview, 11 September 1994, Washington, DC.

92. *Los Angeles Times,* 9 November 1993.

93. Rami Khuri, *Mideast Mirror,* 23 November 1993 (Lexus-Nexus Inter Press Service).

94. *Middle East International,* 28 August 1993, p. 12.

95. Toujan al-Faisal interview, 11 September 1994.

96. *al-Ray,* 11 November 1993.

97. Articles on al-Faisal's victory appeared in many international newspapers and magazines, including *al-Sayad,* 29 November 1993; *Arabies,* 84 (December 1993); *al-Majalla,* 12–18 December 1993; *al-Mar'a,* 75 (December 1993); *al-Mujtama' al-madani,* 64 (December 1993); and *Zahrat al-khalij,* December, 1993; *The New York Times,* 9 November 1993 ; *Los Angeles Times* 10 November 1993.

98. *The Washington Post,* 4 February 1994.

99. Toujan al-Faisal, 'Intimidation and Political Participation of Women in the Arab World,' paper delivered at the conference on 'Religion, Culture, and Women's Human Rights in the Muslim World,' sponsored by the Sisterhood is Global Institute and the Center for the Global South, Washington, DC, 10 September 1994.

100. Lexus-Nexus Inter Press Service, 30 March 1994.

101. Toujan al-Faisal interview, 11 September 1994.

Appendix

'They Insult Us ... and We Elect Them!!'*

Toujan al-Faisal

Although we have seen the Rayya wa Sukaynah drama scores of times, we still laugh every time Suhayl al-Babili utters her famous phrase: 'Are we to remain silent while they hang us?' If we ask ourselves why we laugh at this sentence in particular, we find that the secret lies in its twisted logic. In the blatant contradiction between the two parts of this sentence, and in the ridiculing of the mind by even mentioning it. At the same time, we laugh because this illogical idea actually exists and is practiced in many forms under the cover of all kinds of repression and tyranny.

I recall Suhayl al-Babili's sentence every day when I read the many articles in our newspapers describing a woman as being deficient and lacking in religion, that she is rash and is guided by her emotions, that she is a minor all her life and needs a male guardian to run her affairs and keep her on the straight path, that she is so retarded as to be only capable of doing servant's work (correct me if the servant's duties are not confined to cleaning the house, cooking, and serving the other members of the family). In return for these services, a woman's remunerations will only be that she is fed, given shelter and dressed. It is permissible to beat her if she disobeys her master's instructions. This group of writers unanimously agrees that beating a woman does not hurt her dignity. This is impossible unless the woman is born without any dignity. This is something which does not surprise us from the writers of these articles because they believe that woman was actually born deficient, although God has created the human being in the best of images. Woman's deficiency lies in the fact that she becomes pregnant, gives birth and menstruates. This clearly means that motherhood is the cause of her deficiency!

---

* Translation of the article published in *al-Ray*, 21 September 1989.

In the midst of their vacillations between their claims to knowledge and logic and their adherence to metaphysical concepts and axioms which no logic or reason can accept, these writers have forgotten to tell us whether we should deduce from all this that the barren woman is more complete than the one that is fertile, and whether women who do not menstruate are more complete than the other women.

It goes without saying that holding an argument with these people is futile because their twisted logic will only lead us to byzantine arguments. However, we must draw attention to the duality of the expressions they use and the extent of scorn, which is coupled with slander, to which they resort believing that this is some kind of smartness and cleverness on their part. Some explicitly ridicule the woman who is imprisoned in the house and who has no contact with the outside world because she did not excel in science, politics, and the arts over the past centuries in the same manner that the man excelled – he who has had the chance to be educated, to work, to wage war, and to acquire experience. They try to avoid comparison with those women who have had the same opportunities as men. By doing this, they treat their women unjustly, then ridicule the results of this injustice. This is the group that is not ashamed to tear out one of the eyes of their fellow human beings, and then call him: You the one-eyed.

Others who think that they are cleverer and shrewder try to be polite, by deliberately replacing the words 'deficient, lacking in religion, stupid, lacking in creativity, subservient, incapable, and possessing a physical make-up prepared for menial services' by euphemisms like 'woman's sacred role in taking care of the home and raising future generations,' 'the dominance of the emotions of mercy, love and motherhood,' 'Delicacy and femininity,' and 'respect, chastity and decency.' Because of their fear that these attractive words might not avail, and that a woman might not be deceived by these bright covers, and because of their fear that she might demand her freedom, dignity, and all the rights of the fully competent human being, the same article contains other phrases aimed at intimidating her by the use of slander such as 'the wish to abandon traditions,' 'indifference,' 'wearing transparent or see-through clothes,' 'the turning of woman into a commodity,' 'for fear of wolves,' 'the desire to be left alone with man,' and 'when a man and a woman meet, the devil is the third party to be present,' … and other phrases, which any sane person would agree reflect a sick mentality and sinister intentions on the part of their writer. Such phrases do not reflect the living reality experienced by thousands of women who have gone to work, studied, succeeded, and were also prominent.

The best test to reveal the degree of truth in the alleged respect of those men for the woman, who is to be satisfied with the conditions they have consecrated over the centuries, is to ask them: if the woman's position represents the highest degree of respect, dignity and honor, then what do you say to changing positions? Here we will see and hear all types of condemnation, ridicule and anger which are consistent with the tone of the 'gentleman' they assume.

This is a brief summary of what is being written on the pages of our papers. This is not only a woman's affair; it is a national, political, economic and social issue which concerns us all – men and women – especially since what is taking place is part of the current election process, which we expect will define the image of the Jordanian community for many years to come. Above all, the issue is also a human one which cannot be disregarded anywhere and at any time. The issue can be summarized in the following points:

1. Anyone who believes in the superiority of one group of people over another because of any congenital differences outside the framework of what is scientifically accepted to be a physical or mental disability, such as differences in race or color, is surely a believer in racial discrimination and in all the human practice it entails. Let no one think that this discrimination is confined to woman alone or to people with black, yellow, or red skin. Racial discrimination has more than one thousand colors. It was practised even among whites in Europe under the name of classes and to such an extent that the sons of the upper classes in the Middle Ages claimed that the blood which ran in their veins was different from that of the impoverished classes. That is why they were called 'blue-blooded.'

2. That someone claims his opinion is the only plausible one and his judgement is the only one that should be applied – not because of his superiority in rational debate but because he claims that everything he says enjoys divine support and all his opponents are atheists – heralds ideological dictatorships based

on the concept of priesthood; that is, the existence of mediators between God and man. These dictatorships give themselves the right to practice oppression and terrorism – to the extent of physical liquidation – against all their opponents. This is what happened when the church ruled Europe during the so-called 'dark ages,' and this is what has been happening in Iran since Khomeini came to power. This is also what is implied by the use of the term 'apostate' and that immunity should be given to anybody who sheds the apostate's blood – the expression that we repeatedly hear.

3. Saying that the woman's right to work, and consequently to financial earning, should be confined to a certain category of mankind, and that the other category has to depend on the generosity of the first for its living – in return, of course, for household and personal services that enable the first category to make the earnings – is a call for economic monopoly, entrenchment of capital influence, exploitation of cheap labor, and rejection of honorable competition in learning and work. With the passage of time, this leads to the emergence of a group possessing everything and having the upper hand, and another possessing nothing or very little and living on the charity of the first. If such a situation is accepted and entrenched in any society as a principle for coexistence, then it cannot be confined to the relationship between men and women; it will definitely apply to the relationship between those who possess and those who do not.

4. Saying that the woman's right to her husband's money in return for the services she provides – which in the scale of labor are considered menial jobs – is only to have food, clothes, and accommodation is nothing but acknowledgement of a principle much worse than merely the exploitation of cheap labor; it is the principle of slavery. Only slaves work in return for food and clothes, deprived of the right to use their time and effort in what may secure them a better future. What can we expect from people with such mentality when they deal with issues of labor, at a time when unemployment prevails and one is obliged to make many concessions in order to find one's butter and bread?

5. Applying or accepting the principle of controlling others in an oppressive manner, whether due to physical or moral weakness; curbing freedom of movement for others in a way similar to

house arrest; expulsion from the house, threatening one's security and independence in one's house; and depriving one of one's right to live the rest of one's life with one's children, mean explicit acceptance of the principle of colonialism. Those who do this, therefore, cannot be trusted to be in positions involving political, national, or militant decisions. Rejection of oppression, injustice, and confiscation of liberties is a firm principle; it cannot vary depending on who does injustice to whom and who oppresses whom. Those who do injustice to others cannot raise the banner of liberation; this is not in their favor because they know that all liberation movements are linked to each other whether the other person is an Arab, a Negro, a Vietnamese, or a woman of any color or race.

6. A woman is a member of the man's household. She is either his mother, daughter, sister or wife. Whoever is not entrusted with these people's rights and dignity cannot be entrusted with the rest of her family, and whoever is not entrusted with the members of her household and her family cannot be entrusted with the sons of her homeland.

The parliamentary seats and all seats of decision making and authority are ones of trust befitting only whoever defends right, away from any personal or sectarian gain and regardless of any personal or factional loss.

These are some of the logical inferences which impose themselves upon us when reviewing whatever is written in our newspapers. Although most of what is written is amusing, we view it as seriously as we view comic works of intentional or unintentional social, political, and economic significance. Can anything but a comical play present – within an election campaign carrying all the concerns and hopes of the homeland and calling for all hands to support its young edifice – an election program based on cursing the group that constitutes the majority of voters, promising them all menial positions, consecrating all kinds of sexual rights, including the right of being rewarded by God upon the completion of religion?

Could such a program succeed? The answer lies with women.

If the woman accepts this program and votes for its candidates, she will then really be lacking in mind and religion. These candidates are more acquainted than us with most women. As Spengler has said, there is no dictator who imposes himself on his nation, but these are nations of slaves which make their dictator.

However, if women use their tremendous influence that is not dominated by anyone – thanks to God and the constitution – to pull the rug from under the feet of this group, and pull the seats from under those gentlemen who are leading a luxurious life each served by four women, this would mean that women's silence over this slander and disparagement was neither a sign of satisfaction nor a sign of mental weakness or retardation. It is only the silence of all oppressed human groups until the moment of action comes, in accordance with a poet's saying that 'firmness was born dumb.' Only here all that was published becomes in agreement with the constructive role of the press and becomes worth the time spent in reading it. Only here can all of us – men and women – laugh at all utterances that absent the mind and logic and consecrate all forms of coercion and despotism, and we say to those making these utterances: 'You curse us ... and we elect you!!!'

Index

al-Nasafi, Imam Abdullah, 70, 71
al-Na'sani, Shaykh Badr al-Din, 68
Nasrin, Taslima, 76, 210
nationalism, 21, 43, 54, 82
nationality, rights of, 224
nature, laws of, 9, 105, 119, 128, 146
neocolonialism, 198
networking, role of, 78–103
Nigeria, 86
Nile, irregularities of, 41
Norway, 117
al-Nusufi, 65

oil, 43, 44
Oman, 118
Oran, University of, 195
Organization of Arab Women, 211
Organization of United Jordanian
   Women, 211
oriental despot, concept of, 34, 35
Orpha, Queen, 63
orphans, support for, 180, 181
Ouarda, 189

Pakistan, 1, 8, 10, 22, 24, 84, 85, 87–91,
   98, 117, 127, 161–74, 176, 177, 179, 200
Pakistan People's Party (PPP), 10, 161,
   162, 165
Palestine Liberation Organization, 214
Palestinian women, 212
Parris, Mark, 200
patriarchy, 3, 5, 6–9, 21, 97, 98, 106, 107,
   175, 180; justification of, 79; make-up
   of, 78 personal status laws, 22, 26, 81,
   106, 108, 112, 113, 114, 118, 209, 210,
   212, 220, 224, 227
Philippines, 84
polygamy, 109, 113, 114, 210, 215
population conference, Vatican position
   on, 123–6
population growth, 44, 45
post-modernism, 27–30
poverty, 19, 24; of women, 178
professionals, Algerian: exodus of, 191;
   harassment of, 195
prostitution, 179, 180
public women, 197
purdah, 1, 177

qadis, 37, 40, 217, 218, 220
al-Qidha, Nuh, 216, 222, 224, 225

Qur'an, 37, 38, 52, 58, 65, 67, 69, 73, 107,
   115, 137, 142, 143, 152, 209, 217, 218,
   227; literal interpretation of, 138;
   stance on women, 8
al-Quraysha, Jamal, 227

Rabah, B., 192
racism, 33, 104, 234
Radia, Sultana, 63
Rai music: campaign against, 201;
   defence of, 200
Ramadhan, 153
rape, 161–74, 175, 185, 188–90, 193, 197,
   198; as act of war, 11; as revenge, 170;
   of Afghan women, 178; political, 10;
   stigma of, 179
al-Rashid, Harun, 36
Razi, Najat, 113
Reagan, Ronald, 121, 122
Redeemers, group, 195
refugee women, 11, 153, 154; Afghan, 11,
   176–81; Muslim, 175–83
religion, 40, 91, 193; and secularism, 51–
   60; and women, 91; appeal to, 8, 127;
   as source of women's oppression, 90;
   use of, 218 (in politics, 80); women's
   relationship with, 95
repatriation, 179, 180
Republican Party (US), 122, 123, 126
repudiation of wives, 85, 113
returnee women, 175–83
right wing politics see conservatism
rights, human, 6, 8, 114, 144, 154, 209,
   226 (activism, 139; universality of, 137)
rights of women, 2, 5, 8, 9, 19, 23, 26,
   27–30, 51, 53, 55, 56, 57, 59, 93, 139,
   142, 145, 148, 211, 212; as human
   rights, 154; defined in Islam, 136; in
   Algeria, 184–208; in relation to law, 4;
   in Saudi Arabia, 135–60; in
   workplace, 224; of transmitting
   nationality, 115; official policies on,
   104–32; struggle for, 5; to be protected
   by men, 154; to choose spouse, 84; to
   dress see dress code; to drive cars see
   driving demonstration; to inherit see
   inheritance; to interpret Islamic texts,
   53; to mobility see mobility of women;
   to property ownership, 106, 215; to
   study, 145, 146, 155; to travel see travel
   by women; to vote, 115, 122, 212; to
   work, 143, 145, 194, 199, 235